19-90
JIM LAKER

19-90
JIM LAKER

BRIAN SCOVELL

TEMPUS

First published 2006

Tempus Publishing Limited
The Mill, Brimscombe Port,
Stroud, Gloucestershire, GL5 2QG
www.tempus-publishing.com

British Library Cataloguing in Publication Data.
A catalogue record for this book is available from the British Library.

ISBN 0 7524 3932 4

Typesetting and origination by Tempus Publishing Limited
Printed in Great Britain

CONTENTS

A DEDICATION TO
LILLY LAKER

The idea of writing a book about the record-breaking exploits of Jim Laker came indirectly from his loving and devoted wife Lilly. She said, 'In 2006 it is the fiftieth anniversary of his 19 wickets for 90 runs in the Old Trafford Test in 1956 and the twentieth anniversary of Jim's death on 23 April 1986.

'I wanted to commemorate his achievements because another generation has come along and they won't remember and the memories will fade. Jim was a good man. He was outspoken, a Yorkshireman, and a lot of people have a wrong impression of him.

'The authorities took exception to his book *Over to Me* and he had his membership of the MCC and Surrey withdrawn for a while. Things were different in those days. Cricketers were treated harshly and there was a cruel distinction between professionals and amateurs. Today they are treated completely differently.'

Every twenty-five years or so, English cricket has produced a super-hero. In 1938 it was Sir Leonard Hutton. In 1956 it was Jim Laker. Ian Botham was the man in 1981 and in 2005 it was Andrew Flintoff. They were all Northerners, which supports the theory that Northerners are tougher than Southerners, and with the exception of Flintoff, a thoroughly modest and engaging young man, they were single minded and played the game relentlessly.

All of them set records but Laker's unique record at Old Trafford in 1956 will probably never be beaten. He was a man apart. Some fellow players and critics thought he was rather aloof but those who knew him well liked him and respected him as a man. He put a lot back into cricket and at the Oval they described his years of unpaid service as chairman of cricket at Surrey County Cricket Club as 'outstanding'. He also did a lot of work for charity.

In 1968 he started as a TV cricket commentator, succeeding the late Lord Constantine of Maraval and Nelson, and was on the way to rivalling his Australian friend Richie Benaud as one of the outstanding cricket commentators of the age. Both men shared the same trait – they never used a single word more than they needed.

Jim was a heavy smoker, like many of his contemporaries, including his good friend Ken Barrington, who on 14 March 1981 collapsed and died from a massive heart attack at the age of fifty. A short time later, Jim almost died from an aortic aneurism, the excessive enlargement of a main artery. Five years later he contracted pancreatitis and, to the surprise of his family, his gall bladder was removed. Suddenly he contracted septicaemia and died at the age of sixty-four. 'He died too young,' said Lilly. 'He should have had plenty more years.'

In the early 1960s I worked as the cricket writer on the *Daily Sketch* and one of my tasks was to ghost Jim's column for a year or two. Six months before he was signed up, I wrote, 'This man should be banned for life for what he has done in his book.' That came from the ignorance of youth!

To many, Jim was one of the most friendly men you could meet, with his almost self-deprecating half smile and his dry humour. In his second year with the *Sketch* he was writing his own copy, written in immaculate longhand. He was an educated man of worldly interests and he wasn't totally wrapped up in cricket like so many cricketers. He upset a few people but his heart was in the right place.

One of his leading journalistic colleagues, Alex Bannister, formerly of the *Daily Mail*, now in his mid-nineties, said, 'He was the complete Yorkshireman, often difficult, and there wasn't a better off-spin bowler ever in the history of the game.' England's Ashes winning cricketers were awarded the MBE in the 2006 New Year's Honours List yet the man who achieved the greatest bowling performance of all time was never honoured.

A DEDICATION TO LILLY LAKER

Born in Vienna, Lilly first met Jim in Cairo in 1943 when she was serving in the ATS while he was a corporal in the Royal Ordnance Corps. Much of his time was occupied playing cricket – he wasn't a front-line soldier. Back in London after the Second World War the affair took seven years to lead to marriage in 1951. The vivacious Lilly knew little about cricket but was his most devoted supporter. Their thirty-five years of happy marriage ended tragically but Lilly lives a full life, with her daughters Fiona and Angela and their seven children, close to Salisbury Cathedral. She is very proud of Jim and always will be.

Brian Scovell
Bromley, Kent

ACKNOWLEDGEMENTS

Brian Downing, the former president of Surrey, gave me the impetus to write this book. He had spoken to Lilly Laker and she was keen to commemorate the fiftieth anniversary of Jim's greatest feat of taking an unparalleled 19 for 90 at Old Trafford.

Since then, Brian took a leading part in organising the Lord's Taverners' commemorative dinner at The Brit Oval on 18 September and invited twenty of the finest spin bowlers in the world, including Shane Warne. They all accepted and they support John Edrich's concept of setting up the 'The Laker Spin Scholarship'. A small number of promising young English spin bowlers were chosen to go to Mumbai to be coached each year and the idea is to find spinners worthy of being selected for England. The enthusiasm and drive of Brian and John, Surrey's 2006 president, has given English cricket an opportunity to nurture young spin bowlers and turn them into Test bowlers. And we wish them well.

Lilly and her daughters Fiona and Angela have given me tremendous help in amassing the facts about Jim's extraordinary life and supplying a copious number of photographs and I thank them. It was a pleasant task to interview eight of the remaining nine survivors of the 1956 Laker Test – Peter Richardson, Trevor Bailey and Alan Oakman of England and Colin McDonald, Ron Archer, Neil Harvey, Richie Benaud and Ian Craig. Alan Davidson, who was injured for most of the 1956 series, was another worthy and very helpful interviewee from that tour.

Two important ingredients of the story came from the MCC and the Surrey History Centre. They let me see copies of the minutes in 1960 when Jim had his honorary membership of the MCC withdrawn for seven years and his honorary membership of Surrey taken away for four years. I am grateful to Glenys Williams MPhil, the MCC archivist, historian and deputy curator for her help and also the staff at the SHC for their assistance and giving me permission to publish the relevant material.

Trevor Jones, the Surrey CCC historian, has been an enormous help in the project, giving me access to his books, documents and film, including a copy of the BBC tape on Jim's 19 wickets and I thank him. Also extremely helpful were Doug Insole, Micky Stewart, Sir Alec Bedser, Bill Frindall, David Allen, Dickie Bird, Philip Bailey, joint editor of *Who's Who of Cricketers*, Alex Bannister, Bernie Coleman, Don Carr, Robin Marlar, Keith Fletcher, Tom Graveney, Robin Hobbs, Ray Illingworth, Ray Julian, Roger Knight, Roy McLean, Christopher Martin-Jenkins, Peter Parfitt, Don Shepherd, Brian 'Tonker' Taylor, Peter Walker, John Woodcock, Jeremy Simmonds, Don Crossley, Mike Howard, Graham Massey, Peter Davies, Max Dunbar, David Frost, Tony Brown, Peter Laker, the Rev. Malcolm Lorimer, Keith Hayhurst, Geoff Arnold, Michael Barton, Anne Bickerstaff, Henry Blofeld, Darren Bicknell, Jim Cumbes, Tony Cozier, Colin Evans, Geoff Howarth, Richard Hutton, Arnold Long, Arthur McIntyre, David Montague, Pat Pocock, John Pretlove, Derek Pringle, Jason Ratcliffe, Graham Roope, Paul Sheldon, Raman Subba Row, Betty Surridge, Roy Swetman, David Sydenham, Ron Tindall, David Ward and members of the staff at Surrey CCC, Lancashire CCC and the MCC, also the *Daily Mail* library.

I hope that Brian Downing's vision of finding a few English spin bowlers – even another Jim Laker – will be realised.

Brian Scovell
Bromley, Kent

BIBLIOGRAPHY

Jim Laker: *Spinning Round the World* (Muller, 1957); *Over to Me* (Muller, 1960); *The Australian Tour of 1961* (Muller, 1961); *A Spell from Laker* (Hamlyn, 1979); *Cricket Contrasts* (Stanley Paul, 1985).

Alan Hill: *Jim Laker* (Andre Deutsch).

Tony Lock: *For Surrey and England* (Hodder & Stoughton, 1957). *Who's Who of Cricketers* (Newnes Books, 1984).

Christopher Martin-Jenkins: *World Cricketers* (OUP, 1996).

Bill Frindall: *The Wisden Book of Cricket Records* (Headline, 1993).

Ted Dexter: *Rothmans Book of Test Matches* (Arthur Barker, 1964).

Michael Manley: *A History of West Indian Cricket* (Andre Deutsch, 1988).

David Lemmon: *The Guinness Book of Test Cricket Captains* (Guinness, 1992).

Stephen Green: *Lord's, The Cathedral of Cricket* (Tempus, 2003).

Wisden Annuals 1951, 1957, 1961, 1962, 1963, 1964, 1965, 1969, 1973, 1995, 1996, 2005.

Brian Scovell: *Ken Barrington: A Tribute* (Harrap, 1982); *Sir Clyde Walcott* (Gollanz, 1999); *Not Out – Dickie Bird* (Arthur Barker, 1978).

Richie Benaud: *On Reflection* (Willow, 1984).

Mike Brearley: *Phoenix from the Ashes* (Hodder & Stoughton, 1984).

Henry Blofeld: *The Packer Affair* (Collins, 1978).

Colin Cowdrey: *Autobiography of a Cricketer* (Hodder & Stoughton, 1978).

Godfrey Evans: *The Gloves Are Off* (Hodder & Stoughton, 1960).

Alf Gover: *Long Run* (Pelham, 1991).

Rachael Heyhoe-Flint: *Heyhoe!* (Pelham, 1978).

Stephen Chalke and Derek Hodgson: *Bob Appleyard: No Coward Soul* (Fairfield Books, 2003); *At the Heart of English Cricket: Memoirs of Geoffrey Howard* (Fairfield, 2001).

Brian Johnson: *It's Been a Lot of Fun* (WH Allen, 1974).

Ken Mackay: *Slasher Opens Up* (Pelham, 1964).

Peter May: *A Game Enjoyed* (Stanley Paul, 1985).

Don Mosey: *Laker* (Queen Anne Press, 1989).

Pat Pocock and Patrick Collins: *Percy* (Frost Publications, 1987).

Don Shepherd: *Born to Bowl* (Fairfield, 2004).

E.W. Swanton: *Gubby Allen* (Hutchinson, 1984); *Sort of a Cricket Person* (Collins, 1972).

Freddie Trueman: *Fast Fury* (Stanley Paul, 1961).

Frank Tyson: *Typhoon Called Tyson* (Heinemann, 1961).

Gerald Hudd: *J.C. Laker, His Record Innings by Innings* (ACS Publications, 2005).

Chris Overson: *Tony Lock, His Record Innings by Innings* (ACS Publications, 1997).

ONE

ON A HIGH

OLD TRAFFORD, 31 JULY 1956: ENGLAND *v.* AUSTRALIA
68 OVERS 27 MAIDENS 90 RUNS 19 WICKETS

Just before 5.30 p.m. on Monday 31 July 1956 at Old Trafford, Jim Laker, bowling round the wicket, swivelled round on crossed legs and appealed for lbw against Australian wicketkeeper Len Maddocks. Umpire Frank Lee raised his left index finger. Trevor Bailey, one of England's close fielders, said to Peter Richardson as he turned towards the pavilion, 'You'll not see that again.' Jim had taken 19 wickets for 90 runs, a record, on a doctored pitch that turned into a 'sticky dog', the phrase used in those days to describe a rain-affected, uncovered pitch when the sun came out. Nowadays pitches are totally covered and the sun still comes out even in Manchester.

Jim took ninety-five per cent of the wickets. No batsman and no bowler in the history of the game has monopolised a two-innings match the way Laker did with his mercurial and deadly bowling. India's Vijay Hazare holds the record as a batsman in first-class cricket, achieving 70.77 per cent of the runs for a Rest XI *v.* Hindus in 1943-44 and Brian Lara heads the list for Test batsmen. Lara scored 53.83 per cent of the runs for the West Indies against Sri Lanka in Colombo in 2001-02 (221 out of 390 in the first innings and 130 out of 262) and only two other Test players, South Africa's Jimmy Sinclair and Zimbabwe's Andy Flower, have passed fifty per cent. Sir Donald Bradman's best percentage was thirty-three per cent, mainly because he often didn't have the opportunity to bat a second time. Bradman was at Old Trafford reporting the match for the *Daily Mail* and said, 'I venture to predict that Laker's record will stand for all time.'

Ian Johnson, the scholarly, losing Australian captain, said, 'Laker was the ogre. His bowling is everlasting for his figures are more insuperable than even the batting of Don Bradman. That we succumbed so repeatedly to him is a credit to his bowling rather than an indictment of our batting.'

There were remarkable scenes as Jim took his short-sleeved sweater from the umpire, slung it on his left shoulder and walked off. No-one jumped on him. No-one kissed him and no-one hugged him. Several players shook his hand but not Tony Lock, who was still stunned at not being able to take more than 1 wicket. There was a famous picture of the scene, with Jim striding out, Brian Statham half-heartedly clapping on the right, David Sheppard's hands were about to meet like cymbals on the left and the captain, Peter May, had his hand to his mouth as he turned his head away. Jim had a fraught relationship with May. The picture showed the story.

Jim started to jog towards the wicket gate at the bottom of the steps to the pavilion and, realising he would be on his own, he stopped, intimating that May, or another player, should lead the side in. Someone else motioned to him, pointing. Only then did he turn and run up the steps, with trilby-hatted members leaning forward to pat him on the back. Mike Howard, a young man sitting nearby, recalled fifty years later, 'There was no cheering or shouting as he ran up the steps.' Peter Davies played truant to be there. 'We started queuing at 7.30 in the morning,' he said. 'There was little emotion, particularly from the hero of the day. We sat with our bottles of lemonade, sandwiches and a flask of tea and we hardly moved.' With almost two days washed out through rain and a poor forecast, less than 6,000 people were present and Jim's favourite line in his public speeches years later was, '600,000 have claimed that they were there.'

Jeremy Simmonds from Oakman filled in his scorecard and recalled, 'When I met him at a dinner in 1981 when he was the speaker, he asked me, "Would you like me to sign it?" I said, "Yes please." Jim duly signed and said, "That should be worth a few bob!" As I watched him go off at the end of the game it made me think he didn't really like all the fuss. My lasting impression of Laker and Lock bowling in tandem that day was of being present at two different matches going on at the same time. At the Stretford End, Laker wheeled away in his own unhurried way, bowling with hypnotic flight to a precisely repeated rhythm, imperturbable, relentless and confident in the knowledge that he had the Australians where he wanted them. In contrast, the faster Lock appeared to bowl with that familiar windmill action of his, the more comfortably the Australians played him and the more docile the pitch appeared to be.'

Jim said in his book *Cricket Contrasts*, 'I've never been a demonstrative person. I've always tried to take whatever success came my way, just the same as I accepted the many failures. In moments of triumph, I was credited with being modest and possibly a bit shy. The problem was that when I adopted the same attitude in walking off the field with 0 for 100 it left me open to allegations of disinterest and even on one memorable occasion, of not trying. Which wasn't true.'

Colin McDonald, the Australian who was top scorer in both innings, said, 'In those days we didn't show a lot of emotion. Richie Benaud started that a bit later and everyone followed. But Jim was different. He was a very quiet and humble man. He played it hard, we all played it hard, just as hard as they do today.' McDonald is one of six survivors, along with Richie Benaud, Neil Harvey, Ian Craig, Ron Archer and Len Maddocks. There are only three survivors from the England side, Peter Richardson, Trevor Bailey and Alan Oakman.

One person left the field with a souvenir stump – Emrys Davies, the former Glamorgan player who was standing as umpire in his second and last Test. He stood at the Stretford End in the Australians' first innings and Lee, born near Lord's in 1905, took over that end in their second innings. Lee, one of three cricketing brothers who played for Middlesex and Somerset, was famous for calling South African bowler Geoff Griffin for throwing in the 1960 series in England and he officiated in 29 Tests before he was discarded from the Test list at the age of fifty-seven on the grounds that his hearing had deteriorated.

Davies' first Test as an umpire was in the Second Test at Lord's in the 1956 series when Australia won on a green top that suited the bowling of Keith Miller, who took 10 wickets in the match. He had the stump signed by players of both sides and his son Peter said, 'If I ever had a fire at home and could rescue only one item, it would be that stump.' Oddly, Davies was promptly dropped from the international list and never umpired in Test cricket again. Both umpires at the Old Trafford match were left-hand opening batsmen. Bill Dowling, the Australian manager, filed a complaint about the state of the pitches at Old Trafford and Headingley, which staged the Third Test, and Davies upheld a good proportion of Laker's appeals at Manchester.

Lancashire officials rescued both balls and presented them to Jim. England needed only 40.4 overs to bowl Australia out for 84 in the first innings and only one ball was used in the second innings when 150.2 overs were bowled while the Australians laboured hard and painfully to 205 before England won by an innings and 170 runs. Later Jim's wife Lilly donated the balls to the MCC and they are mounted and placed in a glass cabinet in the Lord's Museum. Footballing memorabilia is now fetching enormous sums but, according to Max Dunbar of Christie's, the most costliest item sold in English cricket, Samuel Britcher's scorebook of 1804-05, was purchased for £90,000. A bat signed by Gary Sobers and others brought in slightly less and one of Bradman's caps fetched £35,000. 'It is very difficult to put a price on the balls used in the 1956 Test match. It is a very specialised market,' he said. 'I would guess around £1,500.' The MCC are coy about the insurance of the balls but the value ought to rise sharply after the fiftieth anniversary of the event.

Back in the dressing room, some of the Australians came in to congratulate him and Ron Archer, one of the survivors, said, 'We didn't stay too long. We were pretty upset about the pitch. We changed and went back to the hotel and the next day Len Maddocks and myself hired a car and drove to York Minster to have a look round. Jim was a lovely bloke and I thought Old Trafford was a lovely ground – except the pitch.'

In Jim's five books about his life he made a point of how much money he made, possibly a sign that, coming from modest means, he felt he should have been paid more. His Test match fee was £75, though Surrey deducted £15 for each of the two county matches he missed through playing at Manchester. Littlewoods Pools and Barclays Bank – he used to work for the bank as a young man – sent cheques of £250 and De La Rue sent one for £190, £10 for each wicket. Another £150 came from three newspaper interviews and he said, 'It showed how commercially naive we were when I signed 1,000 copies of the final scorecard, which sold out very fast at two shillings each with the cash going to my benefit.' Before he was banned by the MCC after his critical book *Over to Me*, he was given a silver salver, presented by Field Marshal Earl Alexander of Tunis. Lord Montgomery of Alamein, another general who conducted the Desert War across North Africa, including Egypt where Jim was stationed as a soldier in the Royal Ordnance Company, sent him an autographed £1 which is now displayed in the Laker Room at The Brit Oval.

It was 8 p.m. when he drove on his own southwards afterwards an interminable number of interviews. Brian Johnston recalled, 'Fortunately Jim took all his wickets from the Stretford End where our cameras were always situated. This meant the viewers got a perfect view of the turning ball unimpeded by the batsman and the keeper. I remember going across to the pavilion to collect him to do a TV interview and he was by far the calmest man on the ground. From his cool, casual air you might have thought he had taken a couple of wickets in a parents' match.'

Jim said, 'I suppose I bowled as well as I have ever done over the past ten years. But the pitch helped me a lot today. If the sun hadn't come out we would have been struggling because the pitch was like an unhelpful pudding. Don't forget a good word about Lockey, who bowled well at the other end without any luck.' Sid Barnes, the eighty-three-year-old former medium-pace bowler who bowled every possible delivery except today's doosra, watched the last rites and he was the previous record holder, with 17 wickets for 159 against South Africa in 1913. The two men shook hands in the car park and Barnes said, 'No bugger ever got all ten when I was at t'other end!'

The M1 hadn't been built and after two hours of crammed driving he stopped at a pub near Lichfield off the A5 for a pint of beer and two stale cheese sandwiches. A dozen or so men were watching the black-and-white television highlights of the match and none of them recognised him. When he arrived at his flat in St John's Wood, near Lord's at 2 a.m., there was a throng of photographers and journalists outside. He posed for pictures and it was difficult to tell who was the most tired, Jim or Lilly. She said, 'I'm sure it started with a pink clockwork rabbit that some friends from Canada sent to us to bring Jim good luck. I told my daughters that it is Daddy's, not yours. Seems silly, I know but when you have your ups and downs, I suppose it is natural to look for a reason for something. Jim is not a superstitious man; apart from having a thing about which of his hundred-odd ties he wears for a particular event, he couldn't care less about which cricket shirt or sweater or flannels he wears. He is an ordinary man and has no fads about food and has no hobbies. But I only wish this job of being a cricketer's wife wasn't such a terribly lonely business. He is often away for ten or twelve days in a row and can be away for up to seven months in the winter. Having your husband in the limelight all the time calls for a lot more hard work than most marriages. The compensations come when he is at home and we have met so many wonderful people I wouldn't otherwise have done.'

Next day Jim had to get up early to drive to the Oval to earn his £15 by playing against the same Australians. Fortunately it rained throughout the day and they let him off early. When the match was resumed next day he went out to bat and Alan Davidson told him he would give him one off the mark. Jim swung, missed and was bowled first ball. But he managed to take 5 more Australian wickets in a drawn game. Ian Craig, who was Australia's youngest Test player at seventeen years and 239 days, played in that match and was bowled cheaply by Eric Bedser. 'It was like facing Jim a couple of days earlier in the Test,' he said. 'Eric was a very similar bowler and he never had the recognition he deserved.'

Colin McDonald, Australia's doughty right-handed opener who toured in England in 1953 and 1956, knew more about the Old Trafford pitch than anyone and he spent almost eight hours resisting the Laker-Lock duo, scoring 89 and 32, or forty-one per cent of the aggregate runs. 'Bradman and Ponsford put up their record stand and Bradman got all the publicity and Ponsford hardly any,' he said. 'It was the same with Laker and Lock. But at least Lock got a mention and I didn't get a look in!

'The pitch was doctored to suit Laker and Lock. I've no doubt about it. It sounds sour grapes now but it's true.' Neil Harvey, another survivor of the Old Trafford holocaust, said, 'We won the Second Test on a green top at Lord's and that suited our quick bowlers. But afterwards Peter May told us, "That's the last one you'll get!" That indicated to us that they were going to prepare pitches for Laker and Lock and that proved to be right. Headingley was a spinners' paradise with Laker and Lock sharing 18 wickets. Jim got 19 at Old Trafford and the Oval pitch turned more than usual in the last Test.'

McDonald described the Old Trafford pitch as 'like Bondi Beach. We played on the same ground in May and it was a typical Old Trafford pitch, fairly dark, grey in colour with a firm surface, which helped the faster bowlers. When we turned up the day before the Test it was yellowy in colour and a lot of marl, about a centimetre high, was piled on it and it wasn't hard. We knew it would start crumbling and whoever won the toss had a great chance of winning. Laker and Lock were great spinners, much better suited to the conditions than ours, Ian Johnson and Richie. Except for his 6 wickets at the same ground in 1961, Richie never really took a lot of wickets in England.

'Old Trafford was a disgrace and we were very upset about it. The Invincibles, the Australian side which won six series in a row, were well past their best and England wanted to win this series to make it three wins in a row, which they did. The pitch was vicious. It started on sand and it finished up on mud. I suppose the Lancashire club was responsible but we wondered whether someone from the MCC put a word in.'

The history of cheating in Ashes series has fluctuated over the years but in this period the Australians were the victims. In the Bodyline series in 1932-33, Douglas Jardine broke the unwritten code of good sportsmanship and in 1956 Ian Johnson's side were cheated out of it, except their batsmen weren't good enough to withstand Laker and Lock. In the 1972 series the Australians responded with Operation Lip Salve, putting fluid on one side of the ball to enable Bob Massie to swing the ball prodigiously both ways. Massie took 16 wickets for 137 runs, the third-best match analysis behind Jim's 19 and Sid Barnes' 17. He rose like a comet and fell like one. Ray Illingworth was England captain and not able to comment on the record, but he leaked enough facts about the case to bring the matter to an abrupt end. On his home ground at Leeds, he led England to an Ashes victory later in the summer on a pitch that ideally suited the individualistic bowling style of Derek Underwood, whose 10 for 82 bowled out Ian Chappell's side twice under 150. Bill Bowes, who refused to bowl bodyline when he played under Jardine, wrote in *Wisden,* 'Not for a moment would one suggest that conditions had been deliberately engineered to produce such a result but the fact remained, that they were least likely to suit the tourists. Their chairman, Mr Brian Sellers, had to give an assurance that the pitch would be up to Test match standard but it was without pace, took spin from the first day and grew progressively more helpful.' Many of these controversies could have been curtailed much earlier if there had been honest talking from the first day but there is a tradition, still existing, that the authorities insist on keeping matters secret to avoid embarrassment.

Sellers was forty-nine in 1956 and served under Gubby Allen's chairmanship on the England Test selection committee until he quit a year before. He was a tough, uncompromising Yorkshireman from Keighley who captained Yorkshire like a tyrant. Dickie Bird's most repeated story was about what happened when he scored his highest score, 181 not out. Sellers greeted him as he returned to the dressing room and said, 'Well played, Dickie lad, but get thee bloody head down, you're in the second team in the next match!'

An inexperienced groundsman had been appointed before the Headingley Test and Sellers would have told him what to do. Normally pitches at Leeds helped medium-fast seam bowlers and they didn't have a lot of pace. Suddenly the ball turned from the first day and the Australians were shocked. Lock and Laker bundled them out twice for 143 and 140, losing by an innings and 42 runs. A kind of freemasonry existed in cricket at the time and none of the leading characters ever sold their stories to the newspapers. They were rich, autocratic men who wanted to run cricket their way and never gave explanations. In 1956 they conspired to ensure an England success in the Ashes and the three central figures were Allen, Sellers and Tommy Burrows, the Lancashire chairman.

The English newspapers carried stories about the alleged pitch doctoring but the stories soon died out. The Suez Crisis dominated the front pages instead. General Gamal Abdel Nasser, the newly appointed President of Egypt, seized the Suez Canal during the Test and it provoked the British invasion of Egypt. By October the mini war had to be aborted after President Eisenhower refused to join in. Sir Walter Monckton, a lawyer and politician who played a big part in the banning of Jim by Surrey CCC and the MCC, was Minister of Defence in the Conservative government and he opposed the war. He resigned as Minister of Defence and was moved to the position of Paymaster General, ironically in the position of co-ordinating the government's information service in Egypt. When Prime Minister Anthony Eden resigned, Monckton's friend Harold Macmillan took over. Monckton finally left the government and became chairman of the Midland Bank and, the following year, chairman of the Iraq Petroleum Company. A cricket lover, Monckton was president of Surrey and president of the MCC. Monckton is the only president of Surrey who served on two occasions.

McDonald lives in Melbourne and believes that pitch doctoring is alien to Australia. 'It happened only once and a curator left the pitch too dry at Melbourne and was worried about the big cracks appearing, so he watered it himself,' he said. 'No-one told him to do it. It doesn't happen here because types of grass and climatic conditions prevent it and each major ground prepares roughly the same pitch. For example, Sydney always takes spin and you can't suddenly produce a green top. In Perth, the pitches are hard and bouncier and so on.'

The most powerful man in English cricket, not just in the 1950s when he was chairman of the selectors for seven years, but right up until he died a pitch's length from the door of the Lord's pavilion on 29 November 1989 at the age of eighty-seven, was Sir George Oswald Browning Allen, CBE, TD, universally known as 'Gubby'. He denied any involvement with the preparation of the three pitches at Headingley, Old Trafford and the Oval in the 1956 series but there was clear evidence that he wielded influence at Old Trafford. Law 7 says, 'Before the toss the ground authority shall be responsible for the selection and preparation of the pitch. During the match the umpires shall control its use and maintenance.' The MCC controlled cricket at the time and no-one admitted that any of their officers, including the chairman of selectors, gave any instructions to the chairman and committee members of the host county and, more importantly, to the groundsman.

The day before the Fourth Test was due to start, Gubby Allen arrived and met Tommy Burrows and Cyril Washbrook, the Lancashire captain who was surprisingly recalled to the England side for the Headingley Test at the age of forty-one. Born in Sydney in 1902, Allen was educated at Eton and Cambridge University, served in the Second World War as an intelligence officer rising to the rank of Lieutenant-Colonel and captained England in Australia in 1936-37 as an amateur when they led 2-0, finally losing 3-2 to Don Bradman's side. A bachelor, he could be said to have married cricket because he lived in a house round the corner from Lord's and spent much of his time there. Bradman was probably his best friend, who said of him, 'His greatest contribution was in the Bodyline series in 1932-33 when he refused to be browbeaten by England's captain Douglas Jardine and risked being sent home rather than bowl bodyline, which he believed was contrary to the well being of the game. His stand displayed courage of the highest order and the cricket world will be forever in his debt.' One of Allen's chief aims in life was to put right what was he thought was wrong with the game and he and Bradman brokered the agreement to ban chuckers in 1961. He introduced many good things, including proposing the admittance of famous cricketers into membership of the MCC as honorary members in 1949. As a lifelong member of the committee, he spoke up for Jim when he was banned for criticising fellow players in a book in 1960 and seven years later he helped to end his ban.

Jim Swanton was another of his best friends and *The Daily Telegraph* cricket correspondent wrote his biography, entitled *Gubby Allen – Man of Cricket*, saying of him, 'No man alive can claim to have played so active and decisive part in the game of cricket as Gubby.' When the selectors met on the Sunday before the Old Trafford Test, Washbrook, who was also a selector, described the pitch as 'similar to the one used the year before when there were 1,300 runs scored and it was a splendid match' after inspecting it himself. Swanton wrote, 'A vast surprise awaited the chairman [Allen] and Washbrook when they went to look at the pitch on the afternoon before the game. Washbrook says that he was astounded by its appearance compared with when he had last seen it eight days before. It wore a pinkish tinge, and Gubby, rubbing his finger on the surface in the traditional fashion, found that it was not firm. The only explanation was that Bert Flack, the groundsman, had applied a dressing after Washbrook had seen it, and that, for some mysterious reason, had been prevented from "washing it in". Thus it had been allowed to "cake" on the top. Was there, at some point, direction from the Lancashire Committee? Flack was a capable groundsman, and if he had dressed the pitch at so late a stage would surely have watered sufficiently to allow the dressing to sink in. When the two selectors were looking at the pitch they were approached by a member of the Lancashire Committee [Burrows] who asked Gubby if he would like a further mowing. To this his reply was, "It wouldn't break my heart. But I must remind you that responsibility for the preparation of the pitch before the match starts is in the hands of the ground authority." Gubby readily admits today that he was unwise to make the remark he did but firmly maintains that by that stage it would have made no difference whether there had been a mowing or not. He believes that the condition of the pitch at Old Trafford was the result of an honest mistake, deriving maybe from a not very knowledgeable member of the Ground Committee who may have prevented watering in the belief that it would decrease its pace. I wish I were so sure. I am inclined to believe that there were some in authority, certainly at Headingley and probably at Old Trafford, who misguidedly aimed to provide pitches that would be helpful to spin, though no doubt they would not have hoped to see the dust rising and the ball turning extravagantly by the second day, as happened in both cases, before rain came to give a different sort of aid to the bowling side. To this extent, the Australians had every cause to think they had been hard done by. The press in both countries strongly condemned both pitches. However, in their attempts to find scapegoats some Australian cricket writers alleged that someone at Lords, or the chairman and his selectors, were responsible. Naturally enough Gubby deeply resented the slur on his reputation. Peter May, who took the next MCC side to Australia two years later, cannot recall Gubby's name being associated with the drama of the two pitches but he added, significantly, "I always felt that the Australians took no action regarding the complaints Freddie Brown [1958-59 tour manager] and I made against their chuckers because they thought they had been 'done' by us over the pitches at Headingley and Old Trafford.'"

Gubby Allen supported the England cause with great passion and in 1956 he came up with a series of inspired selections, recalling Washbrook, the Rev. David Sheppard and Denis Compton. He also saw part of his job as being to talk to chairmen and groundsmen to chivvy them on to achieve the ultimate objective – win the series. Whether it could be called outright cheating is another matter because he was known as a highly principled, Corinthian figure, as he proved in the Bodyline controversy. But what he said that day at Old Trafford went beyond that and his comment must have been seen as an order. Alan Hill, Jim Laker's biographer, reported the comments of Flack, saying Allen turned to the new Lancashire groundsman and said, 'Is this the pitch we're using?' Flack, a jovial man with sideburns, said, 'Yes.' 'Well,' said Allen, 'I am not satisfied.' Allen wanted more grass removed and Burrows said, 'The chairman wants more off. Take a little more off, Bert, and that'll please him.' Flack said to Burrows after Allen had departed, 'That's stupid. The match won't last three days. The surface is not all that well-knit.'

But Flack had to do it and he said later, 'I got my cutter out and went up and down the pitch a couple of times. Then I thought, "Well, why not? If the chairman wants a three-day match, he shall have it."'

He proceeded to give it a second cut. The covers were hauled back in place to prevent the journalists having a look at the bare pitch. If they had seen the state of it they would have written critical reports, even suggesting it resulted from a clandestine conspiracy. Some of the England players strolled over after the three men had gone and one asked, 'Can we have a look?' Bert said, 'Sorry, we're expecting rain.' A Lancashire committeeman said years later, 'Bert was a lovely man but he wasn't terribly well educated. If someone high up gave him an order, he would carry it out. He wouldn't object. Cricket was run very autocratically then.'

Bert died in 2001 at the age of eighty-four and his devoted wife Gladys died at the same age. They lived at the ground and Peter Marron, the present groundsman, said of her, 'I never met anyone more hardworking or conscientious. She had the highest respect from everyone and she could have been one of the great peacemakers of our time. She led by example.' Their ashes were scattered on the square at Old Trafford and, knowing his happy disposition, he would have smiled down as the ceremony took place. Only the ashes of Lancashire players are allowed to be scattered on the square. Lancashire Chaplain Rev. Malcolm Lorimer conducted a short ceremony and Marron said of his old boss, 'I remember him say to me "when I'm wrong, I'm right!" He was a colossus.

'The time that Warne bowled Gatting, the press boys wanted to ask if the pitch was like the Laker one and, within half an hour, Bert had them in stitches, telling them how he made Laker a star. He would have been a lot longer if he'd not seen Geoff Boycott leaving. Geoff had been criticising the Headingley groundsman so Bert went off to have a few words with him. He said, "Oi Boycs! How come you are always slagging people off? You never have anything good to say about anyone." Everyone enjoyed that, believe me. The weather before the 1993 Test when Warne took that wicket was similar to 1956 and the pitch was damp when the game started and the delivery ripped in on Gatting and took him by surprise. The story Bert told about 1956, often repeated and expanded, was about the Nottingham loam they put down and, when it rained, the surface turned to dust.'

Jim inspected the pitch earlier, before the covers came back on and he said, 'I knew it would turn. There was no grass to bind it. It looked good but it wasn't solid.' Back in the pavilion he had a cup of tea with Bradman. 'What do you think of the track?' he asked. 'It's nice and flat, isn't it?' said Bradman. 'It's just what you fellows have been waiting for. They will make a packet of runs out there.' It proved that great players can get things wrong. Jim was reasonably confident he would take wickets on this peculiar pitch but his previous record at Old Trafford was deplorable. His first visit took place in 1948 when he was relegated to twelfth man against Bradman's side. The next year he was left out to allow eighteen-year-old Brian Close to make his debut and that really upset him. He finally played a Test there, against the West Indies in 1950, and took 1 for 86. He admitted, 'I bowled abominably.' Against the Indians in 1952 he was only given 2 overs in the match and in 6 matches there he collected just 8 wickets at a cost of 235 runs. 'Little wonder that thoughts of a world record performance never entered my head in 1956,' he said. Just as worryingly, he was told by the statistician Irving Rosenwater, 'Do you realise that all eleven players in the opposing side has recorded a first class hundred and nine of them have scored a Test century?' 'That should cheer me up,' said Jim.

When the first delivery was bowled, from Ray Lindwall, a supine effort that hardly reached stump high, the Australians realised that they had little chance of winning and only rain could save them. 'There were a few cynical remarks out there,' said Peter Richardson, England's left-handed number one in the order. 'I remember Keith Miller saying, "How did you cook that one up?" I had to admit that the pitch was deliberately tampered with and dust was flying up.' One of the Australians said, 'We've been s—t on!' A renowned humorist, Richardson responded with a few encouraging words as he helped to put on 174 for the first wicket, England's best opening stand against Australia for eighteen years. 'I batted bloody well,' he said.

Richardson, the former Worcestershire farmer now retired and living at Tenterden in Kent, was one of the major pranksters in Laker's time. He remembered one occasion when Jim caught him unawares. 'It was a Test match when Bob Menzies, the Australian Prime Minister, a lovely man, was about to be presented to the two teams in front of the pavilion,' he said. 'It was dragging on and the players were fidgeting and suddenly I discovered water running into the pocket of my team blazer and soaking the leg of my flannels. Jim was squirting the water and he gave me a big wink.'

Jim Swanton, the doyen of the English Press and self-appointed unofficial advisor to a succession of chairmen of selectors, particularly Gubby Allen, was Richardson's main target. Swanton was looked on as rather pompous – he admitted it himself in a number of interviews – and Richardson said, 'I used to write to him every week with Henry Root-style letters signed by various made-up people. I was playing in a county game against Glamorgan at Neath and Tony Lewis and Peter Walker and I were discussing what we should write to him. We concocted a story about a bowler in the Welsh hills who took 155 wickets one season bowled by his right arm and in the same season took 47 wickets with his left. I called him "Dai Bothways". Swanton took it seriously because in the middle of his long Monday morning commentary in *The Daily Telegraph* he wrote about this Welsh phenomenon.

'Another time I was playing with Kent against Hampshire at Canterbury and at lunch Colin Ingleby-Mackenzie, the Hampshire captain who was a mate of Jim's and went on six of his tours abroad, said he had heard Swanton's loud voice from the BBC commentary box while he was on the field. This gave me the chance to take the mick out of him and I went to Bill Copson, one of the umpires and said, "Bill, my concentration is being disturbed at the crease by this loud booming noise at the top end of the ground. What can you do about it?" Bill went to investigate and when the match resumed, he stopped play, walked towards the box and shouted, "Oi! Someone up there is making a lot of noise and upsetting the batsmen. Can the person concerned cut the volume?" Swanton wrote to me a few days later telling me off and criticising my batting.'

Richardson's brief reign as Kent captain ended when the eighteen members of the committee decided that his last prank had gone too far. 'It was on the first day of a county game at Trent Bridge and there was hardly anyone in the crowd,' he said. 'An attendant came in to collect our team sheet for the new electric scoreboard and I had a bit of fun adding the names of Harold Pinter, Harold Macmillan, John Profumo, Arnold Palmer and a couple more spoof ones. The scoreboard operators didn't realise it was a joke and the cricket writers went to town on it in their papers. The following week I was called in to see the committee and the chairman, David Clark, said, "We take a very serious view of this." I said, "And so do I. We haven't won a game for ages and we won this one." Anyway, they decided to take away the captaincy from me and it didn't worry me the slightest. I retired soon after and never regretted it.'

At Old Trafford, Ian Johnson and Richie Benaud bowled 47 overs each but the pitch was too slow on the first day and they were punished. Colin Cowdrey, Richardson's partner, was caught by wicketkeeper Maddocks for 80 off Lindwall and Maddocks only played because the first choice, Gil Langley, woke up to discover that his hand was badly bruised. 'He must have slept awkwardly,' said manager Bill Dowling. Maddocks also dismissed Richardson with a catch off the bowling of Benaud. Richardson's 104 was his first Test century and he bought a few beers for his colleagues back at the hotel later. 'Colin was a very fine opener,' he said. 'I don't know why he was moved down the order. He should have stayed where he was.'

The first five batsmen in the England side were amateurs and it was the first time that had happened since 1899. It didn't help team spirit. The first day's total was 307 for 3, commonplace these days but then it was an exceptional total. Sheppard almost stepped out of the pulpit to go straight into a Test because he played in only 4 matches for Sussex. He was working as a curate in the East End of London when Gubby Allen invited him to join the side, and he rewarded the chairman with a chanceless innings of 113. England's first total of 459 came in 491 minutes and, as *Wisden* noted, 'It was an unusually rapid rate for Test cricket.' Not having a priest in their dressing room, the Australians had to rely on their opener Jimmy Burke to cheer them up. 'He was a great bloke,' said Alan Davidson. 'He loved playing the piano and getting us to join in.

He'd rock the place and it was very sad that he died so young in tragic circumstances.'

Jim's assessment of the pitch on day two was 'a slow moderate turner on which a good county side would probably make 250 against a spin bowler who would hope to capture half a dozen wickets at about ten apiece'. Colin McDonald and Burke put on 48 rather slowly until Jim switched to the Stretford End. McDonald, failing to get far enough forward, nicked an off-spinner from Jim that caught the edge and Tony Lock made the catch at backward square leg. McDonald's 32 turned out to be the top score. He started to leave the crease and stopped, waiting for the umpire to reaffirm his decision. In today's cricket he would have been fined by the ICC referee for showing dissent.

Neil Harvey scored more runs than any Australian batsman of his time except Bradman and was the next man in. Christopher Martin-Jenkins wrote of him, 'The sight of his trim figure coming through the gate – short, stocky, and with his neat, dark hair always capless – invariably spelt danger to opponents.' Harvey took guard, looked round and as Jim padded up to the wicket he bowled a delivery that the victim described thus: 'That Shane Warne delivery that bowled Mike Gatting, well, that wasn't in the same class. It pitched on or about leg and I thought I had it covered but it turned sharply and clipped the off bail. I never faced a better ball than that.'

Jim wrote later, 'I am not being boastful when I said that ball won the series. I was lucky enough to bowl an absolute snorter. Neil stared in disbelief at the pitch. The truth was that I hadn't turned one as sharply or as quickly in all my previous 9 overs. It was just one of those things. We went to tea soon afterwards and they must have been talking about it. At any rate, they panicked when they went back out.' Burke nudged a delivery from Lock to slip and Jim dropped it. Luckily for Jim – Lock had a furious expression on his face – Lock found the edge again and Cowdrey held the catch. It turned out to be his first and only wicket in the Test and it affected his life for the worse. He saw himself as a victim.

Burke's 22 runs made him second highest scorer. 'It seemed to demoralise them and they were bowled out within another thirty-five minutes,' said Jim. Ian Craig was twenty-one, the youngest and brightest in the party, and was being groomed to be the next Australian captain, but his inexperience was soon found out by Jim's relentless attack. 'It was clever bowling,' he said. 'He bowled from different angles, held the ball back a bit and got me with a delivery bowled with a low arm – out lbw. I felt it was a bit short but it wasn't.' When Keith Miller came in he lofted a six off Lock, whose exasperation was showing. Lock was beating the bat regularly but he was speeding up, bowling too wide of the off stump. 'He lost it,' said Richardson.

Oakman took 5 catches in all and he admitted, 'They were pretty easy. We didn't have leg guards, helmets and the rest but Jim was so accurate that you didn't worry too much, particularly on that pitch. I fielded closer than usual and I knew I didn't have much chance of being hit. When we met up afterwards he would always say, "Are you still living on those 5 catches?" He was a very nice man. I'm afraid Lockey disintegrated and it got worse. He didn't get much luck. I put him in the top three fielders of all time. He caught everything.'

When the match started, Oakman was fielding at mid on and Sheppard, a specialist close fielder, was stationed at short square leg. Jim soon suggested they should swap over because Sheppard was out of practice. 'I'd prefer mid on or mid off where I'll have more time to see the ball,' said Sheppard and skipper Peter May agreed. Oakman said, 'Keith Miller looked out to deep square and mid wicket and said to me, "Oakie, that's a dangerous position. If I middle it, they will have to carry you off. Three balls later he pushed forward and I caught him out low by my ankles."'

Oakman was selected as a bits-and-pieces player for the Headingley Test, scored only 4 runs at number three, didn't bowl, held 2 catches and then was promptly dropped. Gubby Allen always insisted on picking class players but he made an exception for this tall and friendly man from Hastings. The Sussex and Warwickshire all-rounder was a sound catcher (he held 594 catches in his career between 1947 and 1968) and he scored 22 centuries in his 21,800 runs. He also took 736 wickets as an off-spin bowler. When the selectors heard that Tom Graveney had reported an injury and wasn't fit, they changed their minds and brought him back. Before the days of mobile phones, none of them knew his telephone number. It was on a Sunday and he wasn't at home or at the club. 'I know,' said Allen. 'Call the police. Ring Hastings Police Station!' Within ten minutes the constabulary found their man. Oakman had a short Test career – 2 very eventful Test matches on scandalously bad pitches.

Jim's fifth sacrificial batsman was the personable left hander Ken Mackay, who had a reputation Down Under of being the most difficult man in the country to dismiss. But he had no idea of how to play Jim, especially in these conditions, and nicked a ball leaving him that was calmly picked up by Oakman. Like McDonald, he stayed at the crease before the umpire gave him out. Ron Archer charged down the pitch and missed a straight ball – effortlessly stumped by Godfrey Evans. 'Don Bradman advised me to go down the pitch to him,' he said with a chuckle. Richie Benaud, number seven of Jim's victims, drove straight to Brian Statham for a duck and Maddocks and Johnson were both bowled. In those mad, reckless thirty-five minutes the Australians lost 8 wickets for 22 runs with Jim's figures reading 9 for 37. His 7 wickets after tea cost 8 runs. It was almost embarrassing. All out 84. 'They appeared to give up,' wrote Leslie Smith in *Wisden*.

Jim showed little emotion as he came in. There were a few hand-shakes and some shouts of 'Well bowled J.C.!' And the crowd clapped and some raised their hats to him in the pavilion. Micky Stewart, the former England manager and captain of Surrey, who was one of his best friends, came up with a good explanation of Jim's languid approach to his sport. 'He greatly admired the South African golfer named Bobby Locke,' he said. 'He got to know him and he copied his style. Locke was a big man and didn't gallop around. He did everything at his own pace and he developed a rhythm and Jim was like that. That was his secret. He never hurried, never looked anxious or strained. People thought he didn't care but he did.'

In the interval, Johnson called for silence and delivered a brief, rousing speech. 'Our honour is at stake,' he said. 'We have got to show some guts.' As Bert Flack appeared, some of his players gestured dismissively. The groundsman asked him, rather superfluously, 'What roller would you like?' Johnson was supposed to have said, 'Please your f—ing self!' That may be apocryphal because he was a gentleman. But he did ask for the lightest roller they had, to prevent any more breakup of the crumbling surface. Johnson refused to comment on the pitch until some time later.

Jim had only bowled 16.4 overs and was keen to restart. Following on 375 behind, the Australians only faced 3 overs from Statham and Bailey before Lock and Laker were brought on by Peter May. As the senior man, Jim opted for the Stretford End. In his third over, McDonald retired with cramp in the knee. 'It wasn't anything,' he said. 'I had surgery on ligaments earlier in my career and I just got on with it.' That brought Harvey in to join the persevering Burke. Jim's version of his first ball to Harvey was, 'I only had two men on the on-side. One of them was Colin Cowdrey at short mid wicket, in much the same position as Bernie Constable had caught Neil in the Surrey match in May. Neil moved into it, making a full toss, and plonked it straight into Colin's hands. I had dismissed the most famous left hander in the world for a pair in the same afternoon and the pitch couldn't be blamed this time.'

Harvey said, 'I couldn't remember him bowling a full toss before. I started going forward but played too soon. There was a picture of me throwing my bat into the air, almost laughing. Two ducks in the same day! We had a drink later and he said, "You've got to take what you can in this game," and he was dead right.' At the close of play Australia were 51 for 1. The Australian journalists wrote scathing articles about the pitch, almost ignoring another reason why their side was shot out for 84. 'They didn't bat particularly well,' said Trevor Bailey. 'They weren't used to playing that type of bowling. They went back instead of going forward. They were hypnotised – Lakerised!'

Some Australian writers used the word 'cheats' and an official of the Lancashire club issued an statement denying that they gave the order to put a large amount of marl onto a very shaven and dried surface to produce a 'result' pitch. But who did it? The people involved are now dead. 'The truth was,' Jim said, 'if the Australians had played only half as badly as they did on that black Friday, they would have saved the match and, as it turned out, the series.'

Lilly arranged to travel to Manchester on Friday night to watch the Saturday play and when she stepped off the train at Warrington, she was met by Jim and a horde of photographers. She said 'Good Lord! What on earth have you been up to? Why are all these people here?' But torrential rain fell in the night and a full house saw only forty-five minutes' play between ten minutes past two and five minutes to three. Strong winds swept across the ground and the Manchester's sky was at its murkiest and most inhospitable. Heavier bails, made of lignum, had to be used instead of the normal ones, which kept being blown off. 'It was a pretty bad summer and it always seemed to rain on Saturdays,' said Craig. The regulations permitted the ends of the pitch to be covered but the rest was sodden. In the three-quarters of an hour's play, Burke was caught round the corner by Lock off Jim for 33, Jim's second victim. Only 6 runs had been added.

Sunday was an atrocious day and the players spent a convivial time in front of log fires in the bar and restaurant of the Lymm Hotel. 'I had to put Lilly on the train to go back home that night so she missed what happened on the final day,' said Jim. 'If we had known what was going to happen she would certainly have stayed on to share in the greatest moment of my career. It was something we both regretted.' The weather was almost as bad on Monday when there were two brief periods of play lasting an hour. It was harder to bowl than bat and Australia took their total to 84 for 2. On the Tuesday, the final day, the clouds were higher but the prospects of a win for England seemed remote. The Australians needed 291 to avoid an innings defeat with 8 wickets in hand. On a sea of mud and marl, even Jim wouldn't have turned the ball. Johnson's players thought there would be a big delay as the ground staff dried out the square but, to their astonishment, the game started only ten minutes late. 'I don't know how it happened,' said Craig, who was one of his side's more heroic batsmen in the second innings. 'Sawdust was everywhere and Ian Johnson even appealed against the excessive amount of sawdust!'

McDonald was able to resume his innings after three days' rest and he and Craig took the total to 112 for 2 at lunch. Almost everyone thought it would end in a draw. But Len Hutton, sitting in the Press box, said, 'England will bowl them out. The sun is coming out.' Jim decided not to join the other players at lunch. He sat in the dressing room alone, relaxing with a beer and a sandwich. 'The clouds were lifting from the Derbyshire hills,' he said. 'And that's a good sign. It was as though someone's prayers were being answered, for an hour of sunshine would obviously bring another dramatic change in the conditions. That was what happened.'

Craig's innings of 38 lasted four hours twenty minutes and he was given out lbw off a similar ball from Jim bowled to him in his first innings, delivered from a low arm. Miller had lost interest, bowled by Jim for 0 and Ken Mackay and Ron Archer were both caught by Oakman off Jim, also for ducks. There were eight ducks in the two Australian innings. Benaud joined the courageous McDonald and, with the sun retreating behind the clouds, they held out to tea for an hour and a quarter, leaving England two hours to take the final 4 wickets. Even Jim admitted that the pitch was 'vicious' at this stage and he dismissed McDonald with his second ball after tea, with the help of another catch by Oakman. Neville Cardus described McDonald's 337-minute innings of 89 as 'the finest played for many years by an Australian in these conditions'.

'The ball was jumping and flying all over the place,' said McDonald. 'A few times I got hit in the chest and arms. I wasn't a great player but an average one, perhaps slightly better than that. It was a bit odd that an opener should play spin well on a sticky dog but it went back to my school days. I spent a lot of time facing the bowling of a teacher who bowled leg breaks in the nets and I learned how to use my feet.' By coincidence, Trevor Bailey had the same experience at school, which explained why he was the best front-foot blocker in the English ranks. 'I had a teacher at Dulwich College by the name of Charles "Father" Marriott, a leg-spinner who played for Lancashire, Cambridge University and Kent, and he spent an awful lot of time bowling to me in the nets.'

Richie Benaud defended gallantly for almost two hours before he was Jim's eighth victim, bowled by a big turner for 18. Jim said years later, 'I was asked thousands of times what went through my mind in the closing stages but I had to say that I was completely relaxed. Odd as it may seem now, I did not even consider the possibilities of taking all 10 wickets. How could I when Tony was fizzing the ball through against nine, ten and jack with venomous lift and spin.' At the time Lock used to bowl with his sleeves buttoned at the wrist, probably to disguise any straightening of the arm to avoid being called for throwing. The Australians thought he infringed the law occasionally. Paul Fitzpatrick of *The Guardian* wrote, 'In 1956 on pitches offering him any assistance and before suspicion had fallen upon his action, he was one of the most lethal bowlers in the game. His action bristled with aggression; his left arm described a full and rapid circle, delivering the ball at a pace that belied his designation as a "slow bowler".'

Jim's ninth victim, Ray Lindwall, was caught by Lock for 8 and Lock never thought of dropping the catch. With a wicket to go, even Laker's renowned calmness had disappeared. His voice was louder, almost screeching as he appealed. Maddocks joined skipper Johnson and they went off for a risky run. Richardson, fielding at extra cover without much work to do, swooped in and threw the wicket down. 'Jim wasn't too happy about that,' said Richardson. 'He used two words, both bleeps, but it wasn't out. The ball went for two extra two runs. I apologised to Peter May and he said, "I'm not bothered about that. All I'm concerned about is getting them out."' In other words, he wouldn't countenance any help for Jim to take the tenth wicket.

At 5.27 p.m. there were roars from around the quarter-filled ground as Maddocks was trapped on the crease by a delivery that turned quickly and hit the knee roll right in front. Laker 19 for 90 from 68 overs, Lock 1 for 106 from 69 overs. Jim's 10 for 53 in the second innings was the first instance of a bowler taking 10 wickets in an innings in a Test match. Only one bowler, India's leg-spin and googly bowler Anil Kumble, has since taken all ten in a Test, against Pakistan at Delhi in 1999 and, ironically, he was one of Surrey's overseas players in 2006, the fiftieth anniversary of Jim's feat.

Jim said, 'It was only during the last two or three hours that it became really difficult. If my performance was unbelievable, then so was Tony's for if the game had been played a million times it would surely have never happened again. Early on he bowled beautifully without any luck at all and beat the bat and the stumps time after time. But as the wickets tumbled at the other end desperation began to creep in and he bowled faster and faster and pitched shorter and shorter. I think I should probably have shown a bit more sympathy towards him than I did at the time. I often thought how I would have felt if the boot had been on the other foot, as it so easily could have been.' The photographers wanted a picture of Jim on the balcony and a few minutes later he came out holding up a glass of Lucozade. By the time he got back in, Lock had changed and gone.

In one of his later books, Jim wrote, 'It was one of the worst exhibitions of batting ever by an Australian side. Batting techniques were quite deplorable with the main fault being that batsmen were pushing forward defensively much too hard at the ball. They made contact with a spinning delivery with the bat often more than a foot ahead of the pad, accelerating the ball towards the close catchers.' Eight of the twenty were caught close in.

Would a modern-day Jim Laker take 19 wickets in a Test? John Woodcock, the former cricket correspondent of *The Times* and former editor of *Wisden* says, 'No-one could do it again. For several reasons, including covered pitches, heavier bats and the forward prop. Trevor Bailey was one of the few in Jim's day who could play forward properly and today's batsmen use the forward prop, putting their front foot just outside the line of the off stump with their bat tucked inside the pad. If the ball hits the pad they can't be given out and it also eliminates the nick from the inside edge towards the short leg fielders. Tony Lock took more than 800 catches and many of them were taken at backward short leg. Today batsmen don't hit the ball that way. They use the sweep much more and it's made it difficult for the off-spin bowlers. Jim's

19 wickets was an astonishing achievement and it is very unlikely to be repeated and certainly not beaten.

'He once wrote to me pointing out that I wrote a large proportion of his wickets were taken at the Oval, which suited spin, but he produced the facts to prove that I was wrong. He was quite sensitive about it.'

Doug Insole, the former Essex captain and room mate of Jim, shares Woodcock's view that there will never be another Laker, 'After Essex were docked 24 points in 1989, a decision that cost them the title, it was decided to do something about poor pitches. They consulted Harry Brind, the Surrey groundsman who had a reputation for making good pitches and he recommended Surrey loam. Within three years nearly every county used loam and their pitches are all the same, so hard that the surface doesn't give much assistance to the finger spinner. There is just one ground that has a name for taking spin, Northamptonshire.

'Even Shane Warne doesn't turn the ball as much on these pitches. When he plays there, he often goes round the wicket bowling into the rough. In 2005 twenty-four batsmen averaged 50 or more in a 16-match championship. In 1956 not one batsman averaged more than 50 and that was in a 28-match championship. Pitches were uncovered then and they helped players improve their techniques. It provided better entertainment. But there were complaints about games ending too soon and commercially it made more sense to cover pitches.'

TWO

DOWN AND OUT

I MAY 1960: J.C. LAKER BOWLED SURREY (FOR FOUR YEARS)
14 JUNE 1960: J.C. LAKER BOWLED MCC (FOR SEVEN YEARS)

Almost four years after he reached the peak of his career Jim found himself isolated and banned from the two organisations who employed him as a cricketer. Surrey County Cricket Club, which gave him the opportunity to reach international standard, and the MCC, which gave him the stage to become one of the game's greatest stars, withdrew his honorary membership. They imposed no limit. It could have been a life ban. He was in disgrace, treated like a leper in certain quarters.

As it turned out, the sentences lasted four years in the case of Surrey and seven years at Lord's, and he was deeply hurt. He wasn't given the right of appeal and he had to work extremely hard to re-establish his reputation. The cause of his sudden downfall was the publication of a book called *Over to Me* in June 1960. It had 233 fairly well-written pages and it cost 16 shillings. Most famous cricketers 'wrote' cricket books and the best-known players like Denis Compton, Fred Trueman, Trevor Bailey and others put their name to several books. There were more cricket books than football books. Jim's first book, called *Spinning Round the World* and published by the same publisher, Frederick Muller Ltd in 1957, was typical of these uncontroversial books. It had chapters called 'Captains of My Times', 'Wives on Tour', '1956 and All That' and 'The Year AD 2000' and it was an easy, informative and prescient read. Most of his prophecies about the way the game would evolve turned out to be true.

But *Over to Me*, one of the better titles, came out in the year after he retired and there were no restraints on him. Test cricketers had a rule in the booklet they were given by the MCC, preventing them commenting or writing about the game, unless they were given permission. It was possible to comment or write about a tour two years later, but again it had to be sanctioned first. But as a retired cricketer Jim could say what he liked. His book, and the pre-launch serialisation in the now-defunct Sunday newspaper *Empire News*, had the effect of bombs going off the outside the Jack Hobbs Gates at the Kennington Oval and the W.G. Grace Gates at Lord's. The committee members at both places were aghast. Some were in favour of disciplinary action.

Most of the players criticised by Jim were amateurs and they included Peter May, Colin Cowdrey and Bill Edrich. May was the highly admired captain of Surrey and England and Jim, or his ghost, wrote, 'Three years ago [in *Spinning Round the World*] when I wrote about Peter May, I said I thought he was a friendly man who had done a fine job for English cricket. Since then, I have been proved wrong to the extent that May has grown away from the rest of the players. He has become aloof and distant. He does not appear to like mixing with his team. He has become almost impossibly hard really to get to know as a person. It was always in May's nature to be shy and quiet but this alone does not explain his modern manner. I believe it all springs from a fear of the Press. He is afraid to do or say anything that might leave himself open to misinterpretation. Any embarrassment brought him by the newspapers was, more often than not, his own fault. One tactless and ill-timed series of articles he wrote for a national paper especially comes to my mind. One of his most recent actions, as I write, is to stop the Saturday Night Club that has long been a feature of our cricket tours. I know May, and the way his mind works, well enough to be convinced that his action is only another sign of his fear of the Press. He is scared that the team will do something, anything, which might bring down criticism. But, good heavens, these are grown men with whom he is dealing. The next step will be to lock them all in their rooms the moment a day's play is over. For the sheer, inborn knack of leadership on the field May was never in the same class with, say, Douglas Jardine or David Sheppard.'

Jim claimed that May only invited him to his bedroom once on the tour of Australia 'and never for a drink and a chat. You could walk into Richie Benaud's room at any time and find half the Australian team there. Which of these approaches do you think bred a better spirit in the team?' Jim also wrote about the time when May called him 'a shirker' at a game at Blackheath. He said of Freddie Brown, the manager of the 1958-59 tour, 'The tour was badly managed. There had been plenty of bad managers in the past, but I find it difficult to match Freddie Brown from my own experience.' Everything he wrote was accurate but the Establishment didn't like it.

Next, he turned to two of May's successors as England captain: 'I think Cowdrey will take over, despite a rumour that has reached my ears that Ted Dexter is a challenger for the job. You can guess my views on this; I don't know what madman started that rumour.' He called Ted Dexter 'the poor man's Trevor Bailey' and Alan Ross, the author and cricket writer, said, 'That was not only cheap, but critical folly.' Jim continued the attack, saying of Cowdrey, 'At the moment I don't think much of his captaincy. He does silly things of the sort that no Test captain can possibly afford.' Of his England teammate Johnny Wardle he wrote, 'He talks a lot of good sense but he is a selfish player, a man who gave an immense amount of trouble to his captain. And he is not a courageous batsman. He is a great fair weather player who will take good care not to be in the line of anything fast.'

One of his most surprising criticisms was aimed at Compton, arguably the most popular cricketer of that era. He said, 'For a man whom I did not, off the field, consider to be especially bright, he showed a fine brain in his play.' Labelling Compton, the man who acted as the mediator in the row over May calling him 'a shirker', as a dimwit was ungenerous and grossly unfair. Jim also accused him of being late for matches, including Test matches, hinting that he was unprofessional.

Not many people who condemned Jim had actually read the book. They were told about the contents, or they were shown the extracts from the *Empire News*, a newspaper directed at a working-class readership, which wasn't normally read in the reading rooms at Lord's or the Oval. The series ran for five weeks and the first shot, published on 22 May, was headlined 'Laker hits Out'. Jim's main target was his former employers, the committee of Surrey County Cricket Club. He accused them of meanness, saying, 'When we won the championship in 1952 we were each presented with a gold watch. Next year it was a silver cigarette box. Both handsome gifts. But the gifts then began to get markedly less handsome. In the years that followed they included a pen and pencil, a leather wallet containing £15 Premium Bonds, a gold-plated cuff-links and a pewter tankard. Will anyone think me grasping if I say that I think the gifts and talent and bonus money were insignificant compared with the story we had written into Surrey's cricket history? Much has been made of the fact that I ignored mention of talent and bonus money in my book. Well, as far as my memory serves me, some players received up to £75 when Surrey tied with Lancashire for the championship in 1950. In the ensuing years, when Surrey won the championship seven times in succession, the championship bonus never approached that figure.

'There were not so many cheers when Jim Laker finally left the Oval last September after playing for Surrey for thirteen years. It is not for me to tell in detail, now, of my record over these years. Sufficient to say that I am proud of it and will never cease to be so. But frankly, I was not so proud of Surrey's farewell to me. It would have been nice to have had a letter of appreciation from the Surrey president [Sir Walter Monckton]. It would have taken little effort. It would have cost no more than a stamp. I got no letter. Indeed, I heard nothing from the Oval beyond the routine things, after I packed my bag for the last time. This was not all. A week after I left, the club held a cocktail party for players and their wives. I was not invited, even though I was still technically on the books until the end of the year. But.... what does it matter? I can only offer only one clue to treatment that seemed to me more than slightly off-hand: I resigned – I didn't wait to be sacked. Presumably that put me in bad odour with Surrey. The officials of the club regard their players in a very casual way. To them the professional would seem to be very much a paid lackey who bowls when he is told to bowl, then, when the match ends, is forgotten until the next. They have little time for you off the field. Once a player has finished his active cricket they could hardly be less interested in them.'

Keith Miller was one of his best friends but Jim, now in a thoroughly sour mood, criticised him for saying, 'I had carefully and luxuriously feathered his nest after having his benefit.' He responded angrily, saying, 'The truth was that I played three more years after my benefit. And all the club allocated me in the shape of that benefit after thirteen years' service in which I helped them win seven titles, was the proceeds of one match and three collections. The gate receipts from that benefit match against Yorkshire at the Oval were £800. Surrey charged me £1,200 in expenses for the match so I lost £400. It was a bad summer and I got only two collections on Wednesday afternoons that yielded a total of £600. Look at the figure and you will see that my net gain from my benefit was no more than £200. In the end my benefit reached £11,000 – a satisfying result, I agree, until I reflect just how paltry was my own club's contribution to it. The truth of the matter was that, six weeks before I played my last game of first-class cricket, I had no job to go to.'

Before the publication he showed some proofs to Doug Insole and Insole said, 'You've come up with some pretty strong stuff.' 'What do you mean?' said Jim. 'About Tayfield being a cheat,' said Insole. He showed it to him. 'I didn't write that,' said Jim. 'He admitted that he hadn't read the proofs before the book was published,' said Insole. Later the subject of who actually wrote the words of *Over to Me* came up. Lilly thought he had written it himself. 'He was always typing away,' she said. But what happened was different. Reg Hayter, the former cricket correspondent of the Pardon's Cricket Reporting Agency and founder of Hayters, the Fleet Street sports agency, acted as an agent and advisor to a number of famous England cricketers whom he met on tours abroad. Jim was one of them and

Reg – whose long cricket reporting career was recognised by the putting up of a commemorative plaque in the media centre at Lord's, the first journalist to be honoured in that way – helped Jim to find a suitable ghost to write the words. Ron Roberts, the highly regarded freelance who covered a number of tours, was the first choice but had other engagements. Not long after Roberts died, at a tragically young age, Hayter submitted the name of Christopher Ford, a rugby and music writer who worked for *The Guardian* and later *The Times*. Ford was selected and he wrote the pungent copy that caused so much offence.

David Frost, a former rugby correspondent of *The Guardian*, was a good friend of Ford's and recalled, 'He wrote beautifully and I thought he would become the cricket correspondent at one time but they preferred John Arlott. Arlott used to write about soccer under the pseudonym "Silchester" and I often subbed his copy and I have to say it wasn't very good. Pretty awful. A good broadcaster but not a good writer.' Ford wasn't a regular cricket ghost writer, otherwise he might have been more choosey about the phrases he used in *Over to Me*. An experienced ghost would say to the subject 'Are you sure you want to see that in print? If not, we can leave that out, or soften it.' Publishers have always used lawyers to check manuscripts to avoid libel actions. But they want provocative views, not mundane ones. Frederick Muller and their staff were seemingly intent on bringing out a contentious book that they hoped would be a bestseller. The first print of 7,000 copies was sold quickly but the flak started appearing and sales dropped away. Sports readers want to read happy, uplifting life stories. They are less keen on bitchy ones. Jim, or his ghost, wrote on page 226, 'There have been moments when I have felt moved to write bitterly in this book but I would not want anyone to think that I harbour any bitterness towards the game of cricket itself. I love the game. It has brought me the life I always dreamed about as a boy. In this, I am one of the world's lucky ones.'

Jim was unlucky when Herbert Montandon 'Monty' Garland-Wells, a former public schoolboy from St Paul's and an Oxford University cricket blue who captained Surrey in 1939, learned the comments of *Over to Me*. 'Monty' became a solicitor and he noticed a paragraph concerning Bill Edrich. He thought it was libellous and told Edrich, one of his friends. In a chapter on the tour of Australia in 1958–59, Jim and his ghost were responsible for these words, 'There are two sorts of pressmen on tour: professional journalists and famous players of the recent past, sometimes even of the present. In the second class we had Johnny Wardle, Bill Edrich and Hugh Tayfield. Just how well they did the job it is for others to judge: the attraction from their viewpoint is the high fee many papers are prepared to offer so that they can print a report under the name of a well-known cricketer. What people seem to overlook is that it takes some skill to do the job well and that some cricket journalists can barely type their own name. I have already mentioned that Wardle, although he was obliged to indulge in some personal criticism, was at least at the cricket. We respected him for that. As far as possible we avoided Edrich and Tayfield, which gives you some idea of what we thought of the truth and relevance of their writings. In many ways it was odd to see two of cricket's most turbulent characters attacking one of the mildest-mannered parties of which I have ever been a member.'

On 13 June, 'Monty', who acted for Edrich, issued a statement on behalf of the publishers that said, 'Frederick Muller Ltd wish to state on behalf of themselves and Mr Laker that Mr Edrich is, in their opinion, a highly responsible and skilled cricket journalist, and that the text of *Over to Me* has been amended to remove any possibility of misunderstanding concerning the matters. The publishers and Mr Laker apologise to Mr Edrich for inconvenience and annoyance that has been caused him.' They also agreed to pay Edrich's legal costs in full settlement of the action. The offensive words were removed from the second print but the harm had been done. What Jim said was true – Edrich hadn't seen every ball of the series and he wasn't a trained cricket journalist. If a similar incident happened today a lawyer of the calibre of the late George Carman would have had a lot of fun in the High Court and the publisher would probably have won the case with the book becoming a bestseller.

Godfrey Evans and Edrich wrote books around this time and Evans pre-empted a possible reprimand from the MCC by writing to Lord's that the excerpts in *The People* did not accord with what was written in the book. He said, 'The headlines were written by the editor and did not always reflect accurately what was contained in the articles. My story was intended to benefit the game and was not written with the intention of being controversial or sensational. It is a genuine record of my career and shows a constructive attitude towards bettering the game.'

Donald Carr probably spent more time on reading cricket books than anyone in the history of English cricket. In 1962 he was appointed assistant secretary of the MCC and he was charged with the responsibility of reading and censuring manuscripts of players. He went on to become secretary of the Test and County Cricket Board until he retired in 1986. 'I took a cautious approach to it,' he said. 'If there was something contentious or objectionable, I would take it out, or change the emphasis. I didn't go for cricketers slanging each other or criticising the Establishment. Most of them kept within the proper limits but some ghost writers, and their publishers, wanted to get as much as they could.' Would he have censured Jim's book had he been in change? He declined to comment, but if it had been drastically pruned it might have saved Jim from being banned.

Viscount Monckton of Brenchley, one of the leading political and legal figures in the land, was president of Surrey County Cricket Club on two occasions, between 1950-52 and 1959-64 and he was also president of the MCC in 1956 when Jim took his 19 wickets at Old Trafford. In 1960 he was still on the committee of the MCC and, according to Sir Alec Bedser, he played a big part in taking Jim's honorary memberships away. Doug Insole, who is the only surviving member of the 1960 MCC Committee, said of Monckton, 'He was a caring, charming man.' Sir Walter Turner Monckton, KCMG, KCVO, MC, QC, was born at Flaxtol, Kent on 17 January 1891 and loved cricket. Educated at Harrow, he kept wicket against Eton at Lord's in 'Fowler's match' of 1910 and in his obituary in *The Times* in January 1965 it said, 'Cricket remained throughout his life one of his main relaxations, and he was fond of following the fortunes of Surrey at the Oval.' He went on to Balliol College, Oxford and made a name for himself with a maiden speech in the Oxford Union, before he became president. Promoted to captain in the First World War, he was awarded the Military Cross for bravery after being gassed. He completed his degree in 1918 and was called to the Bar by the Inner Temple, soon acquiring a large, lucrative and varied practice.

In 1932 he was appointed Attorney General to the Prince of Wales, later King Edward VIII, who was a friend in his Oxford days. He played an important role in the abdication of the King in 1936 and wrote his resignation speech, including the words, 'I found it impossible to carry the heavy burden of my responsibility and to discharge my duties without the help and support of the woman I love.' Monckton also wrote the abdication speech for King Farouk of Egypt. Later in life, a publisher offered him £100,000, a colossal sum, to write a book about the abdication. He turned it down. When he died in 1965, Monckton left £62,000 but there was no suggestion that he ever entertained the thought of accepting the £100,000. He attended the marriage of the Duke and Duchess of Windsor and remained their personal friend and legal adviser and his services to the State were rewarded by being knighted by King George VI. In 2000 Monckton's private papers in ten boxes about the abdication were made public but an eleventh box, including a letter from the Queen Mother describing Mrs Wallis Simpson as the 'lowest of the low' has been kept back under the hundred-year rule, not to be published until 2036.

During the Second World War Monckton was appointed Head of the Propaganda in 1941 in Cairo – Jim was serving as a soldier there at the time but there is no evidence that the two men met – and one of his jobs was to censor news. Godfrey Smith of *The Sunday Times* said of him 'how can anyone possibly be so nice and also sincere?' Promoted to Director General at the Ministry of Information, he turned up one day at his office and put up a notice on his desk saying, 'Have had throat cut this morning. As you can see, only partly successful. Not, strange to say, SI [suicidal intent] but (a) can't speak (b) can't help listening.'

He had just had his throat cauterised to help alleviate the effects of a bad gassing episode.

This small, owlish-looking, bespectacled man rose to some of the highest positions in the land. He was a Tory MP, a close friend of Harold Macmillan, presided over the commission that recast the political future of Central Africa, was Minister of Labour and resigned as Minister of Defence in 1956 over the Suez Crisis. He took over as chairman of the Midland Bank and was credited with the invention of the personal loans scheme. But he still managed to spend a considerable amount of time at the Oval and Lord's. Someone said of him, 'For all his mildness of manner, he was a strong chairman, a man not to be trifled with.'

Within days of the publication of *Over to Me* a meeting of Surrey's Cricket sub committee was held on 11 May 1960 and their members condemned the book without any reservations. Monckton was a highly principled man, a man of Corinthian beliefs, and he was deeply affronted by the contents of the book. He read it and was angry at Jim's criticism of him – branding him as discourteous for not writing to him and thanking him for his services when he retired. On 18 May the full committee, consisting of no less than thirty people, all men, were summoned but among those who offered apologies for absence were the president, Viscount Monckton, Lord Tedder of the RAF, Michael Barton, a former captain, Peter May and Stuart Surridge. Among those who were present included Errol Holmes, another former captain, Lord Ebbisham, Alf Gover, Sir Jack Hobbs, and the secretary, Commander Babb.

Item 4 concerned J.C. Laker and it said, 'Reference to Minute (2) of the Meeting of the Cricket Sub Committee on the 11th May, the Chairman reported that the matter of Laker's recent book had been reported to and considered by the President. The President had read all the contents of this book and had approved the draft of a letter to be sent to Laker. The Committee considered this draft and agreed that it should be sent by hand to Laker forthwith and a copy released to the Press as soon as it was known Laker would receive the letter before publication by the Press. A copy of this letter is enclosed with these Minutes.' It was signed by Maurice Allom, dated 22 June 1960. Allom, a former Cambridge University Blue, played as an amateur with Surrey between 1927-37 and made his name for taking 4 wickets in 5 balls, including a hat-trick, for England against New Zealand in Christchurch in 1929-30.

The letter read:

Dear Laker,

The Surrey Committee has carefully considered your recent book and in particular its attacks upon the MCC, the Surrey Club and a large number of individuals in the cricket world. The Committee particularly deplores your criticisms of many of your teammates and others at the Oval who have worked so hard to ensure the success of your benefit of over £10,000. There have been other books recently that lovers of cricket have regarded as harmful and in bad taste but in the opinion of the Committee, yours has done a greater dis-service [*sic*] to cricket than any of them. In the circumstances, I am instructed to inform you that the right of entry to the Oval given by your Pass has been withdrawn. The Committee feels that it is necessary to make its attitude quite clear to its members and the cricket public. It is therefore sending a copy of his letter to the Press.

Yours truly,

[signed]

B.O. Babb.

Secretary.

That must have been like a bullet in the heart. An hour or so later a reporter from the *Daily Express*, the newspaper Jim wrote for occasionally, called at his house and he said, 'I am very sorry that the club feel they have to do this. I thought any criticisms I did make were fair ones. If you are commissioned to write a book about a Test tour – most of my book was about the last Australian Test series – you must write not as a cricketer but as a writer. I have been blamed because I said that Tony Lock bowled badly. But I had to say this because I really believed it. But I said in the book and I have always said, that Tony is the best in the country. I shall still want to go to the Oval – taking my pass does not stop me paying my half crown at the turnstiles.'

Jim Swanton, the voice of the cricketing Establishment, said 'I have read Laker's book and have no intention of publicising it by a review. It is an ill-humoured piece of writing wherein the author is made to say something either niggling or downright unpleasant about almost everyone in the world of cricket who is mentioned. It is of a kind with various other books that have been concocted by 'ghosts' employed by an agent cashing in, for his client and for himself, on a common taste for malicious gossip. The Surrey Committee has done a service to the game and especially to the average run of self-respecting county cricketers, by taking the extreme action they have deemed necessary against one of their greatest players. How pathetic that Laker will be remembered not so much for his wonderful feats as by this tawdry episode.'

A more balanced view came from Alan Ross, the poet and writer who for worked for *The Observer* for many years. He wrote, 'I doubt whether Laker was always the easiest man to deal with, in the employer-employee situation that is how, I suppose, one has to regard his position vis-à-vis his club: great players rarely are, and Laker, even at the height of his powers, managed, perhaps unconsciously, to suggest a detachment from the proceedings little short of mutinous. Even when bowling out 19 Australians in a Test match he revealed no overt enthusiasm: his demeanour implied that the whole thing was a fearful chore. That was his way. Yet he was one of the great players of our time, a true artist whose variations in flight, trajectory, pace and spin were absorbing to watch, and unquestionably, through the seven years of England's Test supremacy and of Surrey's reign as champions, he will be a key figure. In addition, he is a man of superior intelligence, of prescience, personality and interdependence. Somehow, as so often before with professional cricketers, it all ended in bitterness. Why? The answer lies, I think, in the curiously obsolescent fashion in which professionals, despite many tangible advantages, are still treated. They are not, as should be in the case with a person of Laker's eminence, regarded as part of the upper hierarchy but simply as one of the paid staff for whom, rather as with an NCO, too much knowledge is deemed to be a bad thing. This lack of esteem and confidence develops both ways and it leads to a personal indifference that sometimes borders on the incredible. It is, for example, hard to credit that Laker, when he left the Oval in 1959, received no letter of appreciation from his club, was not invited to the end-of-season cocktail party, nor in any way made to feel that his services had been unusual – and this, apparently, because he had preferred to resign rather than be sacked.

'Unfortunately, Laker damages his case by the uncharitableness of his own comments on fellow players. He quotes Oscar Wilde's "the truth is rarely pure and never simple" to justify a string of personal disparagements sometimes barely short of libel. Towards the end of the book he makes fascinating observations on contemporary players, wickets, tactics, Press relations and most aspects of bowling, including throwing. It makes one wish that professional cricketers would get themselves better literary advisers, with more of an eye on their client's reputation and less of a one on sensation and short-term financial success. Because a cricketer of Laker's qualities has a valid case; he can bring into the open many anomalies, reveal much that should be changed. But a sustained note of professional grousing – however naturally it may come – is an unattractive one.'

Michael Barton, the only survivor on Surrey's 1960 committee, felt it was all unnecessary. 'A lot of people were very upset about it and if he had apologised from the start things might have been different,' he said. Someone who should have protected Jim was his longstanding agent Bagenal Harvey, the pioneer of sports agents. Born in Dublin, the short, stubby publisher – he wore similar glasses and braces to Monckton's – became an agent in 1948 when he met Denis Compton. Noticing a pile of unopened letters in the back of Compton's car, he said, 'What's that?' Compton said, 'Since all this has happened I get hundreds of letters and I can't handle it.' Harvey volunteered to deal with his mail and many of the letters contained offers from companies, including one from Brylcreem. Harvey negotiated a number of deals for Compton and his cut came from a ten per cent deduction from the takings. He was variously known as 'Mister X',

'Mr Ten Percent' and less complimentary names. Soon Harvey signed up most of the biggest names in British sport and in 1961 he acted for Jimmy Hill and the Professional Footballers' Association in the breaking of the wages limit in the Football League. Jim Laker was one of his clients when the Cavaliers, the Sunday cricket celebrity team, was shown on television. In 1969, Harvey won damages from the FA when they claimed he 'had made harmful inroads' into football.

As a friend, Harvey should have given Jim some good advice over the controversial book. But Jim ploughed on into the storm. On 22 May the *Empire News* published another huge article written by their cricket correspondent Bill Bailey in conjunction with Jim, saying, 'Well, let me say this right now: I am completely unrepentant. I do not regret one word I have written. It is not for me to condemn Surrey for the action they have taken. My regret is that the club should have taken such action without asking for a response from me. Even a man on trial for his life is entitled to a hearing.' He claimed that two members of the committee hadn't read the book, only the Press reviews and some members of the club told him they were going to resign from the club. 'I even had a phone call from a Surrey player, who must obviously remain anonymous, asking if he could leave a ticket at the gate for me.' he said.

Four days later the MCC Committee were summoned to a meeting at Lord's and they included Lord Monckton, Gubby Allen, Errol Holmes, the Duke of Norfolk, Freddie Brown, Charles Palmer, Marshal of the RAF Viscount Portal of Hungerford, Maurice Allom, Brian Sellers and Doug Insole. Minute 12 was headed 'J.C. Laker's Book *Over to Me.* The question of J.C. Laker's book and whether, because of the disservice that the contents of this book and the manner in which it was written might be thought to have done to cricket, his Honorary Life Membership of the MCC should be withdrawn was considered. Letters were received from [a name is blacked out because the person is still living] and C.F. Palmer expressing their views were read [both letters were thought to be sympathetic towards Jim and pleaded for clemency].

'Mr M.J.C. Allom reported that there were a number of inaccuracies in the book, many of which related to the staff and officials of the Surrey County Cricket Club. Mr G.O. Allen suggested that rather than withdraw Laker's Honorary Cricket Membership of the Club, the Committee might prefer to issue a Press statement containing a major rebuke to all cricketers who wrote books or articles of a sensational character, criticising their own Committees and fellow players, and pointing out that such writings could result in the withdrawal of Honorary Cricket Membership of the MCC. [In 1960 there were 7,562 full members and 3,003 associate members and 63 people, all men, were made Honorary Life Members.]

'Sir Hubert Ashton, while having the greatest respect for the handling of the situation and the action taken by the Surrey County Cricket Club in withdrawing Laker's pass to the Oval, subscribed to Mr Allen's proposal. In answer to a suggestion that to withdraw Laker's Honorary Cricket Membership of the MCC might create complications concerning other cricketers who had written in a sensational manner, or might do so in the immediate future, the Duke of Norfolk considered that the Committee should deal with each case on its merits as and when it occurred.

'F.G. Mann took the view that Honorary Cricket Membership was a reward for past services and therefore not removable. He did, however, consider that in future it would be advisable to wait, say two years after retirement, before electing Honorary Cricket Members to the Club.' The minutes were signed 'H.S. Altham, President, 14-6-60.' The tone of the meeting was conciliatory and, unlike the Surrey Committee, they wanted a peaceful conclusion. The next day the secretary wrote to Jim requesting him to attend a meeting at Lord's. Nothing was minuted but it appeared to be an initiative from Gubby Allen, who, although considered as a hard individual, was really a compassionate man who understood cricket people more than most. After a lot of hard thinking, Jim decided not to attend but wrote a long letter instead.

That was a mistake. On 14 June, the Committee met again and Minute 8 said, 'After careful consideration of the whole matter a resolution "that the Honorary Membership of the Club conferred on Mr J.C. Laker by the Club on the 13th day of January, 1960, should be terminated forthwith under the provisions of Rule XII (d) was carried nem con and the Secretary was instructed to notify Mr Laker of the decision of the Committee and also to issue a short Press notice on the subject.'" It was noticeable that the MCC, always reckoned to be the more reactionary than Surrey, addressed Jim as 'Mr J.C. Laker' whereas Surrey called him 'Laker'. There was no appeal.

Ray Illingworth, the former England, Yorkshire and Leicestershire captain, said many years later, 'That ban wouldn't have stuck today. The lawyers would have sorted that out.' And most players would agree. Jim was a man ahead of his time. Jim Cumbes, the Lancashire chief executive who played for Lancashire, Surrey, Worcestershire and Warwickshire and played in goal for Tranmere, WBA, Aston Villa and Worcester City, first met him at the Oval in 1962. Now on the other side as an administrator, he felt sympathy for Jim over his indiscretions in *Over to Me*. 'I'm not sure when they introduced a vetting process on books but someone should have looked at Jim's book,' he said. 'It would have saved him a lot of problems. Today it wouldn't have led to being banned. The lawyers would have ensured that.'

Gordon Ross, writing the June edition of *Playfair Cricket Monthly* described Laker's exile from the game as 'a tragedy'. The scorer Roy Webber, reviewing the books of 1960 in the following year's, wrote, 'Laker's book seemed to be the reply he felt unable to make when he was criticised for declining the invitation to tour with the 1958-59 tour to Australia. There is little doubt that it accurately records his ideas and feelings about the latter part of his first-class career. Yet, for a book that aroused so much feeling, it is strikingly lacking in fire [*sic*]. Rather, the reader's reaction is one of sadness that a player who, with his 19 for 90 at Old Trafford, set up the most remarkable bowling record in cricket, who gained virtually all the honours in the game and a hearty benefit to boot, should have found – on this showing – so little happiness in it all. We may suspect that Laker himself, as well as many others, including his friends, wish it had never been written.'

Godfrey Evans's book *The Gloves Are Off* came out at the same time and Webber called it 'never malicious, and was friendly and conversational' but he described Alan Oakman as 'not up to Test standard'. Insole's book, called *Cricket from the Middle*, was published around the same time and *Wisden* called it 'a gem, genuinely funny, yet full of wisdom, surely an anthology piece'. Insole wrote every word himself, that was the difference.

Jim's friends tried to persuade him to apologise and, realising that there was no alternative, he wrote an introduction to his next book, uncontroversially entitled *The Australian Tour of 1961*, saying 'There can be little doubt that the arrival of this book so closely on my last effort will cause a certain amount of eyebrow-raising in many quarters. I have given a great deal of thought to the writing of cricket books and in particular as to why they are written by prominent cricketers and what purpose is served by them. Since the War almost every Test player has been credited with at least one edition on the bookstalls and in great many cases it is extremely questionable what his personal contribution has been towards the book. It is fair to say however great his ambition may be in a journalistic sense, the task of putting together 60-70,000 words, which altogether satisfies a publisher's requirements, is for many cricketers a well-nigh impossible job. It is now that we see the entry of the ghost writer and the hazards that go with it. Without a doubt there is a great art in ghost writing for it means a good deal more than purely to be able to write a cricketer's story: to be successful it must be able to transcribe the thoughts and write exactly as the player would do if he had the time and inclination.

'All this brings me to the great mistake I personally made in *Over to Me*. This book was started with all the goodwill in the world to be written by my own hand, but lacking the time and diligence of a Trevor Bailey, I had before long to summon outside help. At the same time I did spend many long hours in consultation with my ghost but made the cardinal error, due to pressure of time, of not correcting the final proofs and the damage was too late to be repaired. The blame for this must remain purely on my own head. Indeed, I hope I have taken my punishment without attempting to "pass the buck". It is my belief that this had been due to a temperament that did not conform to present-day ideas. Apparently I could walk off a cricket field with 19 wickets to my name without showing a trace of emotion. Up goes the cry then of no interest and a label of a "couldn't-care-less attitude". I could have written a book in full praise of cricket and all the people who go with it but this would have been hypocrisy on my part. Certain people alleged that I had been associated with a sensational book simply to make a lot of money. Any cricketer would be foolish to believe that there is a fortune to be made writing books – the total proceeds from an average cricket book would hardly equal the money received for playing in a Test series. When I realised that the imputation was being widely accepted, I at once wrote to the MCC saying that if they honestly believed this to be the reason I would gladly hand over to them every penny received from the publishers for the furtherance of cricket in any part of the world.'

The sum Jim received from the publisher, less the fee paid to Christopher Ford, was no more than £500 and he claimed that he received a letter from the MCC ignoring the offer and reiterating that his honorary life membership ban still carried on. He admitted that the decision from Lord's was the greater blow 'because I have thoroughly enjoyed my visits to headquarters, both as a player and spectator, and I have received nothing but courtesy and a warm welcome'. This long, rambling apology failed to change the minds of those who imposed the bans and he had to serve four penitent years before the first ban, by Surrey, was lifted. His business interests kept him reasonably busy but he still hankered after playing in the middle. He played in charitable matches for the Lord's Taverners and Sparks, and started to put a lot back into the game.

Laurie Fishlock, his former Surrey colleague, invited him to play for The Forty Club – a worldwide club of 3,500 members aged forty or more who mainly play against schools 'to hand on their expertise' – and he played three matches for them in the early 1960s, taking 6 for 50 in 18 overs at the extremely small ground next to St Dunstan's School, Catford. The previous year Peter May played in the same fixture, scoring an unbeaten 50. But the two men didn't appear together. The feud between them still lingered on. Ninety-five Test players have played for The Forty Club since it was founded in 1936 but in the past ten years the number has dropped to a trickle. Not many modern Test players continue playing after forty which is sad because they could help young cricketers at a crucial time in their lives. Unlike Jim, they earned comparatively high salaries and they have time to spare. As Ken Barrington once said, 'You don't want to be shown up by youngsters half your age!' Barrington, one of Jim's best friends, had his tonsils out in 1962 and he was dropped by England for slow scoring. He joked, 'I am looking forward to satisfying the selectors' edict for attacking cricket. In future I will forget about averages and be known as the Gay Cavalier of the Oval.'

At the start of the 1964 season, after Jim had three seasons Essex as an amateur, the MCC proffered its first olive branch to him. The Lord's Taverners invited him to play against the Old England XI at Lord's on 13 June and Donald Carr recalled, 'I pointed out that there has never been a ban on him playing at Lord's. He could have played for Essex against Middlesex at Lord's but it didn't happen.' Up to then, Jim declined to play for Essex, either at Lord's or the Oval. 'It would be too embarrassing,' he said. 'If I played at the Oval as an amateur I would have had to change upstairs with the amateurs and it might be awkward for Peter May if I had to share a room with him.' Jim took 4 wickets at Lord's in front of a sparse crowd, and his victims included Carr, Insole and Eric Bedser.

Talks behind the scenes at the Oval led to Surrey lifting his Oval ban in the same month. Jim wrote a letter of apology and the committee accepted it. A statement said, 'In view of the letter received by the President [Lord Monckton] from Mr J.C. Laker [a more polite way to address him] in which he has apologised and expressed his regrets for the matter that led to Surrey CCC withdrawing his privileges in May 1960, the committee are glad to announce that these privileges have now been restored to him.' He was soon back, giving advice to the younger players and he eventually joined the General Committee in 1979 and was chairman of the Cricket Committee from 1982 to the time he died in 1986. By then, he had contributed so much that those who were still there totally forgave him for his ill-advised green book *Over to Me*.

It was almost three years before the MCC relented. His honorary life membership was restored and he said, 'I feel that I've been released from a seven-year sentence. I still regard it as the greatest honour in cricket. I was proud to be given the MCC red-and-yellow tie and I only received it a month before the ban was imposed. I kept it in my wardrobe, hoping that one day I would have the right to sport it again.' Like a number of Test players, he spent a lot of time socialising at The Cricketers' Club off Baker Street and that night he turned up to buy a round for his colleagues. Godfrey Evans was there and he said, 'Once Jim had ripped the chips off his shoulders, everybody wanted to talk to him and shake him by the hand. It was a great tribute to a thoroughly nice man.'

THREE

HIS FIRST TEN

Only one off-spin bowler has taken 10 wickets in an innings on two occasions in first-class cricket – Jim Laker in 1956. He might have planned it because it was his benefit year but that is most unlikely because luck went with him both times. Before his 10 for 53 in the epic Old Trafford Test he staged a trailer, taking 10 for 88 against Ian Johnson's Australians. His success gave him a tremendous psychological advantage over the tourists and it lasted throughout the summer. Seventy-seven cricketers have taken 10 wickets in an innings and one of Jim's mentors, Hedley Verity, achieved the best figures, 10 for 10 against Nottinghamshire at Headingley in 1932.

There were several oddities about Jim's 10 for 88 performance on a sweltering hot day on 16 May at the Oval. Fiona, his three-year-old daughter, was ill in the night and her father was up most of the time looking after her. On arrival at the ground he said to Stuart Surridge, 'I don't think I can play.' Surridge, a very persuasive skipper, soon talked him into donning his gear. When Jim took his first 4 wickets, on a perfectly good batting pitch, he asked him if he could come off. It wasn't unusual – Jim often wanted to come off when nothing was happening. 'No Jim,' he said, 'there are more wickets for you in this innings.'

So he carried on, without calling for a drink. There was only one drinks interval per session in those days. He took half his wickets with straight deliveries and he rated his 10 for 88 a far better performance than his 10 for 63 just over two months later. 'The all-ten in Old Trafford was reckoned to be the peak of my career,' he said, 'but from a technical point of view, the earlier one was better. The Oval pitches were good and the ball only turned a little, and not consistently. And although it turned more at one end than the other – and I was fortunate enough to be bowling towards the right end – it was never as difficult as was generally accepted at the time. The five victims dismissed by straight balls were all bamboozled. It wasn't a sticky dog. And Tony Lock bowled more than 30 overs from the other end and took 0 for 100 from 32 in the first innings.'

Lock supported the theory that luck played a part. 'The Aussies were licked by their own deficiencies,' he said. 'And to do it twice was amazing. Twice during 1956 I had the remarkable experience of bowling practically right through an Australian innings without taking a wicket while Jim copped the lot. My combined figures were 88 overs, 42 maidens, 199 runs, no wickets. I wasn't complaining about it. I merely mention the fact in support of my contention that the Aussies largely had themselves to blame for their collapses. Sure, the rub of the green went against them. Nevertheless, I contend that I am a good enough bowler to take a couple of wickets in 88 overs if the pitches were as "impossible" as some people claimed.'

Micky Stewart made his debut two years earlier and has fond memories of Jim. 'I was ten years younger and he was very helpful to me and also Kenny Barrington,' he said. 'But he wasn't everyone's cup of tea. He was very conscious of the fact that the amateurs had their own quarters while the rest of us were down below. It was a circus really, with these ex-Oxford and Cambridge people ordering us around. He didn't enjoy that. He talked to me in a very professional way. For example if you got out he'd say, "You've got to get the runs in the book to win an England cap. Make sure you stay there and get the runs. Build an innings!" Kenny Barrington had problems being bowled through the gate and he spent a lot of time showing him how to stretch his left foot in the right place. He even got friendly with my parents.'

The Oval was a depressing place at the time and with Surrey side running through the other teams the Brown Hats weren't liked. They had a similar approach to the Yorkshire side; hard-bitten, hard competitors who rarely offered any encouragement to younger players. Things hardly changed when Jim took over as chairman of the cricket committee in the mid-1980s. Martin Bicknell, whose benefit year is taking place this summer, recalled in an interview in *Direct Hit* about what it was like in 1985 'There were two dressing rooms, one for the senior players and one for us. Right down in the bowels of the pavilion as well. And I only really knew Micky Stewart and Keith Medlycott. I was chuffed to bits to be on the staff but to be honest the atmosphere was pretty awful. A real Us and Them thing going on – the seniors ran the show, no questions asked. It was only when Dave Gilbert [the Australian coach, now with New South Wales] managed us in the mid-1990s that the divisions stopped and younger players were given the chance to air their views, and to feel part of the team. I think a lot of counties followed on from that, often under the influence of a foreign coach as the mass of serving old pros in the game started to be pushed sideways or out. Now teams are much more at ease with each other and it was much better, so much more democratic.' The building of the £25 million OCS Stand in 2005 with its Living Garden at the rear costing £1 million means the whole ambiance of the ground has changed dramatically. Unlike Wembley Stadium it was completed on time and The Brit Oval is now one of the outstanding cricketing stadiums in the world.

Jim, of course, was one of the first bolshie characters who resented the class distinction in the ranks, which was one of the reasons why he had a reputation of being something of a moaner. He may well have brought in the changes himself but he died early, before he established himself in office. This downbeat side of things was reflected in how the journalists were treated. When Jim was in his heyday, the Press Box on the right of the pavilion was known as 'The Black Hole of Kennington' to some younger, cheeky members. The small room had two rows of sixteen people in each, all crammed in and a black canopy kept out the light and the view of the ball when it was hit high into the air. Some of the older journalists spent most of their time complaining and making cynical remarks about various players. And it must have affected the writings of the journalists.

The Oval was well filled with more than 15,000 spectators on 16 May 1956, when Surridge walked to the middle with Ian Johnson, the thirty-eight-year-old Australian captain who was playing in his final season. Surridge threw the coin up and when it landed on the ground he pointed to Johnson. The cheery Australian laughed, 'You can have last use of that one!' He meant that he felt the ball would turn on the third and final day, suiting his off-spin bowling. With Alec Bedser down with gastritis, the all-rounder Dennis Cox was included and the lively Peter Loader, the tall, fair-haired fast bowler with the high-stepping action, opened the bowling with Surridge. The ball rarely swung and the general view was that Surridge kept his opening bowlers on too long. Jim Burke, the stodgy NSW opener who always had his cap pulled down over one eye, nurdled a few runs with Colin McDonald, the pugnacious right hander who punched anything short to the long boundaries.

At twenty minutes past twelve, with Australia approaching fifty, Surridge took himself off and asked Jim to bowl. Jim bowled economically for forty minutes without looking like taking a wicket and decided to switch to bowl round the wicket. With 62 runs on the wooden scoreboard, Burke was lbw for 28, after missing an attempted sweep. Burke was an occasional off-spinner, not in the class of any of the England bowlers, and Ian Peebles, the former England leg-spinner and writer, said of his action, 'It was like a policeman applying his truncheon to a particularly short offender's head.' During the 1958 chucking series, while Peter May was scoring a brilliant hundred in Sydney, a barracker shouted from The Hill, 'Put Burke on – he can throw straight!' The obdurate Burke had a sad end to his life. After having financial problems and worrying about an imminent hip operation, he shot himself at the age of forty-nine.

Ken 'Slasher' Mackay, similar in style to Burke, came in and immediately gave Laker and Lock confidence with his ungainly attempts to put bat to ball. The gum-chewing Mackay once scored 364 not out and took 10 wickets in a school game in Brisbane and was hailed as a coming superstar. He never quite made it but he was a much-liked and courageous opponent. The England players called him 'Slasher' because he was more of a stonewaller than a hitter. The Surrey CCC account said, 'Mackay pushed deliberately forward for fifty minutes like a boxer jabbing at a punch bag. Four singles he acquired and nothing seemed more probable than that sooner or later Laker would find the edge of his bat. Sure enough he did so with the total at 124 and by then the crowd was dozing off in the afternoon sun, with Mackay as the sedative.'

Jim's description of his dismissal of Harvey – who never wore a cap whatever the temperature – was a brilliant piece of professionalism. 'I always fancied that Neil might be trapped early in his innings, forcing me wide of mid on,' he said. 'He hits against the spin, hoping to find the wide open space there, but sometimes he is apt to miscalculate the strike. Accordingly, I put a fielder at short mid wicket, about three or four yards deeper than the normal forward short leg would be. Neil had reached thirteen when he turned me to leg. He didn't get on top of his shot and instead he sent a catch straight to my posted fielder Bernie Constable.' McDonald was on 89 after 3 hours and 35 minutes and Jim said, 'He was apt to commit himself to his stroke a little early and when I tried him with my "straighty" he prodded out as though he expected the ball to turn into the bat. It didn't, it nicked the outside edge and young Roy Swetman took the chance at the wicket.' The official version was that Swetman, who resembled a jockey in size and still wears his England blazer on occasions, held it on the third attempt.

'I don't know about that,' he said. He is only one of the three survivors in the Surrey side in that historic game. The others are David Fletcher, who lives in Gunnislake, and Loader, who lives in Perth. 'I didn't really get to know Jim,' said Swetman. 'He was a very fine bowler but he was a funny bloke, not a mixer. He was a typical Yorkshireman. I respected and liked only four Yorkshiremen in cricket – Billy Sutcliffe, Willie Watson, Phil Sharpe and Mike Smedley. Jim never went for drink after close of play. He would drive home. In October we used to go to Christchurch for a few days of golf and it was a very enjoyable bunfight but he never went. Although he did mellow later in life.

'He didn't say a lot on the field. We had six batsmen, four bowlers and a wicketkeeper and everyone was a specialist. And we got on with it. When Lock and Laker were bowling together we often bowled more than twenty overs an hour and when we played against Gloucestershire, who had three spinners including "Bomber" Wells and Cec Cook, they bowled more overs an hour than that and our bats were red hot. I get annoyed today when players gather round for a chat after every over. Stuart Surridge wouldn't tolerate that.'

Keith Miller, the number five batsmen, used his reach to counter Jim's turn and Jim was tiring rapidly in the heat after bowling 40 overs on the trot. Wicketkeeper Len Maddocks, the number six, had a reputation of scoring most of his runs from cover drives and just as he was playing himself in, reaching a patient 12, Jim gave an extra tweak and the ball went through the gate to bowl him. Surridge was thinking of taking the new ball but the wicket of Maddocks convinced him to retain Jim's services. Jim's spirits rose as he went in for tea. He had a cigarette and a cup of tea.

The 1956 touring side were light on batsmen of quality and Ray Lindwall, seven in the order, was bowled for a duck in the same way. Ian Johnson was the next to go, caught by Swetman off a straight delivery for 0. 'He could drift the ball away as well,' said Micky Stewart. 'He didn't like the quicker bowlers lifting the seam because it did damage to his bowling finger. Peter Loader was about the only one who went in for it in the Surrey team.'

When he was younger, Jim always carried a cricket ball, flexing his fingers around it. He said, 'I haven't got a particularly big hand so I had to hold the ball securely and had to practise and practise by stretching my fingers. I used the orthodox grip for the off-break as recommended in the MCC coaching manual but the position of the ball was different. I held the ball across the seam and believed I could spin it more sharply that way though my method was very hard on the fingers. The manual method is to hold the ball with the seam practically vertical alongside the index finger. Coaches advocated spin first and then accuracy but later that changed. As a result we are breeding a race of accurate bowlers who never mastered the art of spin. They became defensive bowlers.' That mistake was made for many years, until more innovative coaches, like Australia's Terry Jenner, insisted that spin should be paramount.

Trevor Bailey reckoned Jim was one of the first spin bowlers who always experimented with the angle of delivery, either from round or over the wicket. 'He used the width of the crease on either side,' he said. Jim used mental exercises before bowling each delivery. 'I didn't believe in being mechanical,' he said. 'I tried to discipline myself into putting thought into every ball I bowled. When I walked back to my mark I would say "I'll try a quicker one, well up to him" or "I'll give him a flighty one, held back a bit"'and so on. You have to conserve energy and be patient. It is no good spinning your fingers off with every ball. One way to attack is to roll up a few balls without genuinely spinning, then flick one through which will bite and trap the unsuspecting batsman.' He did that perfectly against the Australians at the Oval.

He had good advice for spinners who went on the defensive when the conditions didn't suit them. 'Attack is the best form of defence,' he said. 'You have to keep bowling two or three times an over to spin the ball, not just bowl straight. In my time I literally spun my finger to the bone and that's why Tony Lock and I sometimes spun the ball and made it turn at the Oval when others couldn't. They used to talk about the pitch breaking up — that's rubbish. Often other bowlers never tried to give the ball a real tweak. My right index finger was much longer than the one of my other hand and it was subject to arthritis, particularly in the cold weather. That year [1956] we started using ultrasonic ray treatment introduced from the Continent and it improved the finger temporarily. But the only way for me to ensure maximum movement in the finger was to keep bowling. The more you bowl, the finger became more torn and sore. I came to expect that at least three times a season.' When his skipper asked him to bowl wide of the off stump to slow the scoring rate he would politely disagree and carry on: 'If I did that, I would lose control or bowl too wide.'

As it was early May, it was unlikely he was having trouble with his fingers, especially as it was an exceptionally hot day. Seven wickets were down with the bulk of the third session still remaining. The spectators were rousing themselves. There was polite applause when the wickets fell, and also at the end of each over. They clapped the runs of the Australian batsmen, too. They were supporting their own side but the tradition prevailed that they were supporting the game of cricket as well. The arrival of limited-overs cricket early in the 1960s brought a significant change and a new breed of supporters were noisier, more demonstrative and they were fans of one side, not both.

Alan Davidson, nine in the order, was a better batsman than Maddocks, Lindwall and Johnson and he averaged 32 in first-class cricket. He decided to hit out and took two towering sixes off Jim over long on. After reaching 21 in a quarter of an hour, he was caught at second slip by Peter May. Two to go. Pat Crawford, the tall fast bowler, hit Jim for six and, going for another, nicked the ball onto the stumps – bowled for 16. Being hit for three sixes in a short space of time was a rare sight for Jim but according to Micky Stewart, there were four batsmen who regularly hit his bowling. 'I'd put Bill Edrich top of the list,' he said. 'Bill always thought Jim wasn't the bravest when someone got after him. Next to him was Ken Grieves, the Australian who played for Lancashire around that time. Ken was the best sweeper of the time and he always put his front leg outside the line of the off stump, making it impossible to be given out lbw. Another one was Arnold Hamer, who played for Yorkshire and Derbyshire. Not many people heard of him but he always got stuck into our bowling and he was a tremendously powerful striker of the ball. Finally I'd include Denis Compton. He knew how to handle Jim, particularly with his sweep. But there weren't many.'

Nine men out, all dismissed by Jim. The last man was Jackie 'Chucker' Wilson, a slow left-arm spin bowler averaging 5.74 with the bat and out for a duck in his only innings of the tour. Miller was past his fifty, farming the bowling to protect the last man, and he started hitting out against the bowling of Lock. He skied a high ball into the covers and Jim thought it might have been his catch. It would have caused a problem – what would happen if he dropped it? 'It sailed over my head, thankfully,' he said in *Spinning Around the World*. 'It went to Dennis Cox's territory at extra cover and he got under the ball well enough but grassed it. To this day, I cannot figure out whether he did it on purpose.'

Like at Old Trafford, Lock was losing his temper and Surridge shouted at him, 'Bowl tighter, for goodness' sake, Tony.' Lock recalled in his first book *For Surrey and England*, 'The skipper and I were still exchanging some heated words in the leg trap when the next over was due to be bowled. Keith promptly withdrew from the wicket and he looked at us like a headmaster and, in heavy tones, he said, "Really, if you two don't stop needling each other, I'll have to report you to the umpire!" Coming from Miller that was rich. But we were not sure whether he was serious or not, so we signed the peace treaty.' Wilson managed to survive for almost half an hour and Miller said to Laker, 'Well, you won't get all ten!' Jim said, 'Once before Keith had denied me a breakthrough when at Leeds in 1948, keeping the strike so that I couldn't get at Neil Harvey in his debut series.'

But with the total on 259, Jim bowled another straight one and Wilson edged a simple catch to Swetman. He bowled 46 overs from the pavilion end, interrupted only by lunch and tea and his 10 for 88 was the first time a Surrey bowler took all ten against the Australians since 1878 when Edward D'Oyley Barratt, a slow left-arm bowler from Stockton-on-Tees took 10 for 43 in 29 overs. Barratt, who qualified to play for Surrey by residence and died at Kennington at the age of forty-seven, was presented with a cheque for £5. The Surrey committee gave Jim much more for his ten – £50 and the match ball. There were no raucous celebrations when the 1956 match ended and only one or two Surrey players shook Jim's hand as they walked off. Miller was left on 59, Lock's figures were 0 for 100 and Surrey's openers Fletcher and Tom Clark put on 34 without loss in the final half-hour. Crawford only bowled 1 over and Johnson took the new ball, rubbed it into the ground and bowled the last 3 overs himself. Johnson replaced Lindwall with Davison, bowling in his slower style.

Bill O'Reilly, one of Australia's greatest slow-medium spin bowlers, then working as a journalist, coined some apt phrases about Jim's performance. He said, 'He smothered the Australian batsmen with his science. His perfectly pitched off-spinners took just enough turn to encourage doubt and flat-footed loitering. This was the day when the thoroughbred came thundering out of the ruck.' Johnson, Australia's spinning thoroughbred, wasn't up to the class of the Surrey champion and he made a mistake copying Jim's very long spell. Bowling slower, and giving the ball more air, he bowled for five-and-a-quarter hours with only one short break of twenty-five minutes. The official Surrey report said, 'Generally he was comfortably played for he hardly turned a ball.' He allowed Lindwall to bowl just 2 overs and Crawford 1 and he bowled 60.3 overs with a return of 6 for 168. Miller had a bad back and wasn't fit to bowl. Davidson bowled 44 overs and took 3 for 101. Constable, notoriously suspect against genuine pace, benefited from the slower bowling and scored 109 in Surrey's first-innings 347. Jim revelled in a seventh-wicket stand with him, taking a rapid and rustic 43 off Johnson, Davidson and the under-used Wilson. Jim Swanton reported, 'A greater contrast in styles could not be imagined. There was Constable, sweeping, gliding and stepping away to cut, while Laker drove at almost everything, long hops included, with that grandiloquent backlift and flourish of the follow through.'

Facing a deficit of 88, the Australian openers put on 56 before an animated Lock proceeded to take the first 6 wickets, raising expectations of an all ten to set alongside the one achieved by his great rival. 'I was suffering from reaction,' admitted Jim. Surridge changed the bowlers over, giving Lock the best end, and Jim made no objection. Burke was out for 20, caught and bowled by Lock and McDonald fell for a Laker catch in the gully for 45. In a spell of 23.1 overs, costing 36 runs, Lock captured 7 for 49 as the Australians collapsed to 107. Jim slipped in to finish his colleague's hopes of a full house, trapping Mackay lbw for 4. 'As soon as Lock began to bowl straighter and to a fuller length, he had the Australians in continual distress,' wrote Swanton. Denys Rowbotham, *The Guardian's* poetical cricket correspondent, caught the mood, writing, 'Lock's blood was up as soon as he saw the first ball rear angrily at Burke. Thereafter all the colour drained from the Australians' cheeks. They wore the haggard look of a cornered foe.' On the third day Surrey needed 20 to win and they achieved it in 15 overs against the hitherto-ignored Lindwall and Crawford. It was Surrey's first victory over the Australians for forty-four years.

Jim's performance ensured his Test place in the First Test at Trent Bridge and he took 6 cheap wickets to Lock's 4 in a drawn game that England would have won but for rain. He had praise for Burke, who batted 4 hours for his unbeaten 58 before he dismissed him with a catch taken by Lock behind square. It was Burke's twenty-sixth birthday and there were joyous celebrations back in the hotel. 'Both sides socialised throughout the series,' said Johnson. 'It was one of the friendliest series for a long time.'

The selectors preferred Johnny Wardle to Lock for the Second Test at Lord's and Lock was mortified, so much so that he went down with severe stomach pains and finished up at St Mary's Hospital. Watching from his television, Lock observed, 'Our batting let us down.' Half of them failed to reach double figures as thirty-six-year-old Miller, restored to fitness, bowled 70 overs for his 10 for 152. Umpire Frank Lee said, 'It was one of the finest fast bowling performances ever.' 'Their bowlers moved the ball more than ours and they won on merit,' said Jim, who took 3 wickets in a low scoring game. Benaud, coming in at seven, played his finest Test innings to score 97.

Jim thought the pitch at Headingley on the eve of the Third Test was 'a normal Headingley pitch, with a bit of grass on it'. But Lock had a different view. 'It's dry and dusty,' he said. He was right. A new groundsman had taken over and he had different instructions. Johnson later described the Leeds pitch as 'worse than the one on which Jim Laker took 19 for 90'. Peter May won the toss – he won four out of five in that series – and Gubby Allen's insistence on recalling the forty-three-year-old Cyril Washbrook, one of the selectors, proved correct as the stocky Lancastrian sweated and grunted to 98. May's classy 101 bolstered the innings up to 325 and the Australians were in trouble. They were bowled out for 143 and 140, losing by an innings and 42 runs. 'The ball did all sorts of things,' said Johnson. One delivery from Jim rolled along the ground to bowl Burke. Known as 'Pinocchio' because of his looks, Burke just about summoned a rueful smile. Miller, unable to bowl again after his knee swelled following his exertions at Lord's, played two courageous, long innings in the gathering gloom. On the last day Jim bowled a lifter and the ball struck him on the glove, and bounced towards Trueman in the leg trap. Trueman was going the wrong way but turned and dived to take a Lock-like catch. 'That was one of the best I've ever seen,' said Jim. May had seven, sometimes eight, fielders close in and the catching of the England team that year was stupendous, better than the catching of the 2005 Ashes winners. Jim's match analysis was 11 for 113 and Lock's 7 for 81. Jim led the team in to somewhat muted applause from a home crowd 'welcoming' back one of their own, a man who preferred to play for the enemy,

Surrey's despised Brown Hats. Before the start of play a Yorkshireman entrepreneur named William Harrison told him, 'If you take 3 wickets before lunch I'll give you £50.' Jim knew he was on a cert and the cheque was handed over with a congratulatory shake of the hand.

The year 1956 was still in the decade of Brylcreem – it started when Denis Compton was given a contract to advertise their product in 1947 – and that season the company put up a silver cup and £100 for the best bowling performance of the season. Jim's 10 for 88 was an early pacemaker until another Yorkshireman, Ken Smales, who later became secretary of Nottingham Forest Football Club, took over the baton with 10 for 66 for Nottinghamshire against Gloucestershire at Stroud. On 10 July, in the championship match at Blackheath two days before the start of the Third Test at Leeds, Lock lowered the bar by taking 10 for 54 against Kent. Lock was 12 runs ahead of Smales in the list and was favourite to win the prizes. Jim had rested his finger in the Blackheath game, which was played on a pitch that yielded turn and venomous lift, enabling Lock to finish with an aggregate of 16 for 83. Three weeks later Jim beat and totally frustrated Lock by a head with his record-breaking analysis of 51.2-23-53-10. There was just 1 run, twenty-two yards, between them. It typified Lock's cricket life – second best to J.C. Laker.

Before his great 10-wicket hauls against the Australians, Jim had enjoyed another phenomenal day six years previously. It was called 'the slaughter of the innocents' and even Jim was embarrassed by it. At the start of the 1950 season he was selected for an England side to take on The Rest at the Park Avenue ground in Bradford, only a few miles from his birthplace at Frizinghall. He was on trial as much as the Varsity students who were called up for The Rest XI after four up-and-down appearances in the England side. Against Don Bradman's world champions in 1948, he started reasonably well at Trent Bridge, top scoring with 63 and dismissing Sid Barnes, Arthur Morris and Keith Miller. But at Lord's he took only two wickets for 128 and at Headingley he had an awful Test as the Australians stormed to 404 for 3 to win, conceding 206 runs in the match. The next summer he was selected for only one Test and performed moderately in the drawn game against the New Zealanders. He was also left out of the tour to South Africa.

With a possible tour to Australia with the MCC in 1950-51 looming he needed some good performances. On 31 May 1950, he recorded the fourth-best bowling return in *Wisden's* category of 'Outstanding Bowling Analyses' of 14-12-2-8 and if he hadn't given a run to get Eric Bedser off the mark he would have halved his runs to 1. His achievement beat the record of Edmund Peate, a Yorkshireman born at Holbeck, near Leeds, who took 8 for 5 against Surrey in 1883. Peate, a slow left-arm spin bowler, had a fierce temper and *Who's Who of Cricketers* said of him, 'His sudden departure from county cricket while in his prime was caused by Lord Hawke's determination to rid the Yorkshire team of its more unruly elements.'

The *Daily Mail* correspondent Alex Bannister wrote, 'Modest 28-year-old Jim Laker's world-beating and incredible feat of taking eight wickets for two runs, which routed The Rest at Bradford yesterday, is a crushing blow to England's team building hopes. Leaving aside the facts we already knew – that Laker is the best off-spinner and Hutton is the master batsman – the trial so far has produced only unpalatable and negative results. Three young men from Cambridge University and Donald Carr, Oxford's captain, came a sad cropper on a gluepot, and proved they are woefully short of first class practice on a turning pitch. The inexperience of the Fenners-nursed Sheppard, Doggart and May was shown up by the comparison with the two professionals, Don Kenyon and Eric Bedser. They, though they did not score runs, at least middled the ball. The others, frankly, had no answer to Laker's spin, rendered deadly by the sunshine following rain.' Up until the morning, there were twenty-four hours of non-stop rain.

The Cambridge trio, plus John Dewes who played in the England side, had to ask for leave to attend the Bradford match during preparations for their university tripos examinations. Norman Yardley won the toss and made the inevitable decision to field. He allowed Trevor Bailey to bowl 6 overs at the start, during which the Essex all-rounder dismissed Sheppard lbw, before bringing on Jim. The strong wind whipped across the ground and the scarce spectators, tightly wrapped with their collars turned up, had plenty to applaud. There is nothing more pleasurable to the average Yorkshireman than seeing Southern-born Cambridge and Oxford University-educated amateurs humiliated. Jim had Hubert Doggart lbw for 2 and May was caught by Hutton for a duck in his first over. Carr followed in his second over for a duck, caught by Bailey.

Donald Bryce Carr, to give him his full name, born in Wiesbaden and the father of a cricketing Army officer, made his name as an administrator with MCC and the Test and County Cricket Board as much as a batsman and captain of Derbyshire for nineteen years. Now eighty, he recalled the ghastly day with some typical humour. 'I was pretty cross with the batsman at the other end,' he said. 'Don Kenyon refused a run on at least two or three occasions, which would have enabled me to avoid facing Jim's bowling. Each time he shouted, "No, no, get back." They were easy runs I can tell you. I decided to have a whack and hit the ball high into the air and was caught, by Trevor Bailey if I remember, for a duck. Don was a professional and I was an amateur. I was paid expenses but as I was secretary of Derbyshire CCC I was paid by the club. Later I became a good friend of Don's and we would laugh about it. The pitch was a wet turner and I am afraid we were out of our depth. I got to know Jim very well over the year and I liked the old boy. He was a good man. We were bowled out for 27, a total that I always remember, not just for that but because Derbyshire dismissed Middlesex for that score after they were 13 for 9. Alan Moss and Don Bennett doubled the score, which at the time was the lowest score for Middlesex.'

Kenyon batted for an hour for a top score of 7. A sharply turning off-break caught his top glove and before the ball fell to the ground, Godfrey Evans darted in front of the startled Worcestershire opener and snatched the ball just as it was about to land. 'He couldn't believe it,' said Evans. There were three more batsmen out for ducks, Dick Spooner, Roley Jenkins and Bob Berry all to Jim, and Eric Bedser stepped back on his crease to become an lbw victim, for 3. Alec Bedser, fielding at mid off, had dropped a few yards back when his twin brother came in and Jim kindly bowled a full toss, giving Eric a run to get off the mark. Alec laughed. 'Yes, I think it was deliberate,' said Alec. 'My brother was a very good all-rounder and if Jim hadn't been in the Surrey side he would have been a regular. He was good enough to take 833 wickets in his first-class career, and he scored 14,716 runs, including ten centuries.'

Jim's eighth and last wicket was a brilliant caught and bowled off the Derbyshire bowler Les Jackson, who was one of the higher scorers with 5. Evans conceded 3 byes, there was 1 leg bye and 1 wide, not from Jim. In the discussions afterwards Alex Bannister raised the subject of the Bedsers conspiring to give Eric a run, saying, 'That's probably been the only favour Jim granted to a fellow bowler.' Jim responded, 'Well, it would have been less expensive if I hadn't given Eric the run!'

Dewes had a close up of the 110-minute annihilation and he said, 'The great feature of Jim's day was the way the ball turned and lifted. He bowled faster than usual and he was at the batsmen all the time.' Billy Griffith, the late MCC secretary, writing in *The Cricketer*, wrote, 'Here there was the smack of a first-class county side in conflict with a scratch Saturday side eleven. The forward defensive shot, almost a reflect action of a young trialist at the beginning of an innings, becomes the desperate means by which he hopes to get off the mark. To play such a stroke at Bradford against Laker was pure suicide.' Bruce Harris, the *Evening Standard* cricket writer, wrote, 'Laker pitched an attacking length with a precision George Macaulay and Hedley Verity would have applauded. The ball, twisting and hopping all over the place, needed a fly swatter rather than a bat to control it.' Jim Swanton decried the fixture, calling it 'worthless', but praised Laker. 'He utilised a quite hateful pitch excellently,' he wrote. 'He spun the ball prodigiously and dropped it on the spot every time. If Laker has a rival as the best of the kind in the country, I do not know his name.'

With the venom disappearing, easing the pitch, Hutton's immaculate batting technique enabled England to score 229 in their first innings. The correspondent in *Wisden* wrote, 'Hutton made 85 out of 155 in two hours and gave a dazzling display of batsmanship on a still difficult pitch.' Facing 202 runs to make England bat again, The Rest lost Sheppard, bowled by Jim, and Eric Hollies, the Warwickshire leg-spin and googly bowler took over, claiming 6 for 28 in The Rest's total of 113. England won by an innings and 89 runs before lunch on the second day. Jim took 2 for 44 off 18 overs, giving him a match aggregate of 10 for 46. A junior reporter piped up from the throng of journalists and asked, 'Are these your best bowling figures, Mr Laker?'

Jim spent the rest of the day with his sister Margaret at her home in Baildon. Jim said, 'There was nothing really special about it. It's a funny game, cricket. One day you are on top of the world. Next day you get nought for plenty.' A week later Jim found out the truth of that old cliché. Picked for the First Test against the West Indies at Old Trafford he took 0 for 43 in the first innings and 1 for 43 in the second and although England won by 202 runs, he was dropped for the rest of the series. Few people understood how someone could rout an England 'B' side and fail against the senior side a few days later when the Lancashire committee ordered a pitch to suit the spinners. The committee told their groundsman to use less water and more rolling and the pitch started to crumble later in the game. Alf Valentine took 8 wickets at a much higher cost than Jim's tally at Bradford – 104 runs from 50 overs. There were some peculiar selections around that time. For the next Test at Lord's the selectors chose three spin bowlers who all moved the ball away from the bat, Jenkins, Berry and Johnny Wardle. Alf Valentine and Sonny Ramadhin shared 18 wickets and won a famous victory. By the end of the series, won by the West Indies 3-1, the selectors recruited three more bowlers who moved the ball to the off – Eric Hollies, Lancashire's slow left-armer Malcolm Hilton and Kent's leg-spinner Doug Wright. They used twenty-five players in the four-Test series to the twelve of the West Indies. Even more shameful were the positions of the respective bowlers in the national averages. Top came Lancashire's off-spin bowler Roy Tattersall with 193 wickets at 13.59. He hadn't been chosen. Fourth was Jim's 166 wickets at 15.32, Wardle came eighth with 174 at 16.71, Hilton ninth with 135 at 16.79, Hollies thirteenth with 144 at 18.84, Wright at twenty-sixth with 151 at 20.79, Bob Berry at fortieth with 79 at 22.41 and the other England bowler was Roley Jenkins at fifty-third with 132 at 24.53. There must have been a rule in 1950 to exclude the country's two best off-spinners, Tattersall and Laker. Or maybe it was because of something Jim said.

That winter the selectors preferred Brian Close for the winter tour to Australia. Close took just 20 wickets that summer at 19 apiece. No wonder Jim was pretty bitter.

FOUR

TWO REMARKABLE LADIES

Most successful men have a forceful, inspiring mother and James Charles Laker was lucky to have one. In his brilliantly researched book *Jim Laker* author Alan Hill wrote of her, 'Ellen Kane, of Lincolnshire stock, hurtled through life as if carried on a roller coaster at the fair. Mercurial in temperament, she evinced a particular dislike for rigid rules. Injustice of any kind incurred her considerable wrath. Conversely, as with many dominant and attractive women, she was not invulnerable to the charms of men. And her independent status was put severely at risk when Charles Henry Laker arrived on the Yorkshire scene from Sussex.'

Her determination explained why Jim Laker lived his life the way he did – he followed his mother's lead and refused to bow down to anyone. Though she had no certificates to back it, Ellen taught in poor schools around Bradford and proved a powerful force for good in the lives of hundreds of her pupils, who included her only son. It was a tangled story. Ellen married at the age of twenty to James Henry Kane, a journeyman printer, and they had three girls, Mary, known as Mollie, Margaret and Doreen. When he was thirty-four, James upset the rest of the family – perhaps he had an affair on the side or may have stolen sheep – and was excommunicated. He was packed off to Australia and they never heard from him again. Hill called her 'a lady with a huge personality with massive energy.' It was very doubtful that she curtailed her love-making activities and when Charles Laker, a stonemason from Breeding, in Sussex, turned up to work on the construction of the Bradford Town Hall they entered into a serious relationship that led to the arrival of two more children, Susie, and six years later Jim. The boy, subject to strict discipline yet fawned over, was born in a terraced house at 36 Norwood Road in Frizinghall on 9 February 1922. Ellen called him James after her husband and Charles after the boy's father. Charles Laker, who was related to a well-known cricketer of the same name in Sussex in the nineteenth century, was something of a con man and when the locals thought he looked like the famous film cowboy Tom Mix he used to sign autographs 'Tom Mix, the man on the range'. Two years after Jim's birth Charles vanished. Ellen had to convince her neighbours and her employers at the school that she was the aunt of Susie and Jim, not their mother, and this deception carried on for some years. (In the early 1920s for a mother to have two children born out of wedlock was looked on as shameful but eighty-four years later the Office of National Statistics showed a record of four out of ten babies were born to unmarried mothers in 2004. They expect the watershed of fifty per cent will be reached in 2010.)

She taught at the Calverley Church School and her teaching skills helped Jim to become one of the brightest pupils in her class. His writing was way ahead of the other children and his ability in that field never deserted him. If he was asked for his autograph when he became famous, his signature was always clearly readable, written in such a way that it showed his character. Later in life he told people that he never knew his father but around 1980 he was given some shattering news from Peter Parfitt, the former Middlesex and England left-handed bats-man who now lives in Norfolk. At the time he ran an upmarket pub near Skipton and he signed Laker up to speak at a sportsmen's dinner. A registrar who lived in Barnoldswick, not far away, told Parfitt that he knew where Laker's father was buried. He drove Parfitt to the cemetery at a tiny village called Ghyll and picked out the gravestone to reveal that Charles Laker had died in 1931 and there were two women named on the gravestone. One was Annie Sutcliffe, who died in 1959 and was reckoned to be Charles' common law wife. The other, Elizabeth Halstead, was thought to be Annie's daughter. 'When I first rang Jim to give him the news there was silence at the other end of the line and I thought, "Christ, that's my dinner up the creek with the speaker not going,"' said Parfitt. 'After a while, Jim grunted, "I don't know about that" and put the phone down. I spoke to him again a few days later and he agreed to come and I picked him up from Leeds station. "I'd like to see the grave," he said. I drove him there and when we got there he said, "I never knew him but he must have been a bit of a bugger!" Snow covered the cemetery and Jim took out a camera and took some pictures. I gather that Jim's three older sisters never told him about Charlie and how he did a moonlight. So with Charlie not marrying his mother, Jim must have been illegitimate, not that it matters these days.'

At school, Laker junior was said to be 'a straightforward, popular boy, above average intelligence and a good sport'. His interest in cricket was fostered by the deputy head and the sports master and they appointed him captain in the knock-up games in the playground. His first bat came from coupons from buying sweets and he recalled in his book *Cricket Contrasts*, 'It took weeks and weeks of chewing through halfpenny packets of gelatine lozenges to collect the necessary one hundred coupons.' The players used an assortment of balls but rarely proper cricket balls. 'We played our imaginary Test matches all through the day in the holidays,' he said. He won a scholarship at Salts High School at the age of ten and the family moved to a nicer place at Baildon. A third man in Ellen's life, Bert Jordan, moved in as her live-in lover and he filled the role of absent father.

She encouraged her son to have a full, rounded life and Jim became a chorister at St Barnabas' church before becoming a boy soprano and soloist in the Salts High School choir. He played a host of sports, including table tennis, tennis and football as well as cricket. Though not fast over the ground, he had the ability to beat opponents in his midfield role in the school football side. After the school matches, he would rush off to Valley Parade to watch Bradford City. One of his opponents at school was Len Shackleton, the Newcastle and England forward who was renowned for his ball skills and cheek.

Jim was a quick bowler from his early days – 'I was very nasty,' he once said – and in one school house match he had figures of 6 for o with the other side dismissed for just 1 run. He developed an interest in spin bowling when he became firm friends with a freelance journalist named Harry Dolphin who was fifteen years older. Dolphin, a non-smoker and teetotaller, turned the ball prodigiously and Laker said he 'learnt more about the game than any of the great players I met in later years'. After being paid a larger-than-usual fee from the *Bradford Telegraph & Argus*, he paid for his prodigy to travel down to London with him for a cricketing day out at Hyde Park. They pitched stumps on a suitable spot and played cricket through the day before catching a train back home. The *Bradford Telegraph & Argus* employed the legendary cricket writer Dick Williamson, who later became a good friend of Laker. The much-loved Williamson knew more facts about football and cricket than Leslie Welch the memory man and he was always testing Laker and his friends. Dolphin drowned in 1940 when his troopship was torpedoed on the way to the Middle East.

Jim's best mate was his sister Susie and she bowled and batted to him for hours on end and gave every encouragement to the budding sportsman. When he was sixteen he passed the school certificate examination, gaining five credits, and Ellen paid out £2 5s for a Herbert Sutcliffe bat in his shop in the centre of Leeds as a reward. She also signed him up for coaching at Herbert's indoor school at Headingley and he was coached by three former Yorkshire players, Benny Wilson, who wasn't a household name and two who were, George Hirst and the revered Emmott Robinson. Born in Hinckley, Leicestershire, Neville Cardus wrote of Emmott 'as a heap of Yorkshire clay into whom the Lord breathed life in order to bowl at the pavilion end.' When Laker was serving in the Army in Egypt he received a three page letter from Emmott without any punctuation. 'Hitler has buggered up the whole thing,' he wrote. With coaches like this, Laker knew he was on the way to fame. His batting improved and when he started playing for Saltaire in the Bradford League he filled the key position of four in the batting order. Sutcliffe, one of the game's immortals, said, 'Laker will make a name for himself.' When Laker made his first-class debut, he told him, 'What a pity your mother never lived for this day. She really was a remarkable woman.'

Sutcliffe was the opening partner of Jack Hobbs in many of his 54 Tests and his Test average of 60.73 was bettered by only Sir Don Bradman, Graeme Pollock and George Headley. He spoke with a Yorkshire accent but when he joined the Army in the Second World War he did an Alf Ramsey and spoke with a posh voice. After the war he became a Test selector and administrator and gave good counsel to Laker in his burgeoning career.

Laker admitted, 'I wasn't a budding world beater' when he started out playing for Saltaire at the age of sixteen. He played 50 matches, scoring 526 runs, including just one century, and took 79 wickets, not cheaply. He had big hands and bowled mainly quick, although he was capable of bowling almost every type of delivery. These were very modest figures compared to the record of the great medium-pace bowler Sydney Barnes who took 904 wickets in his nine years at Saltaire between 1915 and 1923. Christopher Martin-Jenkins said of him in his monumental work *World Cricketers*, 'A large proportion both of those who watched and of those who played against Sydney Barnes, especially on the big occasions, have no hesitation in naming this dark, brooding, gaunt, eventually cadaverous faced man as the best bowler ever. According to his biography his overall total in all cricket was 6,229 wickets at 8.33 in a career stretching into his mid-sixties. He captured all ten wickets in an innings seven times.'

Laker's total of taking all 10 wickets in first-class cricket was just two, one in the 1956 Test and for Surrey against Australia in the same year. Which was the better tally? Most of Barnes' all tens were taken in league cricket, which wasn't classed as first-class. Barnes played in only 27 Tests, taking 189 wickets at 16.43 in his Test career, which ended when he was forty. Sir Don Bradman was indisputably the greatest batsman of all time and Sir Garfield Sobers was the unchallenged king of the all-rounders. But the discussion over which bowler was the best will never be resolved. Laker lost five years at the start of his career when he served in the Army and, at the highest level, in the world series between England and Australia, he achieved the finest figures of all. The cantankerous Barnes had brief periods with Warwickshire and Lancashire only to return to the leagues. He played in leagues in Staffordshire, Lancashire and Bradford and also represented Wales. Laker was too young to play in the same side as Barnes but he met him a couple of times. The first occasion was when Barnes was guesting for Saltaire when he was sixty-four and Laker said, 'His control was still remarkable.' Raman Subba Row, the former Surrey colleague of Laker and lifelong friend, used the same word about Jim Laker. Asked what Laker's greatest asset was, he said, 'Control. He knew what he was doing and he dictated to the batsmen and didn't allow them to dictate to him. He had this beautiful, easy action, left arm high in the air and he gave the ball a great tweak. Some people said the ball fizzed through the air with a loud noise but I must say I didn't hear it.'

Laker's ambition was firstly to play for Saltaire and then Yorkshire, and he fulfilled only half of his objective. He made his debut for his local side at the age of sixteen and his mentor Archie Burgoyne, the secretary of Saltaire Cricket Club, helped his prodigy to attend a trial at the Headingley nets. Burgoyne devoted his long life to Saltaire Cricket Club, right up to his death at the age of ninety-five and he said of his favourite pupil, 'Jimmy was a grand lad, always willing and conscientious in everything he did.' The name Saltaire comes from the Victorian textiles philanthropist Sir Titus Salt who built a settlement including textile mills on the river Aire in 1853 'to transform the squalid hovels around Bradford to a place where the working man can enjoy a decent life without alcohol'. These mills have now been converted to one of the country's finest art sanctuaries.

John Nash, the gentlemanly secretary of Yorkshire CCC, sent Laker a postcard offering him 10s a day plus the tram fare for the trip to Headingley. Laker wrote, 'There were about seventy colts on parade and just as soon as the coaches began to put us through our paces I realised that at least half of them were far better players than I was. Some of them – notably Harry Halliday, who had already made a name for himself as a schoolboy star and was in the Yorkshire first team at eighteen, Willie Watson, Vic Wilson, Ken Fiddling and John

Lawrence – were obviously in an altogether different class from me. I went away convinced that I would never ever be good enough to play for Yorkshire.'

After the Second World War and when Laker had established himself in the Surrey and England side, Len Hutton said to him, 'You know, you ought to be playing for us, not Surrey. What about it?' Laker replied 'It's too late now. I'm settled in London.' A now-dead Yorkshire chairman also approached him, repeating the invitation. Again he refused. But, born in Yorkshire, he was still eligible to play for them. Every time he played in Yorkshire, the crowd responded to him. 'Yet for some reason there has been a strange feeling of unease among Yorkshire's committee men,' he said. 'I have been in the committee room drinking with friends but I was never invited there officially.'

His time in the Bradford League hardened him as a man and a cricketer and he recalled, 'Whenever I watched club cricket in the South I was struck by the older players' benevolent attitude towards the younger ones. They tended to look much more kindly on a boy coming in to bat than they do in the tough, competitive atmosphere of the Bradford League. If I went in to bat and the opposition's professional was bowling, he saw me as the chance of a cheap wicket and the cash collection he was looking forward to. If I was bowling, he would be looking to seize the opportunity of scoring some easy runs towards the half century that would put a few more bob in the kitty. In that kind of cricket, you have to battle to survive, and that has never done anybody any harm.'

The philosophy up North, particularly in Yorkshire, is to knock down the egos of young players whereas in other parts of the country experienced players try to raise their confidence. Many Yorkshire colts have been ruined by this unsympathetic approach and only those with strong personalities forced themselves on to the professional staff. This selfish attitude extends to drinking. Many well-known Yorkshire cricketers were renowned for not buying a drink. 'I wouldn't include Jim Laker in that,' said Subba Row. 'Jim was a generous man.' Over the Pennines, Lancastrians are different and they are usually ready to buy a round. Peter Richardson said, 'The ones from South Yorkshire aren't English! They're from a different breed. But I got on well with them. In fact, I can't really say there wasn't one cricketer I played with which I didn't get on well. Johnny Wardle gave a few problems but I liked him. He was one of my golfing partners. I put him next to Jim as the best slow bowlers I've ever seen.'

In his final years Laker blamed the decline of standards in league cricket on limited-overs cricket. 'The restrictions have made spin bowlers almost extinct,' he said. 'They have reared a whole genera-tion of defensive, medium-paced, leg-stump bowlers.' Indian, Pakistan and Sri Lankan cricketers have swelled the ranks of Bradford League clubs in recent years but they have yet to produce a Muralitharan, a Bishen Bedi or a Abdul Qadir.

In 1939 Laker started work as a clerk at the Barclays Bank in Bradford, earning £5 a month. On Saturdays he worked until 1.30 p.m. in the summer and it was a mad dash to his league games to get there on time. He said, 'There was a war going on and though a good many of my friends had gone forever, I couldn't wait for the call. The calling up age was twenty and it took a good deal of persuasion before I finally managed to convince my mother that I should volunteer. Then, having given a false age, nineteen, I was soon on my way to do eight weeks' infantry training at Earl Shilton in Leicestershire. That was followed by a posting to Chilwell at Nottinghamshire, where, it was said, anyone with real ability at football or cricket was set for the duration.

'When she learned I was kitted out with tropical kit and waiting to sail to Egypt, my mother was distraught. Much to my embarrassment, she spent all her time pounding the doors of every officer she could find complaining about the injustice of an underage solider being despatched overseas with such haste. I was much relieved that her efforts were all in vain because I was secretly looking forward to the adventures that lay ahead.' His mother knew many young men whom she taught who were killed in the First World War and she feared losing her only son. She didn't need to worry. He had a non- combative role in the Second World War and spent more time playing ball games than contributing to the victory of the Allies.

He was away from home for almost four years and early on he mas-tered the art of bowling off-spin and it changed his life. Three hundred young men boarded the SS *Mooltan* in Glasgow, one of twenty ships in a convoy escorted by an aircraft carrier, a battleship and destroyers on the way to the Middle East and the Far East. The convoy docked at Freetown and Durban and the journey took eight weeks before the soldiers disembarked at Port Said. Being on a cramped, ancient vessel was almost worse than being imprisoned at Parkhurst – the 300 shared six toilets and twenty washbasins and there was also the fear of being torpedoed. Laker's football flourished and he was soon playing for the British Army side in Egypt, alongside Tom Finney, Willie Telfer and George Male, all household names in British football.

In 1942 he started playing cricket in Cairo. There were no grass pitches in north Africa. The matches, of a high standard, had to be played on matting pitches and that opened the door for Laker to a new, exciting life. 'I started to experiment with bowling a few off-spinners,' he said. 'Harry Dolphin had suggested it a few years earlier and now, at the age of twenty-three I practised at every opportunity. There were no coaches to help, no manuals to study as I became a self-taught off-spin bowler in the shadows of the Sphinx and the pyramids. To my utter amazement, I was soon turning the ball quite prodigiously on the coconut strips. Wickets galore came my way in inter-unit games and one haul of 8 for 30 at the famed Gezira Sporting Club earned me a place in all the representative matches. This meant I was rubbing shoulders with a host of eminent cricketers like Dudley Nourse, Bert Sutcliffe, Don Taylor, Tom Pritchard, Peter Smith, Norman Yardley, Tom Dollery and George Emmett.'

He was selected for the 'England' side against 'Australia' in front of 10,000 servicemen and again performed well. He scored several centuries and recorded exceptional bowling returns against Test-class batsmen who struggled against his classy off-spin bowling in very helpful, spinning conditions. Pritchard, the New Zealand fast bowler who played for Warwickshire, made a pertinent point about Laker's bowling technique. He said, 'He used to spend hours pushing a cricket ball between his spinning finger and middle finger until he was able to spread them far enough to settle the ball at the base of the fingers. This enabled him to get extra purchase and spin the ball more.' It transformed him into a top quality spinner but it also brought serious problems. When he bowled a long spell, his index finger became sore, with the skin being rubbed painfully, and over the years that finger became arthritic. In his latter years he never bowled without experiencing pain.

With Germany collapsing, he was anxious to return home and in April 1945 his name came out in draw for berths on a ship returning home to England. It gave him the chance of having a four-week break in England. Bert Jordan, his stepfather, had died and his mother was forced to move to a small house close to Valley Parade. She was sixty-seven but still did teaching as a supply teacher and rode a motor cycle. It was a blissfully happy reunion but he thought she looked tired. She was still rushing about and she had just refereed a school football match. As the holiday neared the end, she suggested to Jim it would be a good idea to visit one of Jim's elder sisters Doreen in Eastbourne to get some clean sea air. 'Perhaps she had a premonition because she insisted on accompanying me to the station,' said Jim. Before he returned, she had collapsed and died from a massive heart attack. She had saved up £1,000 worth of assets and left them all to her son.

The Army gave him two more weeks' leave and with the Second World War over he expected to be demobbed straight away. But he was ordered to return to his unit and that stopped him playing cricket in Yorkshire for the rest of the summer. 'It was the most frustrating period in my life,' said Laker. One of his Army colleagues wrote to the secretary at Yorkshire CCC recommending his friend as a potential county player and was bluntly informed that 'we have sufficient bowlers of that type'. Ellis Robinson, the veteran spinner who later moved to Somerset in 1950, was still on the staff and Frank Smailes, who was picked for England against Australia at Old Trafford in 1938 only for the match to be rained off, was ready to resume his challenge for an England place. In 1939 Smailes took 10 for 47 against Derbyshire and played one Test, against India at Lord's in 1946 when he scored 25 and took 3 for 62. Also waiting for a chance in Yorkshire's champion side – they won the title seven times in the 1930s before Surrey repeated the feat in the 1950s – were Arthur Booth, who topped the county's bowling averages in 1946, Allan Mason and Johnny Wardle. The door was firmly shut on

Laker when Maurice Leyland, long-serving coach after his distinguished playing cricket, said, 'I'm afraid we haven't got room for him.'

When Laker eventually returned to England he was billeted in Folkestone in the middle of a hard winter. Eventually his persistence earned him a desk job at the War Office but no accommodation. He explained his predicament to another Army friend, Colin Harris, who lived in Forest Hill, south London, and Harris offered him a room as a lodger. Up to this time it was common for young men to seek lodgings in other people's houses when they left their family home seeking work. They couldn't afford flats so they had to live with a family. In many ways it was preferable to living on their own. These days a third of the population live alone and that is much less enjoyable. Laker loved his new quarters and he remained there for the next five years. He applied to Barclays Bank Ltd for a post in London and was given the go ahead. He had a counter-offer, from a General Palmer, the organiser of the Army cricket side. Laker was a sergeant when he left the Army and Palmer offered him a commission with the promise of regular cricket with the Army.

Peter Smith, the Essex all-rounder who played with him in Egypt, arranged a trial for him at Essex but he had to withdraw because of a sore finger. His friend Harris took him along to nearby Catford Cricket Club and the shy Yorkshireman was signed on straight away. Laker took 10 for 21 against Bromley, one of the bigger clubs in the Kent League, and scored plenty of runs as an opener. His opening partner was Arthur Phebey, two years younger and born just round the corner from the ground. Phebey became a close friend and went on to have a successful career with Kent. Les Todd, another opener with Kent, also played for Catford and so did Les Ames, Kent's wicket-keeper-batsman and long-serving secretary. 'Jim was obviously special,' said Phebey. 'He had a good temperament and did not appear to get peeved if luck ran against him.' Not losing his temper on the field was one of Laker's greatest assets. Trevor Bailey said of him, 'I played with and against him many times and he never queried a decision with an umpire.' Peter Richardson said, 'Although he didn't get on with Tony Lock it never got to a confrontation. Locky was the opposite to Jim.

He would get worked up, give his opponents the stare and gestured and postured.'

Catford was one of the most sociable cricket clubs in London and big-name players taking part in benefit matches used to stay through the night drinking. Laker enjoyed a drink but he never stayed up all night. 'He was what I call an intelligent drinker,' said Bailey. 'He knew when he had had enough.' Laker's reputation spread around the county and in the summer of 1946 Andrew Kempton, the Catford president who had a long association with Surrey CCC, told his colleagues at the Oval, 'This lad is worth a contract.' Laker was invited to attend a trial, along with the tall South Australian left-arm spinner John McMahon from Balakhari. In charge of the trial was the forty-one-year-old Errol Reginald Thorold Holmes, a former Oxford University Blue and amateur who succeeded Douglas Jardine as Surrey captain between 1934-38 and 1947-48. 'He was the biggest snob I ever met,' said Laker. 'On this day we caught him on a turner and I found the gap between his bat and his front pad a few times and he kept being bowled.' Holmes was very excited. 'Not many experienced county bowlers have made me look so foolish,' he said. 'There is room for both of you here.' McMahon was turned into a slow bowler who specialised in chinamen and googlies. Tony Lock, born in 1929 from Limpsfield, had appeared on the scene and soon deposed him in the first team. McMahon left for Somerset in 1953 and three years later, the year of Laker, he took 103 wickets in his most successful season.

Holmes made critiques of the players under him and in 1947 the only man who escaped criticism was Laker. 'A real find,' he wrote in the bound minute book of the cricket sub committee. 'He is a finished cricketer and will never let you down. Full of guts and a through Yorkshireman, who is very popular with the rest of the Surrey side.' The use of the word 'guts' was important because a Surrey captain, Peter May, accused Laker of 'not trying' in a county game at Blackheath eleven years later. Richardson said, 'PBH and Jim didn't really get on because Peter felt he always had an escape clause. If he wasn't successful on a certain day when things went against him, he would say his arthritic finger was troubling him.'

Holmes made some interesting comments about the rest of the Surrey staff of that time. He wrote, 'Gover is finished and will only do harm to himself and his county by carrying on. Lock is very young and very pleased with himself but he has possibilities. At the beginning of the year I found Bedser AV rather swollen headed but with firm handling this will not recur. But firm handling is essential.' One of the best anecdotes about Holmes concerned a game against Essex when Alf Gover was bowling Surrey to victory. Two wickets remained and a delivery from Gover hit the number nine batsmen in the mouth with a bouncer which came off the glove. The batsman had to retire and to the surprise of Surrey's fielders, Holmes waved his players in, accepting the draw. Gover protested and Holmes, universally known as a Corinthian, said, 'We couldn't possibly take advantage of their misfortune.'

Laker's debut for Surrey was against the Combined Services team that included several Test stars including Donald Carr, the England and Derbyshire captain, John Dewes, the Middlesex batsman, Bill Voce, the Nottingham and England bowler who partnered Harold Larwood in the Bodyline series and Reg Perks who, in the words of Richardson who played with him for a while at Worcestershire, 'was one of the best of his type in county cricket'. Laker's first victim was Worcestershire's Don Kenyon, who was a prolific post-war run-getter – caught Arthur McIntyre bowled Laker. In the second innings, Laker bowled Kenyon cheaply and he finished the game with a pat on the back from his captain, with 6 wickets at 20 apiece.

'Don was very fine player,' recalled McIntyre. 'It was a good wicket to get. I met Jim the previous year in that game in Rome between Norman Yardley's Middle East Forces against the Central Mediterranean Forces. Both sides were full of good county players and a few Test players, including Bert Sutcliffe, Don Taylor, Tom Dollery and George Emmett.' McIntyre, the Surrey wicketkeeper between 1938-63, played 3 Tests himself and was one of the most consistent keepers of his era. Now eighty-seven and living in Lymington, he has vivid memories of the occasion. 'Jim was on the losing side,' he said. 'He was a good bowler then, a little quicker than most off-spinners on matting wickets.'

Laker recalled in his book *Cricket Contrasts*, 'For most of us, it was the first time we had flown and what a baptism it turned out to be. We were cramped in total darkness in the bomb bays of a wartime Liberator bomber, which took five hours to find Italy and a small runway at Foggia. And as if that was not bad enough, we were then bounced around in the back of a truck for what seemed an eternity before finally checking in at our destination. I met Arthur McIntyre who was to keep wicket to me for Surrey for so many years.

'Apart from the fact that we played on a matting stretched tight over a concrete base that produced a wicket that was lively in the extreme, my memories of the game are fairly vague. I do recall that we got a hammering and there were grave doubts about the legality of two of my wickets, both lbw to the disgust of the batsmen. Strangely, I have a much clearer recollection of our visit to the Opera House in Rome where we went to see the great Gigli singing in *Cavalleria Rusticana*. Don Taylor, Bert Sutcliffe and myself missed our flight back to Cairo and decided to have a look at Naples. We slept where we could and discovered the only decent food was in the New Zealand NCO's Club where my Yorkshire accent was a big problem as I was masquerading as a warrant officer from Wanganui in New Zealand. Cash was running short and our leave overdue when we dropped in at a Naples airfield and found an old Dakota about to take some cases of fruit to Egypt. Perched on orange boxes and feeling horribly airsick, we finally made it back to Cairo via Malta and Tobruk.'

Laker made two more appearances for Surrey at the end of the 1946 season, a second encounter with the Combined Services and a match against Hampshire at Kingston. The counties nearly always appointed amateurs as captain and in that year Surrey's committee, all amateurs, must have had collective brainstorms because they appointed Nigel Harvie Bennett, a thirty-four-year-old lower-order batsman who wasn't worth a place in the side. Bennett, a former public schoolboy at Stowe School, played 31 matches in the Surrey senior side with an batting average of 16. In his biography of Laker, Alan Hill wrote, 'Bennett's appointment was considered to have been made by accident. Bennett was unheard of in first-class cricket or even minor county cricket. The widely held theory was that Surrey had intended offering the post to Leo Bennett, a top-class cricketer with county experience. By some mischance the invitation was received, to his immense surprise, by the other Bennett.' At the game at Kingston, Bennett went up to Laker at the start and said, 'Now, which end would you like, Laker?' Laker hadn't bowled quick since 1943. Bedser wasn't available and Alf Gover and Eddie Watts were Surrey's opening bowlers, and they were highly amused. 'What's the matter?' said Bennett, 'Don't you want to bowl?' Laker said, 'Yes of course but the fact is I'm an off-spinner.' 'But you bowl quick, too, don't you?' said Bennett. Alf was given the new ball and Laker said, 'Alf's face was a picture.'

When Jim was called to bowl his nervousness showed and he started to come in to bowl before Gover was ready in his position at short leg. Gover was still putting his sweater on when Jim bowled an off-break to Rodney Exton, a twenty-year-old all-rounder from Clifton School who appeared in 4 matches for Hampshire. Exton stretched forward and the ball shot towards Gover, whose sweater was still round his head. The ball hit Gover just above the knee and, with the shock of the impact, he crossed his legs leaving the ball lodged between his knees. 'Howzat?' he shouted and the umpire signalled out. 'That's a blinder Alf!' said Jim.

In August, Surrey offered him a contract with terms of £6 a week through the winter, supplemented by match money in the summer. He promptly resigned at Barclays and concentrated on working on his fitness in one of the coldest winters of all time, 1946–47. 'Having taken the plunge,' he said, 'I was determined to succeed and figured that the way ahead lay in assiduous practice and rigorous training. A number 58 tram from Forest Hill to Dulwich and from there a 37 bus to Wandsworth took me week in week out through the winter to Alf Gover's famous cricket school.' Gover's school had gas lamps and gas heaters and the trainees needed to keep moving to prevent the risk of frostbite. Alf was one of the greatest characters ever in cricket. He called everyone 'old boy' in a posh voice and there were countless hilarious times when Laker, his friend Phebey and Ken Barrington used to turn up together. During Laker's first visit, Gover insisted on giving his prodigy's bowling action a thorough check up 'just to sort one or two things out'. Laker already had an ideal action. Gover's school was demolished after Laker's death and replaced by flats. It was the end of a era.

Every season today's players normally have several pairs of shoes that are supplied by their sponsors, but Jim wore the first pair he had at Saltaire all through the Second World War and up until the tour to the West Indies in 1947-48. Before the age of e-mails, Gover sent regular telegrams to him around the Caribbean and in one he wrote, 'Well played, trust the boots are OK.' Jim said later, 'I was very fond of those boots but they were so heavy that it affected my running. Alf and the other players used to make comments about my slowness between the pitch and I had to get rid of them. I was paying a fortune in excess baggage during my travels around the world.'

Despite marriage going out of business these days, the sport of cricket is still holding faith with the ancient ceremony. Most of Michael Vaughan's Ashes winning side were happily married with families and a high proportion of England cricketers through the ages have been fathered by cricketers. Jim was blessed by a wonderful, stimulating marriage to Lilly – which was sadly curtailed to only thirty-five years when he died at the age of sixty-four.

Lilly, a petite, intelligent brunette with a lively mind, was brought up in Vienna and in 1938, when Austria was annexed by Germany, her family dispersed and she went to live in Egypt. Jim's love affair with her had an unusual and long-winded courtship. They first met in Cairo in 1943 when they served in the Royal Army Ordnance Corps. 'I was in the ATS and I finished up being a staff sergeant,' she said. On their first date, Jim invited her to watch a cricket match at the Gezira Club and she agreed to submit herself to this strange game. After a while, she said, 'I thought English people were supposed to be fair. How is it proper for eleven men to play against two?'

When the Second World War ended the friendship did too and in 1950, with both living in London – he was residing with friends at Forest Hill, south of the river Thames and she was living north of the river at Hampstead – a mutual acquaintance who was with them in

Cairo arranged an invitation to both parties to attend a Middle East Services' reunion in central London. Unbeknown to them, neither invitee knew the other was coming so it came as a pleasant surprise when they met up again. 'Are you engaged to anyone?' asked the forthright Lilly. 'No,' said Jim, 'What about you?' 'Nor me,' Lilly said. 'How about dinner one evening?' asked Jim. 'No, make it lunch, on a Thursday,' said Lilly. Years later, Lilly said, 'I am outspoken – like Jim!' She gave the England and Surrey cricketer her telephone number and six months passed before Jim rang it. The lunch was held at the Star and Garter Hotel near Putney Bridge and it went well. They discussed their respective love lives and Jim revealed that in the previous five years he had proposed to three women and each said yes. The planned marriages were broken off apparently and at the age of twenty-eight he was now ready to settle down.

Lilly was working for Dr Wand, the Bishop of London's Reconstruction Fund at Fulham Palace and after the meal – no extravagance because food rationing had just been lifted – Jim escorted her back to her office. She recalled later, 'Jim was surprised and quite impressed at my spacious room at the palace. Jim thought the palace was like the Hammersmith Palais.' In the summer of 1950 they went out regularly, to Lyons Corner Houses, visits to the cinema and on 19 August, watching Jim taking wickets for Surrey against Middlesex at Lord's. It was her first visit to Lord's and the crowd was much larger than present-day crowds at local derby matches. She found the occasion rather uninspiring. Denis Compton was one of Jim's 8 victims, which cost 165 runs from 59 overs. Lilly realised that her man was a big name in his sport.

His name appeared in the newspapers every day and there were long accounts of his performance at Bradford when he took 8 wickets for only 2 runs. He took 166 wickets, averaging 15.32, and was fourth in the national bowling averages. He topped the Surrey averages with 142 wickets at 14.54 and helped Surrey to share joint-top place in the Championship with Lancashire. He expected to play in the Test series against the West Indies but the selectors gave him a single Test, against Old Trafford in June when his tally of 1 for 86 off 31 overs was hardly a harbinger for his 1956 successes. Still, he thought he deserved a place in the England squad for the tour to Australia that winter and when Brian Close, the brash nineteen-year-old left hander from Yorkshire whose bowling was well short of Test standard, was preferred he went into a long, lingering sulk.

He soon perked up when Leslie Ames invited him to join the Commonwealth tour of India. He told his friends, 'It's as strong as the England team, if not stronger.' He enjoyed the excitement and passion of sub-continent cricket. He said, 'Every day countless people of all ages came up to me and said "excuse me sir, can you please sign for me?" They love their cricket out there.' Alcohol would have helped the boring hours in hotels but except for functions provided by the British High Commissioner and his staff, there was none. Back in his shared rooms he sat down to write long letters to Lilly. She said, 'He wrote every day and I wrote back every day.' Just before Christmas he was advised to return home after a sinus condition. Bombay, next to the sea, didn't cause any problems but he found places like Lucknow, Patiala, Poona and Baroda very polluted. Even someone brought up in smoke-laden Bradford, still harbouring many 'satanic mills', couldn't tolerate the fumes.

He returned home by ship in time for Christmas and brought a large holdall of handbags, knick-knacks and embroidery. Lilly was suitably impressed. The next day – still travelling by public transport because he had yet to buy a car despite playing for his country – he brought another holdall, filled with linen, towels and other items for setting up a home. 'Well,' he said. 'I wasn't sure whether you would say yes.' Weighing down the second holdall was a large brass plaque containing the names of the two sides. The surname of Frank Worrell was spelt 'Worrel'. She suggested a September wedding, outside of the cricket season but the canny Yorkshireman opted for a registrar wedding in March, 'because of my income tax position' he explained. Jim didn't buy an engagement ring. 'I didn't mind,' said Lilly. 'The wedding ring is the ring that counts.'

They were married at Kensington Registry Office on 27 March 1951. He was twenty-nine, a good age for a man who was close to reaching his sporting peak. There was no best man and only a handful of guests. One of them was Michael Barton, who was one of his first skippers at Surrey. Now in his nineties, he still has nice memories of the day: 'He made a very fine speech and I wasn't surprised by his later success as a TV commentator. At first meeting Jim gave the impression of being a blunt Yorkshireman. But this was misleading. He was in fact a very sensitive man. The sensitivity was perhaps magnified by certain difficulties in life about which we knew nothing. He was extremely intelligent, both as a person and as a bowler.'

The newpapers reported the happy occasion and Jim told Lilly not to reveal their honeymoon plans. They had a booking at a medium-sized hotel in Bournemouth and Lilly remembered that he told her not to accompany him into the dining room on the first night and a fellow guest said, 'Isn't it awful, all these newly married couples in the place.' Lilly said, 'Our wedding picture was on the front page of the evening newspaper but he still thought we were not to behave like newlyweds!' Scrabble was one of their favourites games but that was dispensed with during the brief honeymoon. She still plays bridge every week with friends and calls it 'my mental exercise'. She also visits her local swimming pool three times a week to do exercises and with thirty steps to go up to her flat, she is very fit. 'Jim was very patriotic,' she said. 'He was very proud of his country.' Jim was a staunch Conservative and when he first came to London he joined the Young Conservatives. Maybe he was interested in the female members? After a long day's work, either in cricket or commentating, he loved sprawling out in the family's huge and very comfortable settee and two armchairs.

Jim's love for their daughters Angela and Fiona was expressed in many ways, even by taking them to sports events when he was working. 'I remember sitting in the press box at Chelmsford when Dad was commentating at a Sunday League game,' said Fiona, who was a fine tennis player. He used to take her and sister Angela, now a teacher, to Stamford Bridge when they were young. 'He would take us to games at Fulham and Barnsley as well but Angela was the Chelsea fan,' said Fiona, who lives with her husband Philip, a farmer, and her children at Winterbourne Earls, Wiltshire.

'He was a hero to me, a loving father and a brilliant man,' she said. 'He read bedtime stories and sang to us and one of his favourites was 'Albert the Lion'. He drove us to school and on Sundays he would take us to cricket. It was part of our life. I played tennis to a reasonable standard and he chauffeured me to training and to tournaments. I grew up at the same time as Buster and Linda Mottram and Sue Barker and I went to a school in Wimbledon, not far from the All England Club. We always had treats, like visits to the Battersea Funfair and similar places and he took the family on wonderful holidays abroad, including Australia, South Africa, Cyprus and the West Indies. He loved Christmas and was the first person to be up in the morning. No-one had a better and more loving father and our grandchildren idolised him.'

Angela shared Jim's love of Chelsea and they had two seats in the west stand at Stamford Bridge. 'Between the ages of eight and around fourteen, we were regulars and our favourite player was Charlie Cooke. I sent in my autograph book for him to sign and it never came back. Dad rang someone up at the club and said they thought it went to the wrong address. Peter Osgood and Alan Hudson were our other favourites. It was the time of flair players, a bit different to what happens today.'

Angela thinks Fiona and her were 'Daddy's girls'. 'Yes, he did spoil us a bit but we weren't perfect. When he had to exercise discipline, he never shouted or raised his voice. He put over an air of quiet authority. He spoke wise assuring words and we took notice. A lot of boys came round to the house to take us out and he was very tolerant. He used to organise the ball games in the garden and often took part himself. We used to cut out job adverts in the newspapers and give it to him as a joke. "You ought to get a proper job," we told him. For a long time we didn't realise how good he was because he never spoke about his achievements.'

Brought up in a family with four sisters and a father he hardly knew, Jim lived much of his life in a female-dominated household but if he was disappointed at not having a son, he never admitted it. He had four grandsons and three granddaughters and Lilly said, 'Unfortunately, he never saw the two youngest.' It was a family to be proud of and Lilly, who lives in an elegant seventeenth-century flat near Salisbury Cathedral, sees them regularly. John Bradman, the son of Sir Don Bradman, changed his name to avoid the excesses of fame and lived to regret it. Now he is back to 'Bradman'. Jim was careful to protect him and his family from the celebrity cult and they are intensely proud of his father's name and his achievements.

Jim usually took the family's pet, a Labrador named Toffee, on daily walks and he never went in for guard dogs. In 1977 burglars broke into a downstairs window at his home in Putney, stealing most of his valuable memorabilia. 'It was a very foggy night,' said Lilly. 'Jim said to the policeman in charge, "he must have been a cricket lover." But the officer said, "No, he is a thief." Jim's engraved silver mugs, which he treasured, were taken and that upset him. Some other mugs, less valuable, were found on Wandsworth Common.'

There are only two Lakers who have played first-class cricket in this country – Jim, the best, and Peter Guy Laker, born in Hurstpierpoint on 5 December 1926, who played 2 matches for Sussex in 1948-49, the also-ran. He too was a spin bowler, a leg-spinner, and his main claim to fame was being cricket correspondent of the *Daily Mirror* between 1968 and 1985 when Jim was working for the BBC. He also reported two Test series in the 1950s before becoming a sub-editor until 1968.

Peter Laker is a tall, thin and very amusing man who was an expert on 'two up' – throwing a coin down on the ground and trying to land another one on the first one. Jim, too, was a bit of a gambler. Cricketers, and cricket commentators, have plenty of spare time on their jobs and diversions like gambling help fill the time. Jim was a modest backer of horses and when he won he usually walked off with his winnings rather than risk losing them. As Charles Laker, Jim's father, came from Wisborough Green, a few miles from Hurstpierpoint, it is possible the two men were related but Peter Laker, who now lives in Ilton in Somerset said, 'I'm related to Freddie Laker, the man who owned the airline and we come from the other branch of the family. Freddie used to live in Chailey and there are a number of Lakers in Shipley in Sussex, which is a coincidence because Jim was born near to Shipley of Yorkshire and his father is buried near Skipton.' Both cricketing Lakers met Freddie Laker, who died in February 2006 at the age of eighty-three, on different occasions and Lilly has several pictures of Jim and Freddie together and one with her and the pair after arriving from a flight to Barbados.

Peter Laker was playing for Taunton Fourth XI up until two years ago when he stopped playing at the age of seventy-eight. 'Jim was a great bloke,' he said. 'The word I would use of him was "taciturn". He was always helpful and I remember an occasion when the *Mirror* wanted me to do a piece about his 19 for 90 and I tracked him down on holiday in Sardinia. Some people would turn you down but he chatted away and the best line, which I always remember, was about Tony Lock. He told me that Tony Lock was so upset at taking only 1 wicket at Old Trafford he changed and drove home after the game, not even congratulating Jim. And the next month he didn't speak to him.

'Then he did me a very good turn in 1969 when I was at a hotel near Manchester late on Sunday evening when I had a call about Tom Graveney playing a benefit game at Luton on the Sunday of the Test match. I went into the bar and Jim was there. I asked him what happened and he told me the story how Tony Hunt, the business-man and chairman of Luton Town FC, met Colin McDonald, the Australian batsman and Tom at the Cricketers' Club and Tony offered Tom £1,000 to play. Again, a lot of Test cricketers would have said they didn't know much about it but Jim knew my deadline was fast approaching.'

Tom Graveney now has clear memories of that day. 'I asked Alec Bedser, the chairman of the selectors, whether I could play at Luton and he said no. But it was a lot of money, seventeen per cent of my total benefit fund and they didn't make fortunes out of benefits in those days. So I played. The disciplinary sub committee of the Test and County Cricket Board decided to ban me for the next three Tests and it turned out to be my last Test. Well, I was forty-two! But I scored 75 and took a catch at third slip to dismiss Roy Fredericks off the bowling of John Snow.' The peerless Graveney OBE played in 79 Tests between 1951 and 1969, scoring 4,882 runs at 44.38. He joined Jim on the BBC commentating team for the next fourteen years. 'Terrific man,' he said. 'And what a good commentator. He never said more than necessary, like Richie Benaud. They let the picture tell the story and then add the bits the viewers didn't know. These days it's far too much talking.'

Trevor Bailey, Peter Richardson and Alan Oakman were the only survivors of the 1956 Old Trafford Test and Graveney said, 'There are only six left from the eighteen players who took part in the 1953 Ashes-winning side, Alec Bedser, Trevor, Reg Simpson, Fred Trueman, Roy Tattersall and myself.' It provokes a thought that cricketers die before footballers because *The Sunday Times* featured a picture of the twenty players in England's squad in the 1958 World Cup in Sweden and only four had died, Eddie Hopkinson, Eddie Clamp, Johnny Haynes and Billy Wright. In their playing days most cricketers were heavy smokers, including Jim, Brian Statham, Fred Trueman, Trevor Bailey, Denis Compton, Frank Tyson and many more and those who played for the Rothman's Cavaliers on Sundays were given free samples, whereas not so many footballers smoked incessantly. Was smoking a reason? Sitting in those cramped dressing rooms, puffing away and creating a fug must have played a part. Said Graveney, 'Like the film stars, the cricketers smoked in that era. Brian Statham smoked and when the Lancashire committee voted in favour of a smoking ban in the committee room, he resigned in protest. I gave up at five. I went on a cubs' week with my brother Ken and he used to buy Woodbine's so I tried one and didn't like it.' The professionals smoked, the amateurs, like Peter May, Colin Cowdrey and David Sheppard, didn't.'

Jim played an important part to help Lilly to get her family reunited after the end of the Second World War. She hadn't heard from her parents for several years and one day a card from them arrived via the Red Cross. Her father had worked on a farm in Nimes, in the South of France, during the Second World War and later lived in Paris. It came as a tremendous relief that they were still alive and Lilly applied to the Home Office to allow them to live in England. She said, 'Jim had to vouch that they would not be a financial burden to the State. There was a law that a British citizen could apply to be joined by aged parents providing they are self-sufficient and happily that was the case.'

After Jim died, Surrey CCC and the Lord's Taverners made Lilly an honorary life member and she supported some of their functions. When John Stephenson became Secretary of the MCC, he invited her to attend Test matches at Lord's in his box. Lilly said, 'He and

Karen, his wife, lived in a house close to Lord's but they also had a home outside Salisbury. When John retired they went to Wiltshire and I got the idea to stage a charity cricket match at the South Wilts ground and I invited him to join my organising committee, which he did. He did terrifically well to get a team together. We had half a dozen people on the committee and it took almost a year to organise it. Another friend and neighbour, Leslie Thomas, the author, who was a friend of Jim, joined the committee and helped to recruit several celebrities including Rory Bremner, who was the star of the day. I wrote letters seeking sponsorship and Surrey CCC and Barclays Bank sent cheques, among others. I was particularly pleased about Barclays because Colin Cowdrey was connected with Barclays, as well as Jim. We took a £2,500 net from the match and encouraged by that we arranged another one, which brought in £2,300. Sir Edward Heath, who was a Lord's Taverner, came along and shook everyone's hand. When I went to Salisbury I did voluntary work for a number of charities including the Red Cross, raising around £10,000, half from the cricket matches in 1998–99. It was my way of thanking the Red Cross for finding her parents. I couldn't have raised this money without my cricket connection. Thank you Jim! He took my father to a cricket match at the Oval and how much he understood is another story!' It was a very creditable effort from a lady in her late seventies.

Jim kept his public life separate from his family life and, for her part, she never intruded into his professional work unless he invited her to a match or a function. He called her 'my mate', according Don Mosey, the former BBC commentator who wrote a personal life of Jim in 1987. 'I have known many cricket wives and none more devoted than Lilly Laker,' he wrote. 'Jim, a no-nonsense and occasionally irascible companion in his man's world, was a different character within his own home environment. He adored his grandchildren and his daughters and never regretted that he didn't have a son. He knew only too well the burdens imposed on the male descendants and was content that his record would never be an albatross round the neck of a son. Lilly wasn't a cricket wife in the sense that she understood the game well or even enjoyed it but she did enjoy the friendships of other wives, particularly the Surrey wives.'

Lady Dorothy Hutton was one of her best friends and when their husbands died, they went on a number of foreign holidays, including a cruise round the Baltic to St Petersburg. 'Dorothy lived very close, at Kingston Hill, and she was very knowledgeable about cricket,' said Lilly. 'We had many things in common.' When Lady Dorothy and Barbara Watson, wife of Willie Watson, the England and Yorkshire left-handed batsman who was one of the last sportsmen to have represented his country at both cricket and football, took Lilly on her first visit to the pavilion at Headingley the order was that hats had to be worn and she observed it. A lifelong non-conformer, she wasn't wearing a hat on a subsequent visit when The Queen visited a Test match at the Oval and she still has the picture to prove it.

Jim was one of *Wisden's* Five Cricketers of the Year in 1951, taking 149 wickets with an average of 17.99, and a friend in New Zealand invited him to become the player-coach of Auckland. He soon accepted because he saw it as a chance of taking Lilly, some compensation for a proper honeymoon. They spent five months in one of the world's friendliest countries and they made many friends. They stayed with the parents of Don Taylor, a Kiwi Test player who played with Jim in Egypt. They paid £4 a week for a bed, breakfast and dinner and when Lilly took a job with an insurance company it gave them an opportunity to save some money. Jim proved to be a popular figure and was looked on as a fine ambassador. One of his pupils was John Sparling, the New Zealand off-break bowler who toured England in 1958.

He played in four matches for Auckland and he captured 24 wickets at 15.79 apiece and was voted Bowler of the Year in the *New Zealand Cricket Almanack*. He helped turn an average side into one of the best in the country and the magazine reported, 'his accuracy and control of spin were decided assets.' The departing flight from Auckland to Sydney was undertaken in a flying boat, a slow and cumbersome way of travel but they still enjoyed the experience. 'We went on a pilgrimage around Australia, making sure that Jim visited as many cricket grounds as possible,' said Lilly.

They joined their old friends Ray Lindwall and his wife and they travelled together on the SS *Stratheden* through the Suez Canal to England. Peter Iles, a grade bowler, wrote to Lilly when Jim died in 1986, saying, 'Jim volunteered to do much extra work to foster junior cricket. Contacts he made with players while he was with us continued long after that, both at top level among men representing New Zealand or playing for English counties, or at lower levels among young New Zealanders visiting England. Throughout his career he always had time to talk to old friends from Yorkshire, or his Army days, whenever their paths crossed.

'In addition to his many after-dinner speaking engagements of a formal nature, he spent a great deal of time travelling widely, without payment, to more obscure cricketing backwaters with which an old friend, and sometimes a mere chance acquaintance, might be associated. At official functions at Lord's or the Oval I have seen him spend more time with relatively unknown guests than with the celebrities on parade from cricket, other sports and the world of entertainment. Jim had an almost perfect recall for details of his cricketing life and this was not only invaluable as a raconteur but was a key factor in his common touch. But he not only remembered names and faces, he had a genuine interest in the lives of the people he had met. He was not only a good talker, but he was a good listener as well.'

After Don Mosey sent his manuscript of his book on Jim to Lilly, she wrote back, 'Judging by the 350 letters I had after he died and by the obituary notices in the newspapers, he was not an unpopular man. He did like to "stir it up" but there was never any malice in it. He was also a very cautious and careful person and not hasty in making a decision. For instance, he was engaged to be married three times to three different ladies before me!'

FIVE

SIGNING UP FOR
THE BROWN HATS

Jim Laker made a spectacular jump from Catford CC to England inside a year during 1947, known as the Golden Year of English cricket when Denis Compton set a succession of batting records. In his first season with Surrey he was capped on 26 August and, two weeks later, he finished up top of the county's bowling averages with 79 wickets at 17.97. He said jubilantly to Pat Gibson, who wrote the words of his book *Cricket Contrasts*, 'To crown a remarkable first season I was a late selection for the MCC tour of the West Indies under Gubby Allen. I was on my way.' He was twenty-five, young for a spin bowler. But he had been lucky in the Second World War. Being sent to Cairo as a non-combatant, it gave him plenty of time to play cricket and football with a number of highly skilled international-class performers. When county cricket resumed, the ranks were filled with elderly amateurs and professionals in their thirties who played before 1939. There was a dearth of younger cricketers who had played top-class cricket during the hostilities. Some were killed and the most notable victim was Captain Hedley Verity of England and Yorkshire who was shot in the chest and later died in Caserta, Italy in 1943. He had one of the purest bowling actions of any of the great slow bowlers and he was a hero to Jim Laker.

In the First World War soldiers were told what to do by their public school-educated leaders and few rebelled. But after VE Day Winston

Churchill was voted out and his successor Clement Attlee strove to carry out the promises that had been ignored by a previous generation of politicians. Laker was like his mother Ellen – he stood up for himself and he refused to doff his cap to the employers who travelled first class and stayed in four and five-star hotels. The professionals had to pay their own way to the mainline stations to collect their third-class rail tickets and had to stay in cheap hotels and be given tiny meal allowances. The amateurs' dressing room was upstairs, much bigger, and the professionals' room smaller and sparse. It was flagrant class distinction and Laker rebelled against it. Dave Fletcher, one of their survivors of this era, said of Laker, 'He was always his own boss.'

In pre-war years, the pitches at the Oval were beautiful to bat on under the supervision of the club's groundsman, 'Bosser' Martin. By 1947 Martin had been replaced by Bert Lock, a friendly man who, like the incoming captain Stuart Surridge, preferred 'result' pitches. The order came to cut down on the mowing of the ground, making it difficult for the batsmen to reach the boundary. Lock had been an off-spinner and he lived at the Oval. There wasn't a more dedicated groundsman in the country in those years and Micky Stewart recalled, 'I played for three seasons out there before I saw a score of more than 300. Pitches used to go by lunch on the first day.' The pluperfect pitches of pre-war years deteriorated, basically because the War Office gave the order to turn the ground into a concentration camp for prisoners of war – except that there were no prisoners. An AA battery was built and the damage to the topsoil was immense.

The other Bert, Bert Flack, was another 'result' groundsman, as the Australians discovered to their cost in 1956. Laker's ability to spin the ball sharply on the flattest of pitches, honed by his four years playing on matting in Egypt, was revealed in August when the Surrey players caught the Southern Railway train to Portsmouth Harbour station. The last stage of the journey passed alongside the United Services ground, which boasted one of the best seaming pitches in the country, well suited to Hampshire's medium-pace bowlers. Errol Holmes won the toss and Gover and Alec Bedser, who were both on

99 wickets, were keenly expecting the result of their personal contest. Instead Laker took 2 wickets in succession on three occasions, finishing with 8 for 55.

At Bradford, on home soil, Laker and Eric Bedser routed Yorkshire, bidding for a sixth successive championship, on a pitch rated by the Press as 'a sticky dog.' Brian Sellers, the irascible Yorkshire captain, was taken aback by a delivery from Laker that spat off the wet pitch and turned past the shoulder of the startled skipper. As Laker was about to bowl the next ball, Sellers shaped to pull the ball to leg and was astonished to see it go straight on to hit middle stump – it was Laker's disguised straight ball. Sellers let out a stream of oaths. Bill Bowes, who was playing his final season for Yorkshire, said, 'Jim knows where he comes from.' Denis Compton completed his record of 3,816 runs in 1947, helping Middlesex to win the championship but when he played for the South of England against Sir Pelham Warner's XI in the Hastings Festival, almost a Test trial, Laker got him out and took a hat-trick in an 8-wicket match haul. Laker's reward was a place in the MCC squad for the tour of the West Indies that winter.

Apparently umpire Frank Chester advised Gubby Allen that Laker should go because he thought he was the best attacking off-spin bowler in the country. Jim always looked on Chester as the number one umpire, saying, 'He set new standards and changed the whole conception of what an umpire should be. As a raw recruit to the first-class game I recall asking him one day if it was true that umpires should give the doubt to the batsmen. He looked positively shaken. "Doubt?" he said. "There is never any doubt."' In a Test match later, trying to hook a bouncer from Keith Miller, not really the best man to take on, Jim felt a slight touch as the ball went into the wicketkeeper's gloves. There were no appeals and in the next over Jim stood next to Chester. The umpire whispered into his ear and said, 'You were a lucky lad!' After scoring four centuries for Worcestershire at the age of eighteen, Chester was called to the front line in Northern France and had a hand blown off. He stood in only 48 Tests in his thirty-three years as a top umpire.

England's tour to the West Indies (the name MCC was used because it was the controlling body) was a shattering experience for the younger players. Jim Swanton told the selectors that his friend Gubby Allen, the most powerful man in English cricket in the second half of the century, should be selected to captain the side although he was forty-five. Either him or Walter Robins or Erroll Holmes, who were also amateurs, both aged forty-one. There was no thought of appointing a professional. Karl Nunes, the first West Indian Test captain in 1928, had visited London as President of the Board to plead to the MCC to send a weakened side because he insisted that West Indies cricket was in a poor state. 'Gubby felt that we were hoodwinked,' said Swanton.

England's best players, including Len Hutton, Denis Compton, Bill Edrich, Cyril Washbrook, Norman Yardley, Reg Simpson, Harold Gimblett, Alec Bedser, Doug Wright and Eric Hollies were left out. Allen was duly appointed captain and manager and was England's oldest captain since W.G. Grace in 1899. These days England touring sides are accompanied by up to fifteen trainers, coaches, administrators, press advisers and physios. Allen did the lot. After injuring a calf on the storm-tossed voyage to Bridgetown on the 4,500-ton, near empty banana boat named *Tetela*, Allen commandeered two heat lamps and treated himself, and the growing number of other stricken players, in his bedroom.

The players were packed three at a time into tiny cabins and most of them were sick. Winston Place, the Lancashire batsman, hardly came out of his cabin in ten days, saying, 'Get a gun and put me down. I can't stand any more of this.' The tour proved to be a disaster from the start. As the players lined up for a picture at Euston Station ready to board a train to Liverpool dock, most of them were wearing long mackintoshes and trilbies. Laker, bare headed and wearing a heavy overcoat, totally unsuited for the constant 85-90-degree heat in the Caribbean, said, 'We looked like CIA operatives!' He wrote a postcard to his sister saying, 'We're going to play the best pitches in the world and I don't expect to do much out here.' He was wrong. The fledging off-spinner was the find of the tour and Swanton wrote in *The Daily Telegraph*, 'Not often has a young cricketer made a happier introduction to the best class.' Laker had figures of 7 for 103 in the West Indies first innings in the Test in Barbados. One of his victims was George

Headley, the first black man to captain the West Indies. Headley was thirty-eight at the time and was past his best. He tried to sweep and edged the ball into his stumps.

Cricket in the Caribbean was in a chaotic state with each country or colony demanding their preferred candidate to be the Test captain. They came up with an odd compromise – Headley to be captain in the First Test in Barbados and the Fourth Test in Jamaica, Jeffrey Stollmeyer as skipper in Trinidad in the second match and John Goddard, a white Barbadian, captain in the third in British Guiana before it became Guyana. Headley damaged his back in his second innings and played no further part in the series.

The West Indies had three of the greatest cricketers of all time in their side, the three Ws, Frank Worrell, whom C.L.R. James called 'the finest cricketing brain of his time', Everton Weekes, the record-breaking right-hand batsman and Clyde Walcott, who hit the ball harder than anyone and, as Laker said, 'It was like an unseeded tennis player in Wimbledon taking on the favourite.' Swanton and Crawford White of the *Daily Express* had to bowl to the England players in the nets because so many were out of action. Hutton was sent out as a reinforcement but Allen's men failed to win a single match. Laker's 18 wickets was the highest aggregate. He bowled 186 overs, much more than anyone else, and he had to keep going despite suffering from strained stomach muscles.

In some quarters George 'Gubby' Oswald Browning Allen CBE was looked on as a tyrant but most of the players who played with him liked him. Peter Richardson said, 'He was one of the best communicators you could meet. When he was manager, he never hid anything. He told the journalists everything. He loved his Bentleys. On one occasion he let me drive it. When we pulled in for petrol there was an awful burning smell. He said, "You've left the handbrake on!" It didn't upset him.' When he was at Eton, Allen was voted the outstanding fast schoolboy bowler in the country and his refusal to carry out Douglas Jardine's orders to bowl Bodyline in the 1932-33 series earned him worldwide respect. He was lauded after his leadership in the West Indies and virtually retired from playing, concentrating on his work in the Stock Exchange.

An even more one-sided encounter now occupied the nation's time in the summer of 1948 – taking on Don Bradman's side, which the new captain Norman Yardley, another amateur, called 'the greatest side that has visited these shores'. Nicknamed 'Lavender' by the cheekier members of the Australian squad, thirty-three-year-old Yardley had just been appointed Yorkshire's captain. Jim was thrust forward as England's biggest threat next to Alec Bedser and he was the first to say, 'I wasn't up to it.' Eight times the Australians recorded scores of 500 or more before the First Test at Nottingham and Jim's bowling took a pounding in the county match at the Oval against Bradman's side. His analysis of 1 for 137 out of a total of 632 was his worst ever and two weeks later, playing for the MCC against the tourists at Lord's, he gave away 127 runs in a score of 552. Nine sixes came off his bowling, mainly into the Tavern side. He was honest, admitting, 'When a batsman came down the wicket to me, I didn't know how to stop him thrashing me. I became flustered, dropped my guard and was wide open to punishment.'

Some spinners have had the yips, the mental state that soldiers faced in the First World War. But to Jim's credit, he kept going, seeking the answer to containing great attacking batsmen. It took a little time but he found it, in the first innings of the First Test at Trent Bridge, by scoring 63, his highest Test score. Coming in at nine, he and Alec Bedser came together at 74 for 8, needing 39 runs to overtake England's lowest total in a Test at Trent Bridge. They added 89 runs in 73 minutes and England were dismissed for 165. Jim had a habit of making self-deprecatory, wry comments about himself and this was another example of it. He said, 'Ray Lindwall dropped one short at me. I went for the hook and the ball went like a rocket, square on the offside for four. I was just a little late on the shot.' He had congratulatory telegrams from one of his sisters Margaret and her husband, a letter from his old school Salts High School, jointly written by the Head Boy and Head Girl and a telegram from George Parkin, his former Head.

His confidence rose by the minute and when he started bowling he had a startling spell of 3 for 22 in 12.4 overs, removing Sid Barnes, Arthur Morris and Keith Miller, for a duck, before Yardley, a moderate cricketer and an average captain, took him off and took the new ball. In that series a new ball was available after only fifty-five overs, virtually handing the series to Australia before a ball was bowled. Lindwall and Miller were always fresh and they were at least 10mph quicker than England's opening bowlers Bill Edrich and Bedser. Bradman was termed Bedser's bunny by the *Daily Express* writer Brian Chapman after being dismissed by him for the third successive time, but only when The Don reached 138. Lindwall and Miller bowled a very high proportion of bouncers and one cricket historian suggested the reason why – the Australians stopped off to play a friendly game in Colombo on the voyage to England and afterwards they discovered the pitch was two yards too long! Laker bowled 55 overs to record 4 for 134 in Australia's 509. Denis Compton's 184, one of his finest masterpieces, failed to prevent England going down by 8 wickets. Miller bounced him in the closing light and attempting to hook, he lost his footing and fell on his wicket.

Jim was ready for the next bout, on his debut at Lord's in the Second Test. He received the usual letter from Lord's giving his instructions but there was no entrance ticket to the ground in the envelope. He was still living in Forest Hill, nine miles south, and with no car – he didn't own one until he was thirty – he carried his huge, leather cricket bag to the Great Western Hotel in Paddington via bus and underground. Next morning, by public transport, he arrived at the Grace Gates at 10.15 a.m. and told two attendants, 'I'm Jim Laker.' The size of his bag might have given a clue but one said, 'Where's your ticket?' 'I haven't been given one,' said Jim. The men were sceptical. But the chief groundsman spotted him and said, 'He's certainly Jim Laker. Denis Compton gave him a hiding here last summer!' The Gloucestershire batsman George Emmett was also held up. He was told, 'We've had three George Emmetts here already this morning.' Sunil Gavaskar and Clive Lloyd are just two of the many famous cricketers who have been rejected at the gates.

An odd fact about the series was that Bradman only won the toss once. He decided to bat and most experts thought he was wrong to bat because the ball swung before lunch and the personable Sid Barnes was caught by Len Hutton at leg slip – a common fielding place of the day that is now almost obsolete – for a duck. Barnes was in the Keith Miller class as a punter and put on £8 to score a century at odds of 15-1. 'I fell for the old con trick,' said Barnes. But when he batted a second time the conditions were ideal and he collected his £120 after scoring 141 and giving Jim's bowling some fearful punishment, including 21 off one over. Barnes wrote, 'Jim's off-spinners were just made for lofted strokes and my final 41 runs came in 12 minutes before holing out to Yardley going for another six.'

Jim had a more reassuring account of the match. 'When the Don first came in I bowled one of my best overs in my career,' he said. 'I was at the Nursery End, which meant that my deliveries had to turn up the considerable slope and Don played for the turn off my first ball and was beaten because it went the other way down the hill. The process was reversed for the next ball. He played for it going away and it broke back at him. Don would have been lbw but he had the faintest of edges. The third and fourth balls also worried Don. As I passed him at the end of the over, he said, "Well bowled, Jim. Thank goodness, that's over. Now we can get on with some batting."' In Jim's next over, Bradman hit his first ball for four and normal service resumed. Jim's meagre 0 for 17 in 7 overs in the first innings was surprisingly low in the circumstances with Bedser bowling 43 overs and Alec Coxon 35. Rain fell to ruin England's remote chances of amassing 596 to win and they were dismissed for 186, losing by 409 runs on a rain-affected pitch. Laker's 2 for 111 in 31.2 overs was deemed to be unsatisfactory and he was one of four others, including Hutton, to be dropped.

In his book *Spinning Around the World*, Jim gave a brilliant analysis of Bradman as a person and a captain. 'You can't reach the very pinnacle of cricket achievement without being single-minded,' he wrote. 'That's why men like Bradman are often erroneously taken as mean types. Bradman was never very talkative but I liked him from the moment I first encountered him. He was never unfriendly, he was simply on the quiet side. I suppose, really, he was shy. I have always believed in the saying that still waters run deep, and that's why I admired Bradman.' He could have been speaking about himself. 'He was as hard as nails,' he went on. 'And it was difficult to fault him as a captain. His attitude was to win in the shortest time by the biggest possible margin. That sounds grim but the public got their value from it. An example of his unrelenting method was graphically shown in a game in which I was batting at number ten against the Australians and Jack Young, the cheerful little left-arm spinner from Middlesex, was the last man. We wanted a fabulous score to win, something like 450, and when Jack joined me, we were still only halfway there. We put on a few runs and Bradman was standing no nonsense.

'He called for the new ball. "All right Ray," he said, walking up to Lindwall, "get this over." I'll never forget it. Lindwall scared our best batsmen in that 1948 series, let alone a rabbit and the colour drained from Jack's face. "What the hell are we going to do now?" said Jack. I said, "Do our best." I hit a single off Ray's first ball and Jack had got into such a state by this time that he advanced down the wicket to meet the next explosive delivery as though he was facing a slow donkey-drop bowler. I shut my eyes. I had awful visions of Jack being struck between the eyes. I needn't have worried. Ray bowled one of full length, Jack played all round it and it was over.' Jim provided a different slant on Bradman's approach, using cunningness instead of aggression. In the Nottingham Test, when Jim scored his career Test highest total of 63 in partnership with Alec Bedser, he told Bill Johnston, the fast medium bowler, 'OK Bill, try tossing them up to Alec and pack the covers.' Johnston could always bowl in his slower style and after carrying on with the block, the forward defensive shot, Bedser was unable to resist and was caught at deep extra cover.

Jim reckoned that Bradman gave him an inferiority complex. 'Yet I never felt like that when I was bowling to Hutton, Compton, Morris, Weekes and other fine batsmen,' he said. 'As I ran up to bowl, Bradman seemed to know what I was going to bowl, know where the ball was going to pitch and know how many runs he was going to score. That was the uncanny impression he gave me.' Earlier in the tour in 1948, against the tourists at the Oval, Bradman came in and said, 'What a wonderful day for the game!' He started off with a three off the first ball he received and his hundred came in just over two hours. Stan Squires, the popular Surrey batsman who died at an early age, went up to him and shook hands and Bradman replied 'Thanks, yes, it's nice to make a few now and again.' In his career Bradman scored a hundred every three innings!

According to Jim, Stan Squires was the first spin bowler to bowl the 'doosra', the leg-break bowled from an off-break action, as demonstrated by Surrey's Saqlain Mushtaq before his highly successful Test career was curtailed by knee surgery in 2004, Sri Lanka's former world record holder Muttiah Muralitharan and a few others. Said Jim, 'Stan was the only man I knew who could bowl it. It was the perfectly disguised ball and Stan would often amuse himself and confuse others by bowling it out in the middle in between the fall of wickets. But he could bowl it only from a standing position, not with a run up, and he never attempted it in a match.'

Jim's inferiority complex probably came from being in the crowd at Headingley in 1930 at the age of eight when Bradman scored 300 in a day. After Bradman was knighted, Laker wrote to him to congratulate him and he wrote back – he always answered letters up to the end of his life – saying, 'I should have been a spectator at Headingley in 1948 but for Godfrey Evans dropping me!' Eight years later, Bradman must have remembered that letter because after Jim's 19 for 90 he went up to him at Old Trafford after the game and said, 'Well, I certainly was a spectator this time, Jim.'

Jim was good friends with Keith 'Nugget' Miller and they often drank together after the end of a day's play. One occasion, at a festival game at the end of the series, Miller told him, 'Don't think we are all as grim as the little man, Jim. I was no part of it.' The Australians were facing a near-Test side against the Leveson-Gower's XI at Scarborough and Miller wanted to have some fun in the middle. Scarborough is one of the smallest grounds in the country and he fancied hitting a few sixes. But Bradman insisted on winning in the shortest time. When Miller came in, the all-rounder took a single and then deliberately threw his wicket away. When Bradman came in, he played his innings as though it was a Test and scored 153, his eleventh century of the summer. His only concession to fun cricket was to bowl the last over and the Yorkshire committee made him an honorary life member of Yorkshire.

In the Lord's Test, Miller insisted that his back wouldn't allow him to bowl so Bradman gave the ball to Johnson. Jim was off the field at the time but he said later, 'Bradman was very piqued about it and his reaction was not to bowl Keith at all in subsequent games until Keith came along and pleaded for him to be given a chance to bowl again.' Miller played as a batsman at Lord's, scoring 4 and 74 and was lbw for 1 to Dick Pollard in the only innings in the rain-ruined Test at Old Trafford. Miller was reinstated as Lindwall's partner in the Fourth Test at Leeds. His 'sentence' had been served.

English cricket has had countless days of shame – a cliché to which the amusing and erudite Brian Chapman laid claim – and the final day of the Headingley Test was right up at the very top of the list. On a still-good batting pitch Yardley declared on 365 for 8, leaving Australia to score a highest-ever total of 404 in 345 minutes but, with only one spinner, Jim, the Aussies swept to victory with the help of a host of dropped catches and misfields. Arthur Morris, with 182, and Bradman, unbeaten on 173 in his final appearance on the ground that he had dominated, were both missed twice. Jim said, 'It was abject surrender.' Bedser said, 'We shouldn't have lost it. But with Jack Young, the Middlesex left-armer, in our side we would have won it but they preferred Ken Cranston.'

Jim admitted he hadn't bowled well, with 93 runs coming off 32 overs without a wicket. 'There was rough outside Arthur Morris's off stump and it was made for me to destroy him,' he recalled. 'But I failed hopelessly to take advantage of it. Our bowling was terrible. A few years later, that great Australian side would have done well to score 200 in the conditions at the end.' Laker and Lock in their prime might have achieved a different result. There were different views of the pitch. Godfrey Evans thought it was crumbling but Morris disagreed. Hutton and Compton had to come on, with Hutton bowling 5 full tosses in 4 overs. The series was won 4-0 and Jim was dropped. It was a merciful decision by the selectors. Bowled out for 52 on another day of shame in the final Test at his own ground, the Oval, England were beaten by an innings and 149 runs. Jim's 9 wickets in the series cost 52.44 but he was still third in the averages.

Eric Hollies, the stocky little thirty-six-year-old Warwickshire leg-spin and googly bowler who played in 13 Tests and took 10 for 49 against Nottinghamshire two years previously, took his place. When Bradman came in at 117 for 1 he was given a standing ovation on his final appearance and the England players stood around, rather aimlessly, as Norman Yardley lifted his cap and called for three cheers. Yardley was standing on what is now known as the 'prohibited zone' of the pitch and Alec Bedser was standing in a similar position at the other end. The umpires shouldn't have allowed it! It is unlikely that the state of the pitch caused Bradman's famous second-ball duck and the general theory was that he had tears in his eyes that affected his judgement not to play forward to a googly. He played back instead. 'I think it contributed to his dismissal without actually causing it,' said Jim. 'It was a bit of both – a good ball, the googly, from Eric Hollies, plus the occasion. I don't care how long a sportsman has been at the top of the tree – there are occasions when the roar of the crowd deeply affects him. For myself, I did not know how to react to the applause when I took my 19 wickets at Old Trafford. I was elated, naturally, but also very disturbed emotionally. Some show it, others are better at hiding it – but we are all susceptible.' If Bradman had scored 4 runs he would have finished with a Test average of 100. His Test average was 99.94 and the next man in the list is South Africa's Graeme Pollock with 60.97. Pollock is a long, long way behind, an indication of the way Bradman dominated the art of batting. Sid Barnes, the irreverent opening batsman, was the first man to be out and rushed back to the dressing room to remove his gear in order to film the proceedings from the balcony. When Bradman arrived back to the away dressing room, Barnes said to him, 'I've filmed your entire innings!'

Most people who talk about the greatest pair of slow bowlers of post-war years, if not all time, start in this order, 'Lock AND Laker.' Surrey named two stands on the right of the pavilion at the Brit Oval 'Lock and Laker.' But alphabetically it should be the other way round. Also, Laker was the older man by seven years, the one who set more records and he did, after all, take 19 wickets in a match. 'I looked up to him,' said Lock. 'I was the youngest player and he was an established player.'

Laker was the leader because he was more intelligent than Lock, had more social skills and was a better, controlled spin bowler. Lock, with a village cricket background, was in awe of the Yorkshireman from the North and tried to compete by being more aggressive and sparky than the laid-back Laker. When he was younger, Lock threw himself enthusiastically into action almost in reckless fashion, encouraging the view that his behaviour was rather immature. This over-excitability throughout most of his career may well have been enhanced by his intake of caffeine. He used to say, 'I was a big coffee drinker.'

Jim was more sophisticated and he was able to mix with business leaders at receptions whereas Lock stood in a corner with his mates. Lock was a bit gauche and although he travelled around the world and was a household name he still retained that quality. Micky Stewart, Surrey's first professional captain, said, 'When he was captain of Leicestershire we were staying in Leicester before a game and Lockey rang me and said, "Michael, you are going to be taken to one of the best restaurants in the district and I will be sending a car round at seven."That wasn't the real Lockey. Everyone knew me as Micky and as a young player Jim told me not to muck around with your name. "It's Micky and you stick to it," said Jim. Anyway, Lockey came round to collect me and we went off to this posh place outside town. After a while, the wine waiter said to him, "Mr Lock, are you ready to order your wine?""Not now," said Lockey. Ten minutes later, the waiter repeated his question. "Later, later," said Lockey. A little later, the waiter came up. "Have you made up your mind, Mr Lock?" he said. Lockey looked up. "Yes," he said. "Red!"

'But he had a heart of gold. He gave my wife Sheila her first Test match ticket and she was delighted. While Jim was smartly dressed and tidy, Lockey was always scruffy, even if he was wearing an expensive suit. On a trip to Rhodesia, as it was, he turned up wearing a mauve suit every day we were there. The hosts arranged for a trip down the Zambesi after visiting the Victoria Falls and we were about to set off when we noticed that Lockey was missing. After a brief search, we left and an hour later, on the way to Monkey Island, I saw him waving from a canoe, still wearing his mauve suit and holding a bottle of gin in one hand and a glass in the other.'

The two great spin bowlers were rivals, not friends in the early years and it was later that Lock realised that being in someone's else shadow wasn't necessarily a cause of lifelong resentment. In their later years they became good friends and he wrote a fulsome tribute to Jim after he died and he told Lilly, 'I wish I hadn't taken that one wicket in the Old Trafford Test.'

Stuart Surridge had to treat the two men differently. He put his arm round Jim to reassure him when things weren't going too well and he often relented when he wanted to change Jim's field. 'Stuart was a very attacking captain he wanted to bring fielders in,' said Stewart. 'But Jim always wanted someone out at cowshot corner, deep long on, just in case someone connected with a big swing. If Stuart tried to insist, Jim would say, "Put yourself on." Stuart nearly always gave in. But with Lock, he was like the ringmaster, giving out orders all the time. Keith Miller once said to me, "I wouldn't talk to my dog the way he treats Lockey!" When Jim died we wondered what would happen with his ashes. Someone suggested that his ashes should be scattered on the outfield at the Oval and I said the best place, cowshot corner, was the right spot! Lilly agreed.'

Lock rarely argued with his captain. He explained, 'My exuberance on the field apparently gave the wrong impression in some quarters. People thought I was too demonstrative in my appeals and gesticulations. I said it stemmed only from keenness. Being unrestrained in my gestures kept me alert and made me try harder.' Lock was born into cricket, on 5 July 1929, son of a useful club cricketer who bowled at a lively pace for Limpsfield Cricket Club, where the future Test star was born. His book *For Surrey and England*, published in 1957, started, 'As long as I can remember, cricket has meant everything to me.' At the age of six he had his picture taken wearing his cricket gear, including pads, gloves and bat. The headmaster of the village school, a Mr Moulding, was a cricketer and the cricket ground where his career started was right next door on the common. 'The square was excellent and we were allowed to have the school nets rigged up on the turf close to the match wickets,' Lock recalled. 'We never had the fear of getting a crack on the head from a ball of good length and we learned to meet the ball with a straight bat instead of backing away and aiming hopeful swipes. This meant we had to strive for accuracy. Mr Moulding would put a white handkerchief on a good length to help accuracy.'

With his background, Lock's development was much quicker than Jim's, who had no father to encourage him. Lock became one of the world's great catchers and his natural skill was improved by playing a game called 'Wall' in the school playground. A boy was stationed in front of a high wall and three others, standing around fifteen yards away, hurled tennis balls at him with the aim of hitting him. The boy scored a point for catching the ball and the three others scored a point if their throw hit the victim. They had another game, throwing balls at a corner of the wall, with the ball coming off in different angles. Fifty years on, the ECB are spending millions of pounds on coaching well-equipped youngsters who lack the motivation of a Lock or Laker. Cricket-loving schoolteachers did that work for nothing and boys like Lock tried harder to get to the top. Jim was lucky to have someone recommend him at the Oval and Tony Lock had the biggest name in cricket to help him – Sir Henry Dudley Gresham Leveson-Gower, the former Surrey captain and president, cricket philanthropist, Test selector and administrator known as 'Shrimp', who lived two miles away at Titsey. With patronage like that, he soon found himself in the Surrey Colts before his fifteenth birthday and he made his first-class debut at the age of seventeen years eight days. He was Surrey's youngest player and no-one has yet broken his record.

'I first recall him as a well-made youngster of sixteen, a head full of red hair, with a quiff falling over his eyes,' wrote Jim in his book *A Spin with Laker*, published in 1979. 'The first time we played together was in a second eleven game at Bristol in 1947 and he was a slow, flighty bowler and bowled with little or no spin, to a deep extra cover and a long off. The pitch was given the sand treatment and it was made for the finger spinner. The ball spun at right angles and it wasn't an exaggeration to say that Lockey dropped four catches in the first hour. I said to the Hon. R.R. Blades, the skipper, "Do the kid a favour and stick him on the boundary, he'll never be a short leg as long as he plays the game." That wasn't the most prophetic remark and we had a lots of laughs repeating it over the years.'

While Jim headed the Surrey bowling averages with 66 wickets in 1947, Lock was doing his National Service with the Royal Artillery in Cornwall and Shropshire. Too much square bashing wrecked his right knee and, at the age of eighteen, he had both cartilages removed. His right leg was the one that landed as he bowled. In his twenty-five years with Surrey, Leicestershire and Western Australia he bowled 271,163 deliveries, mainly when he had pain from his knee. He had his knee strapped up every day but rarely complained. He also had the same problem as Jim about his sore spinning finger and he ripped the ball so hard that there were occasions when the bone was exposed. He was one of the toughest, most courageous cricketers of his time, or at any time. Both men had to miss matches but Lock took more chances with his fitness. 'Someone people thought Jim didn't fancy it whereas Lockey would usually play when injured,' said Stewart. 'He had his knee wrapped up with supporting pieces of equipment and off he went. Most big spinners of the ball played with a damaged bowling finger but I reckon it's twenty years since I last saw one with a callous on his finger. There aren't any spinners now of that type.'

After his National Service, Lock returned to the Oval and he soon realised that he rarely matched the wicket taking skill of Jim. 'We discussed things and I told him he ought to bowl quicker,' said Jim. 'I spent the best part of two weeks in the nets, showing him how to spin the ball, explaining what he had to get his fingers round it and give it a flick and warning that if he was really going to spin it, it would hurt because he would get sore fingers.' That wasn't the act of a bitter rival, it was an act of kindness. That winter Lock took a winter job with the Allders Indoor Cricket School in Croydon as a coach. The roof was much lower than any other cricket school in the country, even lower than Alf Gover's in Wandsworth, and Lock had to bowl much quicker to avoid hitting the roof. By the time he returned to the Oval for pre-season practice the other players noticed that his action had completed changed. There was a jerk in the arm when he delivered the ball. Sir Alec Bedser said, 'Lockey bowled his first ball in the nets, to Jack Parker, and the ball landed on Jack's front foot at a very brisk pace. Jack said, "You've f—ing thrown that!" Lockey couldn't argue with that. He carried on in that style and it took a couple of years before an umpire did anything about it.'

A diplomatic Jim said, 'I wasn't quite sure whether his delivery was illegal but it was certainly very close to the mark. He would certainly have been banned in present times.' He was wrong – since the ICC introduced a five per cent tolerance in spin bowling actions Lock would have probably got away with it. The threat to the apprehensive batsmen came with a jerk of the arm, which came over much quicker. Lock was now bowling medium-fast and was no longer a slow bowler. In 1952 he topped Surrey's championship averages with 116 wickets at 16.53 to Jim's 86 at 16.87 and it was Surrey's first championship success in their run of seven titles in a row. Lock made his Test debut against India at Old Trafford and the first time he touched the ball he made a catch from Alec Bedser's bowling off Vinoo Mankad. Most of the cricketers in England were talking about Lock's action and when Doug Insole had his middle stump flattened, he said, 'I agree I'm out, but was I bowled or run out?' As a quicker one from Lock smacked into the gloves of wicketkeeper Arthur McIntyre, Keith Miller shouted, 'Strike one!' In May umpire Fred Price no-balled him on three occasions for throwing against the hapless Indians. 'I felt like exploding,' said Lock. 'He never warned me. One of the first things you learn in cricket is to accept the umpire's decisions as final. It's a waste of time to argue.' There was a big crowd and there was so much barracking that Price had to sit down to wait for the noise to subside. Surridge calmed the furious Lock, saying, 'No other umpire has done that so don't get upset and lose control.'

Lock and Laker played together in the Fourth and Fifth Tests in 1953 and played key roles in regaining the Ashes in the final Test after there had been four draws. According to the Australian captain Lindsay Hassett, groundsman Bert Lock prepared a special, dry pitch ideally suited for the spin bowlers; 'It was a different proposition from that on which the two county games were played and Lock and Laker proved far too good for our batsmen. They captured 9 wickets for 120 runs from 37 overs. That was in marked contrast to their performance in the two matches against Australia when their combined analyses read

4 for 252 from 74 overs.' In the away dressing room, the Australians opened bottle after bottle of champagne and Hassett threw his glass into the large clock. Others joined in and soon the floor was covered with broken glass. It cost Surrey a good sum to clean up afterwards. Bedser took 39 wickets in the series, one more than the rest of the England bowlers and just over half a century later he said, 'The 2005 Ashes win was very similar to 1953, except that none of our players got a parade in London and didn't get a medal.'

Every season during the championship-winning years there was a battle between Lock and Laker to be first past the 100-wicket mark. Jim believed that Lock's 'new' action helped improve his own form. 'I had to try harder to stay ahead of him,' he said. Both Surrey spin bowlers were selected for the MCC tour of the West Indies in 1953-54 and they took 14 wickets each against some of the greatest batsmen in the world. But whereas Lock was no-balled and disgraced, Jim did a reasonable job. He dismissed Clyde Walcott for his 1,000th first-class wicket and his bowling average was 33.50, high by his standards, but well under Lock's 51.28. Walcott was convinced that the lbw decision was at fault and he said to Jim, 'That would have missed all three.' Jim replied, 'I only asked because it would be my 1,000th!' 'I struck up an early friendship with Jim,' said Walcott. 'He had the dry sense of humour of a Yorkshireman and we were constantly ribbing each other. He got me out 13 times, 11 in Tests and I suppose I was his bunny, the same way Arthur Morris was Alec Bedser's bunny.'

Jim gave blood for England's cause on a slow pitch in Port of Spain in the Fourth Test. Batting alongside Fred Trueman, England's greatest living Yorkshireman, said, 'I've assessed the situation, Jim lad, thee take Frank King and I'll take Worrell.' Facing a short ball from the much faster King, Jim was struck above the eye and needed stitches. He had to go to hospital later and with the final Test six days ahead, against King on a faster, bouncier pitch at Sabina Park in Kingston, he thought his chances of being retained in the side were fading. But Len Hutton wanted him to play and he relented. His second innings performance of 4 for 71 in 50 overs was hailed as a 'beautifully controlled exhibition of high-class spin bowling' by *The Times*.

Tour reports on players are still on the secret list but twelve years later details of Hutton's report on Jim appeared in *The Cricketer* and he was livid. The relevant parts said, 'He is an extremely fine bowler but he has a tendency to be afraid of certain batsmen instead of adopting the attitude, "I am a better bowler than you are a batsman." When a good batsman is at the wicket he is inclined to indicate his unwillingness to bowl. Laker should be considered in committee before future selection for overseas tours.' That probably kept him out of the next tour to Australia. Both Lock and Trueman had critical reports, neither of which was leaked, and Lock blamed some incidents on 'the sarcastic and nasty comments' about them by senior players. It was a controversial tour with a riot at Kingston when J.K. Holt was unfairly given out and Jamaican Prime Minister Michael Manley wrote, 'Lock's bowling showed as much hostility as any quick bowler that has ever lived.'

In the First Test the revered veteran George Headley had his career ended at the age of forty-four by a fast throw from Lock and as he returned to the pavilion he said 'Dis ain't cricket, man, dis is war!' 'It was the most blatant throw I've ever seen,' said Walcott. Something had to be done and, in the Second Test in Barbados, umpire Harold Walcott, uncle of Clyde, no-balled Lock, nicknamed 'Shylock' by the Bajan supporters, from square leg. The batsman was seventeen-year-old Garfield Sobers. 'I was a bit late on it,' he said. 'I'd removed my gloves before I heard the call. When I spoke to Lockey later he told me, "I've changed, I'm now bowling properly."' But in the next game, against Barbados, he was no-balled again, by umpire Cortez Jordan and Harold Walcott. Today a bowler who is 'called' is taken out of the game for his action to be remodelled. Lock had to sort it out himself and it wasn't until the tour to New Zealand in 1958-59 when he saw a film of his action taken by the New Zealander bowler Harry Cave that he realised he had been flouting the laws. He finally reverted back to his original action from when he was in his teens. The amateur administrators were shamefully slow to act against the chuckers and Jim came out with a cynical observation. He said to David Sheppard, 'Lockey is throwing this year. If I can turn the ball two inches, he is turning it twice as much!'

Jim always produced figures to show that he took more wickets away from the Oval than at his own ground, evidence to be used that Bert Lock's pitches were not specially prepared to suit Lock and Laker. Micky Stewart said, 'None of the pitches were very good, home or away. They were nothing like they are now. At the Oval the pitches started breaking up on the first morning and I remember being hit in the throat by a lifter from Ray Illingworth at ten to twelve! Every ball did something and you had to work on your technique, cushioning the ball, or let it go. Surrey had the best attack in the world and it was hard work to make a total against them. They rarely needed a second new ball.'

Jim was keen to show that he took more wickets at a slightly lower cost at Lord's than at the Oval. The menace of Lock, with his suspect action, and Jim, with his prodigious spin and relentless accuracy, gave Surrey a psychological advantage and this feeling in the away dressing room led to the refrain, 'Ashes to ashes, dust to dust. If Laker doesn't get me, Lockey must.' Often the dust was flying up from both ends of the pitch. There was little dust coming up in the wet summer of 1954 when Surrey, eighth in the table with ten matches remaining, roared through the field to win, finishing 22 points ahead of Yorkshire. Lock and Laker shared 103 wickets, five of the matches ended in two days and one, against Worcestershire, ended on the first day with Worcestershire bowled out for 25 and 40 after Surridge declared on 92 for 3. 'I heard the weather forecast,' explained Surridge.

The public school educated administrators at Lord's were becoming concerned about the activities of Lock and Laker. In their eyes, they considered them as Burke and Hare, the Victorian villains, not as respectable as Fortnum & Mason or Marks & Spencer. They were suspicious of both men – some of them marked them down as 'awkward' – and Jim was picked for only one Test in the inaugural series against Pakistan and Lock was left out completely. From the day Jim was first selected for England to the last Test he was chosen, he could have played 99 Tests. But he only appeared in 46. In that dreary summer of 1954, Lock took 125 wickets at 16 and Jim 135 at 15.17 yet neither was selected for the 1954-55 tour of Australia. In the opening match of the season against the MCC at Lord's, Jim had figures of 15 for 97, good practice for 19 for 90 two years hence.

There were outstanding spin bowlers around, like Wardle, Tattersall, Shepherd, Illingworth and Fred Titmus but were they so much better than Lock and Laker? The Surrey pair only played together in one Test against South Africa in 1955 and they helped to win the rubber, 3–2, at the Oval with Lock having figures of 10 for 101 and Laker 7 for 84. Lock took 216 wickets in the summer, a total only exceeded by Tom Goddard's 238 in 1947. If they had been picked for every Test when they were available they could have finished up with 300 or more wickets instead of their respective figures of 174 wickets at 25.58 (Lock) and 193 at 21.24 (Laker). Together they captured 4,788 wickets. They were wicket machines, ploughing the nation's batsmen into the ground and they complemented each other beautifully. One, the elder, was calm, relentless and unemotional and the younger was excitable, slightly erratic and very dangerous with his quicker deliveries.

Lock and Laker weren't the only stars to be mysteriously dropped for supposed 'offences' by the Lord's hierarchy. Don Crossley, the member of the Cricket Memorabilia Society who was present at the 19 for 90 match, told a fascinating story about Bill Edrich, one of the best all-rounders of his time. He collects autographs and more than twenty years after Jim's record at Old Trafford, he contacted him and asked if he could come round to his house in Putney to sign some books. 'Jim wasn't too friendly,' he said. 'He did it but he came over as a dour Yorkshireman. Not long before Bill Edrich died at his home in Chesham, I visited him and he told me that he was left out of the England side between 1950 and 1953 because he upset Freddie Brown, the England manager, for laying on a party at his bedroom in the team hotel next to Brown's room. I thought it might have been a fanciful story but later I went to Freddie Brown's house in Sudbury. Freddie was very friendly and I asked him about the Edrich story. 'That's true,' said Freddie. 'That dreadful man!' One of John Warr's funniest witticisms was about being invitied to Edrich's fourth wedding – 'I've got a season ticket for your weddings,' he said.

On 23 April 1986 Mickey Stewart attended a St George's Day lunch at a London hotel and also sitting on the table were Bill Edrich, John

Murray, Fred Titmus and Don Bennett. 'When I got home Sheila had a telephone call saying that Jim had died that afternoon at 3.30 p.m.,' he said. 'We were shocked. I'd seen him at the Putney Hospital a day or two early and he was going home. He had to go back into a private hospital in Wimbledon to have his gall bladder removed and no-one thought he was in danger. That night John Murray rang and said, 'Have you heard the news? Bill Edrich has died. He wouldn't be left behind, would he!'

After coming well behind Jim in 1956, Lock was back in front the following summer, topping the bowling averages with 212 wickets at a meagre 12.02 to Jim's 126 at 15.54. He broke the all-ten barrier, taking 10 for 54 against Kent at Blackheath two weeks before Jim's 19 for 90. His match aggregate, 16 for 83, is still a Surrey record. He played a prominent role in England's 3-1 win over the West Indies, taking 18 wickets, 6 of them at the expense of Walcott. Surrey won their seventh championship in succession in 1958, before handing over the baton to Yorkshire. 'There was plenty of aggression out there,' said one player. 'A lot of chitchat but nothing really outwardly confrontational. They didn't like each other although some of players from either side got to know each other on tours.' Jim's 116 wickets at 14.23 helped to earn a place on the tour to Australia at the age of thirty-six. Lock went on the same trip but his knee kept him out of some matches yet still collected 170 wickets at 12.08. In 1959, the year the Jim left the Oval, Lock still took 111 wickets after his second remake of his bowling action. It worked so well that he was able to play first-class cricket for a further ten years – 'without a single objection to his action,' as Jim said.

Lock was very upset at the outcome of his benefit in 1960. He expected to pick up around £10,000, just short of Jim's £11,000, but in a wet summer he received a cheque for £4,700. In an article he blamed Jim, writing, 'I fancy I caught the backwash from his book. He had let his hair down in print on his retirement [in *Over to Me*] and as a result the public weren't exactly enamoured with temperamental star cricketers. I was shocked when my benefit was the smallest benefit for years. I had overcome two crises, the second operation on my knee and the throwing shemozzle, and I was banking on security from a good benefit.' The bald-headed Lock usually fielded without a cap for much of his career with Surrey and that may have contributed to the cancer of the throat of which he died in 1995. 'Jim didn't wear a cap most of the time,' said Stewart. No-one wore sunglasses, or sun cream or helmets.

After Jim's retirement with Surrey in 1959, Lock carried on for three more seasons and he regained his England place in 1961, hitting seven boundaries off Richie Benaud to turn the 'Trueman Test' towards victory at Headingley. The whitish-green piebald pitch, treated with chemicals, was a disgrace and Trueman, frequently bowling unplayable shooters, took 11 for 88. But the pitch at Lord's in the previous Test was even worse and Bill Lawry was struck countless times in his innings of 130, which was hailed as one of the greatest rearguard actions ever played at Lord's. Afterwards, remedial work was done at the Nursery End to eliminate the so-called ridge. Australia won at Lord's, otherwise their board may well have made an official protest. Doctored pitches were much more common in England than in Australia until the ECB introduced the standardisation of firmer, flatter pitches with powers to punish counties who failed to meet the new standards. Not surprisingly, Lock finished up the season with 127 wickets on these dodgy pitches but his average jumped to 28.48 and Surrey finished fifteenth in the championship.

Left out of the 1962-63 tour of Australia – the selectors chose three off-spinners and not one left-armer to confound a previous set of selectors who claimed that English off-spinners would never succeed Down Under! – he went to play for Western Australia. He settled in Perth with his family and became an inspirational, winning captain who transformed one of the weaker cricketing states into one of the best, taking 302 wickets at 23.87. Leicestershire's secretary Mike Turner also signed him to play county cricket between 1965 and 1967 and his figures were even better, 272 wickets at 18.80, taking the county to their highest position for eighty-eight years. Jim wrote, 'In place of the immature medium-paced spinner striving the whole time to pitch on the leg stump and hit the off was a bowler with the smooth, flowing action of a genuine left-arm spinner, making intelligent use of the breeze and capitalising on his thoughtful study of batsmen's weakness. He retained his boyish enthusiasm and the responsibility brought the best from him.'

At the age of thirty-eight, Lock was flown from Perth to the West Indies and played the last two Tests after Fred Titmus had four toes sheared off in a motorboat accident. He scored his highest Test score, 89, to preserve England's 1-0 winning margin at Georgetown despite being struck on the head by a stone. Jim's opinion of him changed, admitting, 'Having been seen to have had precious little in common, apart from a burning desire to take wickets, the passing years brought us closer together and our understanding and friendship became stronger than at any time. In my view, he was never truly appreciated. He was just about the greatest competitor I ever saw. I've seen him bowl 30 overs non-stop with knees and ankles strapped up to such an extent that many wouldn't have tried to walk down the pavilion steps. He had no peers as a short leg fieldsman and caught no less than 830 catches, only beaten by Frank Woolley and W.G. Grace.' The two spin bowlers met again in the Centenary Test in Melbourne in 1977 and they shared a hotel room. Jim later stayed with the Lock family on another visit. The rapprochement of the two complex, great bowlers had finally been achieved. 'I would take a lot of convincing that we ever had any serious rivals,' said Jim.

Lock's halcyon days in Western Australia ended in despair and, according to Micky Stewart, 'he died of a broken heart' on 30 March 1995, a few months older than Jim. After he retired at the age of forty-one he worked as a coach and, in 1980, a fifteen-year-old girl cricketer alleged he had sexually assaulted her. According to Stewart, the allegations became public through a phone-in programme about girls being molested by men. Police investigated her story and in 1994 the case was heard and many of Surrey's former players and committee men contributed around £8,000 to help pay his legal costs. Lock and his family were adamant that the 'incident' hadn't taken place. Most of his colleagues were convinced he was innocent, in the same way that the former Southampton football manager Dave Jones was found not guilty in similar circumstances. But there were others who thought 'there was something in it'. Lock was found not guilty by a 10-2 majority and immediately re-arrested and charged with offences with a ten-year-old. Two months later his wife Audrey died of cancer just before their forty-fifth wedding anniversary. He blamed himself for so much pressure being put on her. By this time he was suffering from cancer of the throat and his elder son Richard said, 'After Mum died, he became unsure of himself. He didn't want to go out in case people recognised him. He shut himself in the house because he was afraid someone would come and get him. The temperature would be 102°F and we'd go round to find the windows and doors locked up and Dad inside.' Stewart said, 'I rang him just before he died and he said he wasn't eating. He was drinking whisky. It was a tragedy, very sad.' The second set of charges were dropped earlier in February and Lock died two months later. Just before he said, 'I suppose when I die it won't be Tony Lock, the greatest left-arm bowler to play for England, but Tony Lock, the guy who was up on sex charges.'

After Jim died, Lock wrote an article about his friend in the Surrey yearbook. This is what he wrote: 'The telephone rings constantly in my house, so it was not out of the ordinary when it rang one morning in the Australian winter. As I picked up the nearest receiver the call was from London and in the next two minutes my world was completely shattered. A gentleman from the BBC was informing me of the death of Jim Laker. The voice at the other end was asking if I could say a few words on this sad event. From memory, I said, "The world may have lost a great cricketer but I have lost a bloody good friend." The rest of the day was fairly hazy. The telephone rang all the time; most of the time my wife answered.

'During dinner that night I placed on the table some beautiful glassware, a gift from J.C. and I thought it appropriate to drink to his memory, followed by a toast to his widow Lilly, hoping she could cope with her tragic loss. I was unable to attend the service so my first visit will be to Lilly on my next visit to England. Naturally my thoughts went back a number of years to when I bowled opposite probably the greatest spin bowler I have ever seen. He used to wander in to bowl and he knew exactly where it was going to land, and the scoreboard would read "caught Lock, bowled Laker." I had the greatest confidence in his ability so I was able to stand very close knowing I wouldn't get hit. If a catch was not held, J.C. would stand there looking at me, one arm folded across his chest, cupping his chin in his other hand. Not a word passed his lips but I would know what he was thinking.

'His feat of taking 8 for 2 during the 1950 Test Trial at Bradford was incredible. Considering he gave his teammate Eric Bedser one to get off the mark, makes it more incredible. His legendary bowling at Old Trafford when he totalled 19 wickets (years later I often wished I had not taken the odd one) and his 10 wickets against the Australians in the same year at the Oval made me admit to myself that he was the greatest. He stayed with me during a visit to Perth and my wife and I decided to have a party consisting of a few of the visiting English team and friends. J.C. decided he would be in charge of the bar and started off with great zest, which lasted all of ten minutes. He retired to a quiet corner and with a slight grin, said, "that's not for me" and became a guest drinker for the rest of the evening. J.C. and I were not always the greatest of friends, or for that matter, even friends for he was a very hard man to get to know, very deep and quiet. Naturally we had the greatest respect for each other's ability but it wasn't until the Centenary Test in Melbourne, when Jim and I shared a room, that we became very close friends. I have no idea how it actually happened but it did and this is why I have such fond memories of that particular match.

'J.C. did not always have the dour Yorkshire spirit when it came to batting. With a pick up that started at extra cover, then in a circular way to the correct position, with monotonous regularity he would drive the ball via the edge of his bat to the boundary between first and second slip. A slight shrug of the shoulders and a slow grin would await the next delivery. He was not the greatest of fielders but when he did take a catch in the gully from my bowling he would say, "Lockey, that's one you owe me. What would be done without me fielding here?" I have thought a great deal about J.C. in the past few months and firmly believe he is not really dead. It was suddenly decided that his services were required on a much higher level and no doubt is now discussing tactics with the great players who went before him. To those of you who saw the great man bowl you were very lucky and, for those of you less fortunate, you have now to put up with very poor imitations. I had the honour of playing cricket with him but more than that, I had the honour to have him as my friend.'

1. *Right:* Young Jim, watched by his proud mother Ellen.

2. *Below middle:* The house in Kirlands Avenue, Baildon, where Jim was happiest as a boy.

3. *Below bottom:* The distinctive Salt School at Shipley where Jim was educated.

4. A pious Jim.

5. Midfielder Jim is front row, second from right.

6. Jim as a mature
fifteen year old.

7. Jim (right) playing for the British Army in Cairo in the Second World War.

8. Pictured on the day when he started work at Barclay's Bank, in Market Street, Bradford on 9 February 1939. Jim was seventeen.

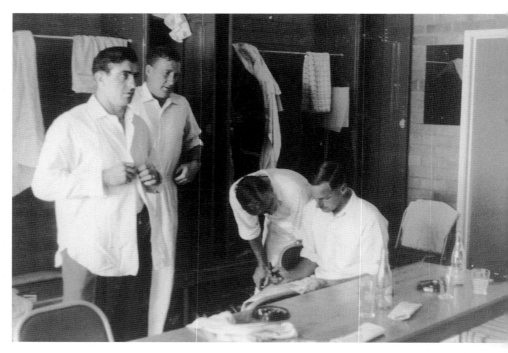

9. Fred Trueman, Jim Laker and Peter Richardson await skipper Peter May's orders.

10. Another Surrey Championship-winning side. From left to right: Alec Bedser, Stuart Surridge, Peter May, Arthur McIntyre, Jim Laker, Peter Loader, Eric Bedser, Tony Lock, Ken Barrington, Micky Stewart and Bernie Constable.

11. Lilly and Jim with friends in New Zealand in 1951.

12. Jim hits a four off Jimmy Gray of Hampshire at the Oval, 5 August 1953. (*Getty Images*)

14. Keith Miller of Australia is bowled out by Jim at the Oval, 2 August 1956. (*Getty Images*)

13. *Opposite page, below:* Jim catches Roy Smith of Somerset from a ball by Lock at the Oval, 16 May 1955. Surrey's off trap is Peter May to the right of Jim, skipper Stuart Surridge and wicketkeeper Arthur McIntyre. (*Getty Images*)

15. The beaten Aussies at Old Trafford 1956 with a smiling Johnson, the skipper, flanked by Keith Miller and Ray Lindwall with Richie Benaud at the rear.

16. Doug Insole (left), an SA official, Peter Richardson (smoking), Jim and Johnny Wardle on the tour of South Africa in 1957.

17. *Above:* Colin Cowdrey, Ian Johnson and Jim Laker.

18. *Right:* Peter May and Jim (smoking) at a fancy dress party in South Africa.

Presented by the Yorkshire CCC to commemorate
his performance for England v The Rest
at Bradford 1950

14 overs, 12 maidens, 2 runs, 8 wickets

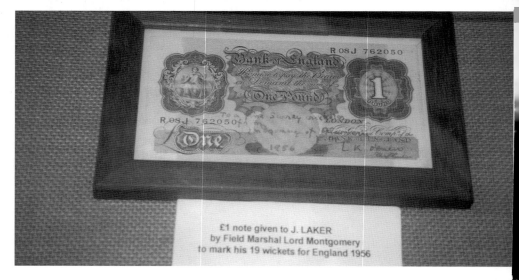

£1 note given to J. LAKER
by Field Marshal Lord Montgomery
to mark his 19 wickets for England 1956

20. The England squad on the way to SA in 1957. From left to right: Colin Cowdrey, Godfrey Evans, Tony Lock, Johnny Wardle, Trevor Bailey, Denis Compton, Jim Laker, Peter May (Captain), J.S. Bevan, Lord Rotherwick, Captain Farrow, Freddie Brown (Manager), Doug Insole, Peter Richardson, Brian Taylor, Alan Oakman, Frank Tyson, Peter Loader, Brian Statham, Jim Parks and George Duckworth (scorer).

19. *Opposite page:* Jim's most prized trophies. The two balls that took 19-90 (top), the ball he took 8-2 with in 1950 (middle) and £1 signed by Field Marshal Lord Montgomery (bottom). (Courtesy of Glenys Williams, Lord's Museum, Marylebone Cricket Club)

21. *Right:* Lord Monkton, twice President at Surrey CCC, voted for Jim Laker's exclusion from membership at the club in 1960.

22. Essex 1962. Laker is seated far left.

23. From left to right: Freddie Laker, Jim Laker, and friend John Powell.

24. Ken and Ann Barrington are seated on the front left-hand side of the picture, Lilly and Jim Laker are seated on the right. Shelia and Micky Stewart are standing far right.

25. English Press v. Australian Press at Harrogate 1978. Back row, from left to right: Jack Fingleton, Ian Chappell, –?–, Kerry Packer, David Lord, Greg Chappell, –?–, –?–, Henry Blofeld, –?–, Scyld Berry, Brian Scovell, –?–, David Frith, Peter MacFarline, Peter Lush, –?–. Front Row: –?–, –?–, –?–, –?–, Geoff Wheeler, Alan Shiel, Wendy Wimbush, John Parker.

26. Jim golfing with Fred Perry in Jamaica.

27. Jim going racing with Willie Rushton.

28. Surrey's Peter Loader, Ron Tindall, Jim Laker, Tony Lock and Ken Barrington meeting up in Australia.

29. Jim as an entertainer.

30. *Above left:* Jim and Lilly at the Piccadilly Hotel in 1966.

31. *Above right:* Groundsman Bert Flack with Jim at Old Trafford.

32. Jim (extreme left, standing) surrounded by other sporting stars.

33. Godfrey Evans and Jim at a question-and-answer session.

34. A happy Jim with Godfrey Evans and Tom Graveney in 1985. Six months later he died.

SIX

THE FINGER OF FATE

David Montague, Surrey's physiotherapist, probably spent more time with Jim than his own family when Jim was at the height of his career. Jim's arthritic finger, the index finger of his bowling hand, increasingly became painful and that hastened his retirement. The corn on the inside of the finger needed continual treatment. When I called at his home in Coulsdon, David was reading *Over to Me*, Jim's second book, published in 1960, which led to his seven-year exile from cricket. It was an extraordinary coincidence and David, who was the first qualified physiotherapist to go on an England tour, said, 'I've been re-reading it after a long time. It certainly caused a bit of a rumpus!'

Chapter one started with a lament about the way Jim was left out of the 1950-51 and 1954-55 tours of Australia before he was eventually selected for the 1958-59 tour, known as the Chucking Tour because three Australian bowlers, Gordon Rorke, Ian Meckiff and Jim Burke, were purged from the game under Law 24, governing the fairness of a delivery. Being overlooked caused Jim a lot of bitterness over the years and he blamed the 'amateur' brigade who made the selecting decisions. He said, 'Playing against Australia gives a player the greatest thrill he can experience, particularly in Australia. Once you have done that, once you have played in a Test match at Sydney or Melbourne, Brisbane or Adelaide, you can die happy.

You really have reached the top of the tree.' It took him twelve years to reach it.

Jim blamed Freddie Brown for his omission from the 1950–51 tour when he was established as England's leading off-spinner and Brown was the England captain. 'They took Brian Close, a nineteen-year-old "discovery" on a hunch,' said Jim. 'In the previous season he took 20 wickets at an average of 19.30 and I had taken 166 wickets at 15.32. The outcome from Close's selection was that he scored 1 run and took 1 wicket in his one Test. To put it mildly, I should have gone. Like a young man who has just been jilted, I jumped at the next thing that came along, which turned out to be a tour to India with a Commonwealth XI.'

Jim wasn't the only outstanding off-spin bowler who was jilted. Roy Tattersall, the Lancashire bowler born in the same year as Jim, took 193 wickets in the 1950 season, topping the averages. But the selectors chose a lopsided spin attack of Close, Doug Wright, Eric Hollies and Bob Berry that didn't include a quality off-spinner. 'I don't think they thought off-spinners would do so well out there,' said Tattersall. 'But when Doug Wright and Trevor Bailey were injured, Brian Statham and I were flown out there and we played in the final Test.' Lilly Laker was a close friend and neighbour of Dorothy Hutton and over one of their lunches, Dorothy brought up the subject of blue eyes. She said Len had a theory that any cricketer with blue eyes would be less successful in Australia because of the light in Australia. 'Well,' said Lilly, 'Jim's eyes were blue!' When the story was related to Roy Tattersall, he said, 'I never heard of that. I don't think it happened. No, it was because they thought it wouldn't turn so much in Australia. Jim was a great bowler and he and I were friendly rivals and we played in the same England side in two Tests. You wouldn't see that today, two off-spinners in the same side.'

Leslie Ames, the Kent and England wicketkeeper, captained the Commonwealth side and when their ship, the *Chusan*, stopped at Port Said, overtaking the MCC's vessel *Stratheden*, which departed a day earlier, Jim asked him about the rumour that Close was preferred to him by the whim of Freddie Brown. Ames was an England selector and he told him, 'Your story is quite true. But you shouldn't have known about it!' Brown was supposed to have said, 'Close is just the man for me. I want him.'

In the summer of 1954 Jim took 135 wickets at 15.17 and thought he would be selected for the winter tour. But, impressed by a performance by Jim McConnon, the thirty-two-year-old Glamorgan off-spinner and Aston Villa centre half, who took 7 for 23 against Surrey at the Oval, the selectors chose him instead. The other off-spin bowler was Yorkshire's Bob Appleyard, whose credentials were supported by his unusual ability to bowl medium-pace cutters when the conditions failed to help the spinners. Peter Walker, McConnon's colleague at Glamorgan, was a great supporter of Jim but he suggested, 'Our Jim had more in the air.' The tall McConnon flighted the ball more than Laker and his fingers were longer and less damaged. But Walker said, 'It was a fallacy that Jim Laker couldn't bowl on hard, fast pitches. Every time he was put to the test he bowled beautifully.' Earlier in the tour, McConnon broke down and failed to play in a single Test. Neither McConnon nor Bob Appleyard had blue eyes.

Brown was still causing Jim problems in the tour in 1958-59 when, as manager, he accused him of being 'a lead swinger'. Before the Fifth Test at Melbourne Jim went down with a fever and said he wouldn't be fit to play. His bowling finger was sore, another reason for him to rest. There was little more than thirty-degree movement in the joint. But Brown told the correspondents, 'Laker has a bit of a chill but the doctor says he is fit to play.' Brown insisted that he should play. David Montague said, 'Jim had a temperature of 103°F and I sat with him through the night before the start of the Test, sponging him down as the sweat poured off him. But he had to play. He took the field with the rest of the team and bowled 30.5 overs in Australia's first innings, taking a highly creditable 4 for 93. But he was back at the hotel in bed by six and it took a lot of out of him. There was a lot of animosity between them and Freddie was getting really p—ed off over Jim's fitness.' In the First Test Jim batted at nine in the order but Peter May dropped him to eleven in the Melbourne Test. 'They at least had the decency to send me in at 11,' said Jim dryly.

Born in Lima, Peru in 1910, Brown was a hard-drinking, pipe-smoking 'amateur' of the tough school who was the all-rounder star of the Cambridge University side. Raman Subba Row, the Cambridge University and Surrey left-handed batsman, broke a bone in his wrist early on in the tour and he expected to be sent home. 'Instead he told me to stick it out, which I thought was a nice gesture,' he said. 'I got on okay with him but some other players didn't, including Jim. Freddie was very brusque and had the approach of pre-war amateurs. By that time things were changing and they were on the way out.' Christopher Martin-Jenkins described Brown as 'burly, red-faced and jolly, with an appearance and mien of an archetypal country squire. A dynamic personality, he was once nicknamed "Ginger" for pluck. There was a force and inspiration about his captaincy that was immortalised in the Sydney barrow boy's cry, "Fine lettuces, fine lettuces! Hearts like Freddie Brown's."'

No-one doubted Brown's courage and his flamboyant white neck-erchief was a symbol of defiance. He was thirty-nine when he stood in for the unavailable Norman Yardley as captain in Australia in 1950-51 and he bowled in two styles, medium fast as first change and used his leg-breaks and googlies later in the innings. He bowled 109 overs and took 18 wickets at 21.61 – only Bedser bowled more – and coming in at six, he scored 218 runs and finished third in the averages. After being on the losing side in the first four Tests, he led the side to England's first win over their major rivals for thirteen years. Arthur Morris, one of the few survivors, said, 'The last time he toured in Australia was in 1932-33 and he hardly played. It was generally thought that he had been chosen as a figurehead, the last of the amateurs and all that. These feelings were soon dispelled because he was one of the great successes of the tour. His personal courage and able leadership and, not least, his fine ability as a cricketer, set an admirable example to his players and gained for him the unstinted admiration of the Australian public and players.'

In his report to the MCC, Brown picked out the conduct of the travelling English journalists as one of the reasons why England had to struggle. 'Even before we had bowled a ball they were on to us, saying that we were lackadaisical, not trying and so on,' he said. 'No cricketer minds criticism provided it is constructive and I do believe that if these cricket writers were to encourage rather than write down England, our side would show up better on the field.' There were some tough journalists in that party but Brown's brusque behaviour didn't help his cause.

One of Brown's edicts on the three-week voyage out to Freemantle for the start of the 1958–59 tour was to tell the players to wear a tie for every meal. Peter Richardson turned up for breakfast without one and was ordered to return to his cabin to change. Richardson was an amateur and a county captain and he liked a joke. So he returned to the table wearing an overcoat and a scarf. Brown also restricted the players' drinking at the Saturday Night Club to one hour but the rule didn't apply to him: he drank whisky galore. There were more than twenty English cricket journalists on the tour and he told the players not to speak to them. The players had cards issued to them and one of the rules forbade any contact with the Press. Peter May, upset at the way he was criticised on the previous tour of South Africa, declined to give any interviews and Brown, not the most diplomatic of men, was put in charge of Press relations. It was a disaster. England were the holders of the Ashes and were favourites to retain them. Richie Benaud's reign as captain started in that series and the odds against his team were 4-1, so some of his colleagues had some big wins as England lost 4-0 in one of the worst, and most boring series of all time.

Ray Lindwall said, 'It was full of incidents, big ones, not little ones, and they were magnified by the England players and the Press of both countries. After one or two failures, May's players should have put their heads down and fought back but they gave up.' May and Cowdrey went in at five and six and May looked shell shocked when he put Australia in on the best batting pitch of the series in the Fourth Test at Adelaide and Benaud's team scored 476 to win by 10 wickets. Jim missed the game through injury after bowling a marathon spell of 46 overs at Sydney when he had figures of 5 for 107 on a painfully slow pitch, of which Fred Trueman said, 'They should have charged it for loitering.' On the same pitch Richie had a match winning aggregate of 9 for 173. Before the previous Test, Brown put pressure on Jim, urging him to play despite the pain. The manager made a terse statement, 'We have named twelve players and the last choice would be Laker or Frank Tyson.' After a net, Jim repeated that he wasn't up to it but Brown delayed the final announcement, upsetting the journalists. Finally, Brown conceded and Tyson was selected and the Northamptonshire fast bowler recorded an unenviable century, 1 for 100 off 28 overs.

In the 1954-55 tour the balding Tyson, dubbed 'Typhoon' Tyson, blew the Australians' hopes away at Sydney with match figures of 10 for 130 and, according to Trevor Bailey, 'At the time no-one bowled faster than Frank. He was really quick!' Geoffrey Howard, the highly approachable manager, brought along an American who loved cricket, Henry Sayens, and he offered the England bowlers 10 US dollars for every wicket. The money went into the Saturday Night Club drinking kitty. In the First Test at Brisbane Hutton was forced to ask the Australians to bat first because he and his co-selectors chose five fast bowlers – probably a record until the West Indian fast bowlers came along thirty years later – and it rebounded like a revolving door crashing into his face. Australia compiled 601 for 8 and England, and Tyson with 1 for 160, went down to an humiliating defeat. Most of Hutton's contemporaries thought he was a cautious man. Peter Richardson said of him, 'He had this odd habit of stopping when you spoke to him, turn his head one way and to the other, looked round in case anyone was within hearing, then made his statement. One day someone said, "Len, what do you reckon of Jim Pressdee [the Glamorgan opener]? I reckon he will become a great player." Hutton looked around and after a few moments, he said, "Not in my lifetime!"'

But Hutton made a brave decision before the Second Test, leaving out his best bowler, Alec Bedser. Tyson recalled, 'I can remember my personal remorse at the omission of Alec and also a sense of frustration caused by my first spell, which was totally unworthy of the man I was replacing.' Soon Tyson and Brian Statham shared 15 wickets to square the rubber 1-1. It was the turn of the Australian players to be humiliated. Ted Dexter told a telling story about Hutton. As a power-ful striker of the ball, Dexter wasn't a great admirer of Hutton's style of batting. He said, 'One day at Melbourne a couple of bouncers whistled past his head. A barracker shouted out, "Why didn't you hook, Hutton?" "It occurred to me," said Len, "that I was doing all right by letting them miss me. I couldn't see myself getting many runs in the local hospital."' Tyson bowled 151 overs, more than any other bowler in the series, and his 28 wickets cost 20.3 and England won the series 3-1.

By the time Tyson returned for the next series in Australia his menace had virtually ended and his 3 wickets cost 64 apiece. Jim came top of the bowling averages, with 15 wickets at 21.20 in 4 Tests. He was apologetic about his absence from the Adelaide Test, saying, 'If I had thought I could do anything to help England win the match, no thought of the future would have stopped me. But I knew the truth. Had I played I would have been letting down England, who most likely would have been landed with a useless passenger.' The Australians wanted to avenge their Lakering at Old Trafford eighteen months earlier and Benaud admitted, 'We tried, but Jim bowled pretty well in difficult circum-stances.' The only time Jim was in trouble was when the mercurial left hander Neil Harvey took 167 off England's bowlers in the Second Test at Melbourne (in those days they played two Tests at Melbourne). Tom Graveney said, 'Neil was the only batsman who sorted Jim out. Jim didn't know where to bowl to him. That was the first time I've ever seen him in trouble once he became a great bowler.'

Brown had to be called 'Manager', not Freddie, on the controversial tour and there was a predicament earlier in the tour about how to address Desmond Eagar, the Hampshire secretary, Brown's assistant manager. Jim remembered, 'We called him Des, or Desmond but the manager wanted him to be known as "Assistant Manager" by the professionals. There weren't too many things for Des to do because George Duckworth did almost everything but after a while we dis-covered that Des handled the cash so we called him "Cash".'

David Montague gave an interesting insight into Benaud's sporting and cricketing ethos, saying, 'Richie gave Jim a lot of advice about how to treat his finger. They were good friends and colleagues. The skin was hard and cracked and we had to pour olive oil and other potions on it to avoid infection. By the end of the tour Jim's finger was twice the size.' Most great sportsmen are characterised by their sportsmanship and Benaud was another example. Real champions have the capacity to help opponents, not try to diminish them. But in *Over to Me* Jim was critical of the antics of the Australian fielders. 'Benaud fell from grace a little in his behaviour when wickets fell,' he told his ghost. 'Almost in the manner of the professional soccer player, he would rush around, all but embracing those concerned. I am all for enthusiasm in its proper place but I felt his conduct did little for the dignity of the game of cricket.' That would read oddly these days but many cricket lovers still feel the same way.

Most of the outstanding spin bowlers of Jim's time used different types of potions to alleviate the problems of sore fingers and Tony Brown, who played against him on many occasions, said, 'David Allen, John Mortimore and myself all had a mixture. David used to mix boracic powder with calamine lotion and pour it down the gap or sometimes, Friar's Balsam. I had a lot of respect for Jim. He certainly had a chequered career and he upset them up at GHQ. Some did and others didn't but Jim was a Yorkshireman. What do you expect? I remember a game at Bristol when I slogged him down the pitch for a six and as I got to the other end he was standing there, with his arms crossed, saying, "Cor, bugger me, they've made the boundaries shorter!"'

David Allen was Jim's successor as the England off-spinner and when he went off on his debutant tour in 1959-60 he received a telegram from him saying, 'Good luck, if you can bowl out there, you can bowl anywhere!' Allen played 39 Tests and, with his big turn, he was able to bowl long stretches. 'I really appreciated Jim's gesture,' he said. 'He always helped young players and I regretted not having a pint with him over a chat but when I got back he was banned by Surrey and the MCC. I didn't see so much of him. I played against him a few times and I was always impressed by the way he could drag out his full armoury. It was educational to see him in action. Some players said he used his sore finger to miss games but I didn't see any evidence of it. In his only tour in Australia the other players said Jim carried the bowling. He was top of the averages. No-one could argue about that.'

Robin Marlar, one of the leading off-spinners between 1951-68 who became a well-read, controversial cricket writer and broadcaster, said, 'Jim got up to some scrapes, many of them over his finger. He used to walk around holding up his finger and Peter May wasn't too happy about it. He introduced me to "newskin", a plastic substance that you wrapped on the finger. It was quick drying and it helped.'

May's players were criticised by the Press over their fitness. Jim said, 'They thought we should have daily sessions of exercises and running. They didn't know what they were talking about. I was a first-class cricketer, supposedly on a high level of fitness. Yet I very much doubt whether I could have completed a lap at the Kennington Oval without pausing for breath. But more to the point, I could bowl and field all day in a Test match without any physical after effects, which is something. I don't imagine a Pirie [Gordon Pine the Olympic runner] and Chataway [Chris Chataway the former MP and Olympic athlete] could do. The cricketer and the ordinary athlete require a different sort of fitness, which must be gained in a different way – a fact that seemed completely to escape our critics.' Sir Alec Bedser still agrees with that now. 'Bowlers only get fit by bowling, not running round the pitch,' said Sir Alec.

May's players were accused of excessive drinking, keeping late hours and going to parties by one correspondent and others joined in. 'I don't know what sort of picture all this must have painted in the minds of people at home,' said Jim. 'It didn't happen and one Australian writer said, "Richardson, Milton, Watson, May, Cowdrey and Graveney wouldn't have had one good drinker among the lot of them!"' But Jim admitted that between games, the players liked a party. 'A lively party is often a good thing in the circumstances,' he said. 'Makes people relax.' One London writer filed a half-term report on the players and it contained a line, 'Laker skipped a match in Launceston to enjoy private pleasures in Hobart.' Jim's explanation was that he did have two days in Tasmania after three-and-a-half weeks' continuous cricket 'and I spent most of the time catching up on my correspondence'. The next morning Jim confronted the journalist. The man went beetroot in the face, stumbling to offer an explanation. 'It was cut and they changed a few bits,' he said. Jim was charitable. He bought the unfortunate man a drink.

There were critical articles about wives and girlfriends joining the players and May was particularly upset about stories concerning his fiancée Virginia Gilligan. Her uncle, Arthur Gilligan, was England's captain in 1924-25 and was a regular visitor to Australia. He and his wife Penny invited Virginia to accompany them to Australia for part of the tour. On her arrival, May scored a century in each innings and Virginia was written up as a welcome addition who had brought luck to her prospective husband. But in his autobiography *A Game Enjoyed* he revealed the other side of the story. He said, 'In April we were engaged but as the tour went on, there were hints that the captain's fiancée was taking up too much of his time. Eventually a piece was written reporting that we had been secretly married. This was really disgraceful and made me very angry. It is all right to look back on it now and have a good laugh. But Virginia's parents, Marjorie and Harold Gilligan, were naturally horrified. They were preparing the wedding at Shamley Green in the following April and they wanted to know what was going on. It upset Virginia and it did not increase my respect for certain members of the Press. I may not have been as at ease with the Press or as forthcoming as my opposite number Richie Benaud, but he was a journalist by profession. I always tried to be helpful when I could and felt let down.' When the wedding took place, several Test players were pictured in the family group, including Tony Lock, Godfrey Evans, the inseparable Bedser twins, Peter Loader, Peter Richardson and Trevor Bailey. Jim did not have an invitation. Jim's view was if their husbands can afford to pay the expenses, well, it's up to them. Not many professional cricketers could afford to do it. He also thought it was a good idea to invite the wives later on these long tours, not at the start.

After the tour of Australia, the MCC had arranged a series in New Zealand and Jim was unwilling to go. He told May that now that John Mortimore, the Gloucestershire off-spinner, had joined the party it would be a sensible plan to let him play against a Kiwi side well under the strength of the Australians. Four players were going to be trimmed from the original party – Godfrey Evans, Tyson and Trevor Bailey, with Jim as the probable fourth. May was reluctant to release Jim. Brian Statham and Peter Loader were out of the Fifth Test because of injuries caused by a traffic accident and the management wanted as strong a squad for the second stage as possible. On the rest day of the Test, May asked Jim to come to his room. 'I don't mind coming up for a drink,' Jim said dryly. Brown was sitting in May's room and as Jim entered, Brown said, 'I want you to go to New Zealand now that Statham and Loader are out of action.' Jim responded, 'I'm not going. I've done most of my packing ready to go home.' Brown was enraged. 'Are you breaking your contract?' he stormed. 'I told you my finger was too bad to continue and I'm not staying on,' he said. Jim Brown tried to contact someone at Lord's and, after several failures, he spoke to an assistant secretary. Jim could hear Brown saying, 'Can't we get Wardle to take over?' Wardle had been selected for the tour but was left out after Yorkshire complained about a series of articles criticising his colleagues were published in the *Daily Mail*. The articles were similar in style to some of the passages in his own book *Over to Me* published two years later and, according to Jim, 'He sold it practically for nothing!' With or without an agent – in those days only a few, including the pioneer Denis Compton, employed an agent – Wardle could have been an all-time great cricketer but his personal frailties stopped him realising his potential. He was probably the best wrist spinner of his time (1946–1968), as good as Tony Lock in his slower version of slow left-arm bowling, a hard-hitting batsman, an outstanding fielder and a man who entertained the crowd with his clowning. In the 1956–57 tour of South Africa he was more successful than Jim, taking 90 wickets at 12.25, including 12 for 89 in the Cape Town Test. Doug Insole, the vice-captain, said, 'It was a very happy tour and Jim and Johnny Wardle, mesmeric with his wrist spin, were a very successful duo. Jim, as a finger spinner, wisely perceived that he wouldn't achieve much turn on these pitches. He concentrated on line, length and flight and did this beautifully.' But once he was blackballed by the MCC and Yorkshire, Wardle's first-class career was finished. He ended playing league cricket and for Cambridgeshire in the Minor Counties.

Jim's summing up of Brown's bid to revive Wardle's career was typical of him, suggesting, 'Knowing how Wardle's stock stood at Lord's, it wasn't very clever.' He had a good relationship with Wardle – a fellow Yorkshireman with a sharp sense of humour. The *Mail* promptly signed Wardle up to 'cover' the tour of Australia. He sat next to his many ghosts and watched every ball. Most famous cricketers who were signed by newspapers were much less conscientious. Keith Miller, for example, often went racing before he would turn up late in the day at the match he was deputed to write on and ask someone, 'Fill me in on what's happened, that's a good chap.' Most of the cricketers earned more from newspapers than their clubs and if they failed to come up with the necessary controversial material the ghost would do it for them. Two others on the tour – Hugh Tayfield, the South African off-spinner bowler who was a rival to Jim and Bill Edrich, the former England batsman who occasionally bowled quick – were employed as critics and Tayfield, not a nice man, did what was required.

Back in May's hotel room in the Melbourne Test, Brown was still trying to get Jim named in the squad for the tour of New Zealand. He arranged an appointment for Jim with a leading specialist in Melbourne, at 8.30 a.m., with a view of proving Jim's fitness. Brown insisted on coming along at the surgery and opened the conversation. 'Excuse me,' said the specialist. 'Don't you think it would be better if Mr Laker tells us about his own finger?' After a thorough examination, the specialist said, 'I sincerely hope you haven't been playing cricket for three or four weeks.' Jim said 'Well, I'm playing at the MCG now!' The specialist said, 'If you keep playing, you will run the risk of doing yourself serious and permanent damage.' Brown had to concede and Jim went back to the hotel to finish his packing. His damning verdict of the manager was contained in *Over to Me* – 'I was aware that there have been plenty of bad managers in the past but I find it difficult to match Freddie Brown from my own experience. He started wrongly and never looked back.' Brown never forgot that and he used his influence to excommunicate Jim at the end of his career.

May was under pressure throughout the tour, yet he claimed the 4-0 drubbing, the worst for thirty-seven years, was 'one of my greatest successes – because at the end of it England and Australia were still speaking to each other'. Sir Don Bradman had a fifth columnist in the England camp. He was the man who talked round the delegates of the other member countries of the then Imperial Cricket Conference, now known as the International Cricket Conference, on the issue of the throwers. At a conference they voted in favour of expelling the bowlers from Test cricket who had suspect bowling. Most of the Australian writers defended their offending bowlers, including Ian Meckiff, whose bowling action was called 'the most blatant throw I've ever seen' by Jim Swanton. Jim Laker told me on a number of occasions that the game would be threatened with extinction if the throwers were allowed to continue. He would be worried today after seeing bowlers like Muralitharan, Shoaib Akhtar and Brett Lee sometimes infringe the law and be exonerated after the ICC introduced a 15-degree tolerance on bent arms for fast bowlers.

But there was one case when he was caught out. Arnold Long, the former Surrey captain who played for the county between 1960 and 1975, said, 'I was sitting alongside some of the other young players watching a county game at the Oval when Jim was fielding at cover and someone said, "Have you seen that? Jim has been marking the Test match pitch!" The game was played on a pitch near the Test pitch and the Test was due to start in a few days' time and, as he walked back and turned as the bowler started to run in, he scuffed a spot on a length with his spikes. They got the binoculars out and you could see it clearly. Later on the groundsman probably rolled it down and it didn't make any difference. Those things used to go on. The ball was always being interfered with and the worst example was the Australian bowler Bob Massie in the 1972 Test at Lord's when he took 16 for 137. I've never seen the ball move like that. The Aussies put lip salve on the ball and

England were a bit late on that one.' Massie is fourth behind Jim's 19 for 90 in the *Wisden* list of 'Most Test Wickets in a Test' – Sid Barnes and the Indian N.D. Hirwani were the others.

English cricket has traditionally fostered myths and misconceptions and Jim was a victim of it when he was excluded from the 1950-51 and 1954-55 tours. The selectors believed that no England off-spinner had succeeded in Australia and never would but in his book *Spinning Around the World* Jim wrote, 'In 1950 I had taken 166 wickets at 15 apiece and made close on 600 runs and those figures weren't enough to gain me a place. I made no bones about it – my non-selection was a bitter disappointment. Neither the selectors nor the critics could convince me that off-spin bowlers were little use Down Under. To that assertion, I replied, "What recognised off-spinner had been to Australia in the past twenty years, in which time conditions and wickets had changed considerably?" Since the Second World War, two of the most prolific wicket-takers in Australia have been Ian Johnson and Geoff Noblett, the first an off-spinner pure and simple, and the second mixing off-breaks and his medium-pace swing bowling. Furthermore, the Australian off-spinner, Jack Iverson, dominated the 1950-51 series. The theory that Australian pitches are too good for the natural spinner is outmoded. Practically all the Australian pitches help the spinners on the last couple of days of a six-day Test.' In the modern era, Shane Warne and Stuart MacGill were regular match winners, particularly at Sydney and, to a lesser extent, Melbourne.

Jim enjoyed most of the aspects of the Commonwealth tour to India, his first to the subcontinent. Afterwards he claimed that his best ever bowling performance was at Bombay, not Bradford when he took 8 for 2 in the Test trial. George Duckworth, the charismatic former Lancashire and England wicketkeeper who played in 24 Tests, was in charge of seven overseas tours as manager, four of them with England's MCC squad and was a long-time friend. Realising that Jim had been snubbed, he invited him to join the Commonwealth squad, which boasted a number of players at the peak of their careers, including Frank Worrell, Jack Ikin, George Emmett, Les Jackson, George Tribe, Bruce Dooland and Sonny Ramadhin. Len Hutton never 'read'

Ramadhin's bowling but, after practising with Ramadhin, Jim soon picked up his disguised off-break. 'In clear light you could see it,' he said. 'But in England with the light not too good and poor sightscreens, it wasn't so easy. With Jim being recruited, the spin attack was probably the strongest ever brought to India – himself, Tribe the left-armer who bowled orthodox and chinamen, Dooland with leg-spin and googlies and Ramadhin, the mystery bowler who baffled England's finest batsmen in the 1950s. The Commonwealth won the series and Jim relished playing on good pitches in India.

There were many funny incidents and, bowling on a beautiful pitch at Poona, he was about to bowl when a rat raced up the pitch and a kite hawk swooped down and snatched it into his beak and soared back into the air. Jim was so surprised that he bowled a double bouncer that was hit to the boundary. Kites are still hovering over cricket grounds in India and they are much more threatening than the pigeons who still frequent the new Oval.

Just after the Second World War, Indian cricket needed patronage from the Maharajahs to keep it going – before it earned billions of rupees a year from TV contracts – and in the game at Patiala George, Tribe was becoming frustrated after being turned down on a countless number of lbws. The Maharajah of Patiala survived through the umpire's indulgence and finally Tribe, who played seven seasons with Northants, lost his temper and grabbed the umpire by the shoulders and shouted, 'Don't be such a bloody fool, have another look!' The startled umpire looked up the pitch and said, 'My word Mr Tribe, you are right.' He raised the finger and said to the Maharajah, 'I'm sorry, Sir, but you are out.' And the Maharajah had to go.

It was a far happier tour than the controversial MCC tour in Australia, which was wracked by disputes, incidents and rows with the manager, Freddie Brown. Monkeys ran about the rooms of the players, mosquitoes bit them and harassed them and not many toilets had running water. Baths were rare and hot water was non-existent. On the field, firecrackers kept going off and the incessant noise often drowned the snicks off the bat, explaining why so many appeals for catches were turned down. A golfing expedition had to be cut short at the fifth hole when a leopard appeared and alcohol was virtually impossible to find.

Jim began suffering from sinus problems and he reckoned it was caused by frequent flights around India. After obtaining permission from Leslie Ames and George Duckworth, he set out on a 1,200-mile train journey and it proved to be the most hazardous experience of his life. He was the only white man among the thousands clinging on to every square inch of the decrepit train, which stopped frequently with or without stations. 'They gave me a knife in case I was attacked but the person who I was going to use it on was myself, or nearly,' he said.

Finally Ames and Duckworth agreed to release Jim from the tour and his last unofficial Test was against a strong Indian side at the Brabourne Stadium, the quaint, Victorian ground named after a former Viceroy of India that sadly no longer stages Test cricket, because it has more charm than any Test venue in the country. On the fourth day, when India were scoring a hundred an hour, Jim bowled almost the whole of the day in temperatures of more than 100°F. There was only one drinks break each session, much different to what happens today. He rated his figures of 64.5 overs, 34 maidens, 88 runs and 5 wickets above his 8 for 2 in the Bradford Test Trial game. 'It was cricket at its hardest,' he said. 'The point is that on a good wicket it is difficult to dislodge a mediocre batsman who is not taking risks – more difficult than it is to get rid of a good batsman on a tricky wicket. Bradford gave me plenty of help and the batsmen were afraid to play shots because they were seeking Test places – but Bombay gave me no help at all.'

The Reuters agency flashed through the details and the *Evening News* carried a short report. Placards around London said 'Tribute to Laker.' Lilly was travelling home on the underground and when she saw it, she was highly concerned before she bought a copy of the newspaper and read the full story. Along with Dick Spooner, the wicketkeeper, and Les Jackson, Jim boarded SS *Canton* had two pleasant weeks recovering on the voyage home, just in time for Christmas. He missed the second, and better, half of the tour but he was longing to return to his family.

One of the worst tours Jim took part in was in South Africa in 1956–57, not so much because of its controversy but for the slowness of the cricket. 'I don't believe the game has ever known a series in which the defensive mentality took precedence over the natural desire to attack,' he said. 'The pace was set on the very first morning of the series at the Wanderers' ground in Johannesburg and it hardly changed all through.'

It was against his cricketing instincts and he didn't enjoy the five-month trip, except for a three-week period in the middle when his family joined him. When the party set off, Jim told one of his friendly cricket journalists that he intended to spend some of his £11,000 benefit proceeds on taking Lilly and her daughters Fiona, aged four, and Angela, aged two. The journalist reported, 'It is the first time I have heard of a complete family visiting an MCC player on tour overseas. Like Colin Cowdrey's bride of a month, Penelope, they sail in January. The wife who will be the longest with her husband this trip is Mrs Valerie Compton, whose parents live in South Africa. She leaves in the *Edinburgh Castle*, the ship in which Denis Compton and the rest of the MCC party sailed from Southampton.'

'There is a of lot nonsense said about wives on cricket tours,' said Doug Insole, who roomed with Jim. 'Most tours I've been on, wives came but I'm not sure whether Lilly was the first to bring her young children. She might have been. Jim was a great family man. The only time wives had been discouraged was when Michael Atherton was England captain and he thought it was a distraction. But in recent years the ECB have paid for the wives to go. Up to then, the players paid for them.'

Insole, who captained Cambridge University, was vice-captain in South Africa and he went on to have a distinguished career as manager of two England tours of Australia, and also had a long stint as an unpaid Test selector and served on several MCC and Essex committees. He wasn't the normal MCC person of that time and is one of the longest, if not the longest, serving members on the council of the FA. He is a bluff, friendly and humorous man who is a fan of West Ham and his comment after the TCCB lost the Packer case in the High Court was typical – 'We've had a good stuffing,' he said. He was eighty on 18 April 2006 and Frank Keating wrote a well merited tribute in *The Guardian* on a popular man who put much more into sport than he took out.

Jim went on two previous visits to Durban, when a troopship made a short stop on the way to the Middle East in 1941 and in 1948-49 when he coached at schools in Durban including the famed Durban High School, the school that has produced a record number of South African Test stars, twenty-nine in all including Barry Richards and Trevor Goddard, among others, almost ten per cent of South Africa's Test players. One of the pupils coached by Jim at Durban High was Goddard, the man who played a big part in ruining the 1956-57 tour with his defensive left-arm medium-paced bowling, pitched just outside the right-handed batsman's leg stump. Another boy who was coached by Jim was Hugh Tayfield, who also played against England eight years later. At the time the pupils were almost exclusively white. Now the majority are from Indian, African or of mixed-race descent. Jim was a firm opponent of apartheid and he said, 'Few of us ever spoke to a black South African the whole time we were there.'

After having a successful tour of the West Indies in the previous winter, he wasn't happy to be left out of the 1948-49 MCC tour of South Africa, led by George Mann, but it was a consolation to be offered six months' coaching in the republic. 'I worked as hard as I've ever done in my life,' he said. 'I was coaching from nine in the morning until seven at night five days a week and playing on Saturdays and Sundays. I had a few days off over Christmas and met a mining manager and his wife who offered to put me up in Johannesburg to watch the Test against Australia. He was from English stock and asked me if I would be prepared to coach some black boys. I was happy to do it and it turned out to be a fascinating experience, meeting about fifty blacks who were all natural athletes and tremendously keen but knowing little or nothing about the game. Only two or three of them would ever have made the grade but one chap – who never moved his feet and smashed the ball to all quarters – wrote to me later to say he had scored a hundred after meeting me.' Not many England players coached black players in South Africa but Jim was one of the first.

Oakman remembers going off to help Jim's coaching sessions with all-white schools. 'He was sponsored by Gallagher's,' he said. 'One day there were about eighty lads standing round this net and I was batting to Jim. He said 'I'll bowl a couple of off-spinners and you can block them. But make sure you miss the third one.' I did what I was told and Jim finished up hitting the wickets countless times. Made me look a pretty awful batsman!'

Before the MCC tour, skippered by Peter May, the players were briefed by Field Marshal Earl Alexander of Tunis, the MCC president. He told them not to mention colour at any time. 'The safest thing to talk about is the British Lions' rugby tour which has just ended,' he said. In several of his books, Jim wrote about an incident on the tour involving Alan Oakman. He said, 'Driving back, quite late, Alan couldn't avoid a man riding his bicycle out from a side turning. The man had his leg broken and was in great pain. Alan, shaken, got out and a crowd gathered. They started asking, "Hello Mr Oakman, you played a bad stroke today... will you sign my book Mr Oakman?" Nobody took any notice of the man lying on the ground. Then a policeman came along. His first question to Alan was, "He was drunk, Mr Oakman, wasn't he?" The policeman then collared a man from the crowd and said, "He was drunk, wasn't he?" The man hadn't seen the victim until that moment and he agreed. A coloured man in the crowd was picked on. "You live near this nigger... he is always drunk, isn't he?" Slowly, fearfully, the man nodded. Once this "justice" was done, the injured man was taken to hospital. Next day Alan went to see the victim and he gave him some money.'

The coloured players, as distinct from black players, have always been keen on cricket because of their Indian origins. 'They are great mimics, and all the funnier for it and there is any plenty of cricketing talent among them,' said Jim. He suggested a game between the England players and a coloured eleven but it never happened. Jim took 25 wickets in the first five warm-up games (that was in an era when there were warm-up games!) and he slowed down to just 2 wickets in the inaugural First Test at Wanderers, which England won by 131 runs. Trevor Bailey countered Goddard's defensive bowling with an equally boring response and as both men bowled a lot of overs, the scoring rate tumbled. It was a rare example of two ultra-professionals cancelling each other out. They bored everyone else but they loved it. 'I thoroughly enjoyed the tour,' said Bailey. 'It was one of the best tours I've been on and I loved the game reserves and the hospitality.'

Most of the excitement came from the South African fast bowlers, Neil Amwin Treharne Adcock and Peter Samuel Heine, who captured 39 wickets between them. Built like Brian Statham but taller, Adcock had pretensions of matching Statham's renowned accuracy and he often hit batsmen's fingers with lifting deliveries. He later became a highly rated radio commentator and was a popular figure. But the 6ft 5in-tall Heine, of Afrikaans extraction, was nasty on the field and Jim said of him, 'His attitude to his job was simple – he bowled at the batsman as often as he bowled at the wicket. He was one of the few cricketers of Dutch extraction we came up against and we called him "the bloody Dutchman". He was a fearsome figure, his black hair straggling over his eyes and a great red streak across the front of his shirt, on which he viciously polished the ball.' Incensed by Trevor Bailey's over use of the forward defensive shot, Heine had frequent and rude exchanges with the England all-rounder, including one priceless one that went like this: 'I want to hit you, Bailey. I want to hit you over the heart.' This was before chest protectors, helmets and the rest of the protective hardware. A bouncer from Heine struck Jim on his shoulder and the scowling Afrikaner shouted, 'Have I hurt you?' Jim responded, 'I'll hit you over the head with the bloody bat if you do that again!' Quite restrained by today's standards! Insole said, 'Jim didn't like the short stuff. He never did. South Africa have never produced a more lethal opening bowling pair than Heine and Adcock. They were fast and dangerous.' Heine wasn't nasty all the time, as Denis Compton discovered. Heine's Test place was being threatened by a fast bowler named Pretorius and the next time he bowled to Compton, he started bouncing the England batsman. 'Sorry about that,' said Heine, 'but I've got to put a bit more in.' 'Don't worry,' said Compton. 'Most of them are finishing over the fine leg boundary!' Insole went on the tour as an amateur. 'Wimpey's took me on with an annual salary of £450 and I was paid £150 expenses on the tour,' he said. 'Several of us were amateurs with part-time jobs and it was very difficult to exist. Jim was looked on as a strong opponent of the idea of the amateur but I never found any semblance of fact to back it.'

In 1962 the status of the amateur was abolished and Jim said, 'It was one of the best things that has happened.' Insole was a member of the sixteen-strong Advisory Cricket Committee that made the decision and among the six who had three Christian names on the committee was Peter May. Many years later when he was an administrator, Insole had the opportunity of examining the minutes concerning players' wages just after the Second World War. 'Denis Compton was the most famous sportsman of the day and he was paid £940 for taking part in the 1946–47 tour of Australia,' he said. 'Denis was a big-name footballer with Arsenal and in the following season the Gunners paid him £200, less than a quarter of what he made from cricket. Now it's the other way round, with Premiership footballers earning fifty times as much as the best-known English cricketers.'

Jim took a hearty dislike to Hugh Tayfield, the off-spinner who out-bowled him in the series. 'Jim had just come back off his record-making feats and was looked on as the all-conquering hero but in South Africa the conditions didn't suit his style of bowling,' said Insole. 'Jim wasn't happy. He took just 11 wickets to Tayfield's 37 and after the Fourth Test at Johannesburg Tayfield was carried off in triumph. He was the national hero.' Women fell for him everywhere he went and he married five of them and divorced all five. He died on 25 February 1994 at the age of sixty-five and in his obituary in the 1995 edition of *Wisden* the writer called him 'a playboy', deservedly so. Tayfield studied Jim's technique and concentrated on accuracy, although he rarely bowled round the wicket. Many of Jim's successes came bowling round the wicket. Jim was a bigger spinner than Tayfield and in one match he bowled 137 deliveries in succession without conceding a run. Both men had the same competitive urge to win. But whereas Jim believed in upholding sporting principles, the ruthless Tayfield sometimes cheated and got away with it. Jim said of him, 'While Heine was rough, Tayfield was smooth as they come. Everyone thought he took more liberties with the laws than sportsmanship allowed.'

Jim thought it started in 1955 when Peter May and Denis Compton, both 'walkers' and fair-play advocates, were on the winning side in the final Test at the Oval. Tayfield claimed he had him lbw before he scored. The umpire ruled against Tayfield and one England player said, 'The South Africans wouldn't have walked if the situation had been reversed, so why was Tayfield so upset?' Do world-class batsmen walk for lbw without an upraised finger from an umpire? According to Jim, he knew of two – Neil Harvey in the First Test at Brisbane in 1958-59 and Ken Barrington at a game at the Oval in 1959.

What really upset Peter May's players in that tour of South African was a shameful incident in the First Test at Johannesburg. Compton drove a delivery from Tayfield firmly towards the bowler and the ball appeared to have landed a foot short as Tayfield caught it and threw it into the air, shouting, 'I've caught it, I've caught it!' Compton said sternly, 'Did you catch it, Hugh?' 'I tell you, I caught it!' said Tayfield. As a sporting man, married to a South African and as Jim said 'not wanting to upset the morning's peace' Compton walked off. Insole was batting at the time and he said, 'It landed two feet short, not one.' The South African captain, Clive van Rynefeld, spoke to Tayfield and then ran after Compton with the intention of calling him back. But Compton shrugged and carried on walking towards the dressing rooms. Van Rynefeld, who was capped by both England and South Africa at rugby and was a lawyer and later a political figure, was acutely embarrassed. 'I tried to tell Denis that it wasn't out but he was the kind of player that if the fielder confirmed it was a catch, he would accept it,' said Insole. 'He was an amazing guy, so likeable. He would walk for nicks behind and if there was a doubt about a catch, he wouldn't leave it to the umpire. He would ask the fielder and expect him to give an honest answer. His "dismissal" went into the book as "Compton caught and bowled Tayfield 32" but we knew better.'

Jim was the bowler when Russell Endean, the South African wicket-keeper who was termed as 'Endless Endean' for his Bailey-like batting performances, was given out 'handled the ball'. Jim turned to the umpire and appealed in a restrained tone, like asking a shop assistant 'How much is that?' The umpire gave Endean out. 'Jim was almost apologising,' said Insole. 'He wasn't a stentorian appealer. It wasn't his style.' In the Third Test at Durban, Tayfield conned another England player out off the last ball of the fourth day. Trevor Bailey had just returned from having treatment on a finger and shouldered arms as Tayfield appealed for a catch 'taken' by the short square leg fielder. Up went the finger and the umpire removed the bails for the end of the session. Bailey stood there, leaning on his bat, as the fielders walked off. Jim thought the standard of umpiring was dreadful. 'The umpires never gave anyone out lbw on the front foot,' he said. He felt that was one of the major reasons why he finished up bottom of the bowling averages with only 11 wickets at 29.45. Another reason was the way May brought him on early in the day to take on the best batsmen, leaving Johnny Wardle, England's most successful bowler with 90 wickets on the tour, knocking out the later batsmen.

Being 2-0 ahead, England should have won the series but slow batting gave the South Africans the opportunity to draw it 2-2. Jim had a good relationship with Trevor Bailey but he was very critical of his batting, saying, 'It was murder to watch, Trevor all but seized up.' Bailey's 80 took six-and-a-half hours in a total of 218 and, with the punishing Roy McLean scoring a century, Insole rescued England with a maiden century. McLean, a clean and powerful hitter, was the only batsman on either side to take chances, which explains why he collected 11 ducks in his 40 Tests. He went on three tours of England and was an outstanding fielder. McLean is one of the few survivors of the South African side and said, 'Jim was very popular with our side. He used to come in our dressing room with Denis Compton and Godfrey and a few others and we had a few drinks and a laugh. Jim would say something funny with a straight face, that was his style. He wasn't bubbly. These close-of-play chats never happen now, unfortunately. A lot of today's players wouldn't have heard of Jim. They don't have a sense of history. I don't think anyone would beat Jim's record, or even equal it. Perhaps if he was playing today he might have taken 20 wickets against Bangladesh or Zimbabwe!'

McLean believes the spinner, particularly the off-spinner of the Laker type, is now being alienated. 'It's all down to money,' he said. 'They want pitches to last five days and the medium pacers and the quicks do all the bowling. And with short boundaries coming in all round the world, the spinner doesn't have much chance. Hugh Tayfield wouldn't be as effective as he was in those days. He bowled close to the stumps and with their heavy bats, they'd sweep him. Jim had more variety and he bowled both sides of the wicket.'

Peter May had an appalling series, averaging 15, but Jim attributed it to 'the rottenest luck imaginable'. Tayfield got him out four times out of ten. Outside of the Tests, May scored four hundreds in succession and averaged 55.31 from 1,270 runs. In the Fourth Test, back at Johannesburg, South Africa realised England were losing their edge and on the final day Tayfield took 9 for 113 to win the game. Insole was the only batsmen in the series to be dismissed by Tayfield and when he reached 68 he pulled Goddard high towards square leg near the boundary and was caught by Tayfield. Insole shared Jim's feelings about the home side's hero and was determined not to be out to him. The Fifth and deciding Test was scheduled at Port Elizabeth and Jim called the relaid pitch 'not fit for a self-respecting village green'. The players were able to stick their fingers into cracks and the ball often scuttled along the ground. Brian Statham would have been playing but he was injured and Johnny Wardle slipped a cartilage in a knee while playing snooker. 'Godfrey Evans gave a performance that I've never seen bettered,' said Insole. 'Tyson was bowling really quick and he had to stand halfway up from his normal position because the ball was keeping so low. But in the first innings he didn't concede a single bye and in the second innings he let 1 bye through. When he was concentrating, at the highest level, Godfrey was unmatched but sometimes playing for Kent his mind would wander a bit.'

Brian 'Tonker' Taylor, the Essex wicketkeeper and later England selector, was the back-up keeper on the tour and played in most of the provincial games. 'Jim was a great guy to be with,' he said. 'He was the biggest spinner of the ball I encountered. Second behind him was Gloucestershire's David Allen. I found it much harder to keep to Jim because the ball was usually coming into the pads, whereas the stock balls of Wardle and Lock went the other way. In one game there was a bit of a spot at one end and he pitched on it five out of six deliveries most overs. He had such good control.'

In the First Test Peter Richardson scored the slowest hundred of all time in 488 minutes and, in the Durban Test, Jackie McGlew beat it, taking 545 minutes. It just about summed up the funereal state of the series. Twenty years later Pakistan's Mudassar Nazar set the current record of 557 minutes, against England at Lahore. Before the Port Elizabeth Test, Jim bet Richardson that he would score more runs than him and he won the two shillings. He scored 6 and 3 against Richardson's 0 and 3. Frank Tyson's 6 for 40 didn't stop England avoiding defeat. A back-foot player, Richardson found himself pinned back on his stumps by the short-pitched bowling of Adcock and Heine. 'I had to stick it out, or tried to,' he said. Not long after Tayfield retired, he was sentenced to jail after being found guilty on embezzlement charges. He went to live in Australia for a while and he had plenty of time to reflect on his personal battle over the world's greatest off-spin bowler, which he won so convincingly. That might have cheered him up.

These days England players have single rooms but pre-1980 there were constant problems caused by upsetting habits like snoring, smoking or failing to tidy the shared room. 'Jim was an ideal room mate,' said Insole. 'And he didn't snore and he didn't smoke too much in the room. He struck me as a good bloke, with a dry sense of humour. He was very tidy and he wasn't a night owl. He'd go out to dinner with friends most nights and kept reasonable hours. We became good friends and I was delighted when he joined Essex at the end of his career. We tried to sign him when he was in Egypt. Peter Smith, who was a very good leg-spin bowler who served with him in the Army, tried to talk him into coming to Chelmsford when the Second World

War was over. But when he moved to London, he said he was committed to sign for Surrey.'

Jim Laker almost failed to go on his first and last tour of Australia in 1958-59 because he took offence to Peter May's accusation that he was a shirker. Early in the summer of 1958 rumours appeared in some of the newspapers saying that he may not be available for the tour. Gubby Allen, the chairman of selectors, asked him if the stories were true. 'No,' he said. 'They've concocted them for some reason.' The rumours arose from his other job, working off-season for a business and he told Allen, 'Providing my employers agree, I was ready, willing and able.' A few weeks later a letter from the MCC arrived asking him if he was available. It was the normal pattern. He wrote back confirming his availability.

To end the speculation, Jim agreed to write an article in one of the Sunday newspapers confirming that he was ready to go on the tour. Today's players can earn up to £300,000 a year for playing for England but the fee paid to the players on the 1958-59 tour was £1,200. The tour was much longer than present ones and lasted six months. Few professional players could turn down an opportunity like that and Jim Swanton claimed the last one to do it was Sid Barnes in 1920 when he was forty-seven. A number of amateur players, including Frank Mann, Norman Yardley, Walter Robins, Errol Holmes, Sir Frederick Jackson and Charles Fry made themselves unavailable for business reasons.

In the Headingley Test Jim took 5 for 17 against the New Zealanders but three days of rain forced him to bowl 60 overs in the final sessions and he was extremely tired. Soon after the end of play, he had to drive to Swansea for Surrey's game against Glamorgan, starting the next day. On the A6 – before the introduction of motorways – May's car broke down and Jim helped him to get it going again. By this time it was 10.30 p.m. and the cars finally arrived at the players' hotel at 3 a.m. Next morning May and his players were hoping to bat but Glamorgan's skipper won the toss and Jim bowled 63 overs in the match. When the three-day match ended, he drove back to London ready for the start of the following day's match at Blackheath. Against Kent he totted up 54 more overs and Surrey lost in acrimonious circumstances.

In *Over to Me* he wrote, 'To add to my tiredness, I was having trouble with my spinning finger. I can't pretend that I bowled especially well against Kent but I certainly did the best I could. This business of trying is not something conscious to a player who has been in cricket as long as I have. I cannot remember ever playing cricket without trying my hardest. As a Yorkshireman, I learned my cricket in the ruthless school of the league and it comes naturally to me to try.'

Jim was given the next match off and Peter May was also excused. Jim had to see the secretary, Commander R.O. Babb, at the Oval and he encountered May. The England captain looked upset. He started talking about the defeat at Blackheath, blaming Jim. 'I don't think you were trying to bowl them out!' said May. Jim was furious. 'You can talk,' he said. 'You were bowled out by a slow full toss!' Jim wrote later, 'Making due allowance for the fact that we were both tired and that May was still irritated by defeat, I saw neither justification nor excuse for his remark. To a professional cricketer, as a reflection on his approach to the game that provided his bread and butter, it was damned near to what the lawyers call slander. It wasn't a remark on the spur of the moment. There was no doubt in my mind that he meant precisely what he said and, because of this, it was not a remark which could be quickly forgotten.

'Naturally, a fairly heated argument followed. Firmly but politely, I asked him to withdraw his remark. He refused to do so. Much as I looked forward to another chance to bother the Australians on their own pitches the thought came uppermost in my mind that I could not play on tour under a captain who had the opinion of my attitude to cricket that May had just shown. I was hurt and angry and I knew that there was only one honest thing to do. I went straight into Commander Babb's office and explained what had happened and told him I was not available for Australia.'

Jim and Peter Barker Howard May, Surrey's captain between 1957 and 1962, never really had a good relationship. Jim's favourite captain at the Oval was Stuart Surridge, of whom he said, 'He went down as a fairly ordinary cricketer, although he took around 500 wickets and took more than 50 catches every season, so you couldn't call him a passenger. But as a captain, a leader of men, he was one of the most dynamic characters ever to set foot on a cricket field. He didn't believe it was possible for Surrey to lose a match. As a result, he made a few mistakes, not very many and was also the greatest retriever of lost causes I've known. And he had the happy, inborn knack of knowing how to handle people. He would shout at Lockey but he know it was useless to shout and bellow at me. All in all, he was a very popular guy, even in the professionals' dressing room.' Surridge had a good sense of humour, too, and if there were rows, as they were occasionally, he would soon smooth them over.

May was more diffident, gentle and sensitive and John Warr, the Middlesex and England all-rounder, said of him, 'Like Sir Jack Hobbs before him, he was a modest man who was almost embarrassed and weighed down by the limelight. He was a great player, a great per-former in the classical tradition.' P.B.H. didn't like confrontations and, as a pupil from Charterhouse, he believed in Corinthian values. In some ways he was out of place mixing with hardened professionals who were constantly pressing for bigger financial rewards. His father flew Sopwith Camel aircraft in the First World War and in peacetime ran a contracting business in Reading. The May brothers, John and Peter, were brought up with various balls in the home and his mother, who died when he was sixteen, was a fine tennis player. His ball sense helped him to become a natural cricketer and by the time he was fourteen, he was scoring hundreds in the first team. His mentor was George Geary, the Leicestershire player who had the biggest hands in cricket, next to the Bedsers, and Geary told his prodigy, 'Keep your head still and stand still as long as you can.' Today's shuffling batsmen ought to follow that advice.

May went into the Navy as a Writer on National Service for two years before he gained a 2.2 in History and Economics at Cambridge University. He was the best known of the group of outstanding England cricketers from Cambridge in the 1950s, including David Sheppard, John Dewes, John Warr and Hubert Doggart. Brian Castor, the Surrey secretary, signed May in 1950 and he was renowned for his loudspeaking announcements including, 'Go away you pigeons. Go to

Lord's!' On one occasion, Dennis Cox limped off the field and Castor rang the dressing room. He asked for the physiotherapist, Sandy Tait. 'Yes, Mr Castor.' 'What's the matter with Cox?' (Dennis Cox, the all-rounder). 'He's got a bad knee, sir.' 'Tell him to run it off.' Next day Cox had a cartilage removed. The Bedsers, Ken Barrington and May all came from Reading, a non-cricketing area. Within a year May was making his Test debut, scoring 138 against South Africa at Headingley, and he captained his country on 41 occasions in six years before illness, reckoned to be caused by stress, shortened his career at the age of thirty-four. He was a wonderful father for his four daughters, one of whom became the European Three-Day-Event Junior Champion in 1979. Under his niceness was a ruthless streak and though he was an amateur, he had the approach of a professional. He could also be very stubborn and Jim found out on a number of occasions.

Commander Babb was a very autocratic man who treated the senior players like serfs, addressing them by their surname. Without making any attempt to persuade Jim to change his mind about going to Australia, Babb said, 'It's your business,' picked up the receiver of his black telephone on his desk and dialled the MCC at Lord's. He asked for the secretary and relayed the information. 'Laker has just told me that he is not available for the tour of Australia,' he said. Then he replaced the receiver. One of the staff at Lord's was asked to telephone the cricket correspondent of the Pardon's Cricket Agency in Fleet Street, and relayed the information. Within minutes a 'snap' was put out to all the national and local newspapers around the country. 'By the time I left the Oval the news was in the stop press of the evening newspapers and on the placards,' said Jim. 'Never had anybody said "Jack Robinson" more quickly. For my part I acted without sufficient thought. In one sense I still believed I was right. In another, one has to put up with a lot of injustice in the course of life. But perhaps I should have laughed and forgotten about May's allegation.

'But to those at Lord's and the Oval – to whose way of thinking I am a professional cricketer, a man who signs a slightly one-sided contract – the position should have looked different. It would have been in character for them to act almost as if I were just a private who had refused to accept an order. But they went to the other extreme. Babb didn't suggest that I should have second thoughts. He didn't even suggest a chat with May and myself over a drink. The man at Lord's acted just as hastily as Babb, without thought. This, after all, was a matter which seemed to be important to English cricket. We wanted to hold on to the Ashes, and the idea was that I might have something to contribute towards the effort to do so.'

Jim felt that if Gubby Allen had been at Lord's that day the matter would have been handled with more sympathy and common sense. Allen might have said to him 'Don't be so silly, we need you!' Next day, 17 July, the back pages of the national newspapers were filled with the news. The headlines of *The Daily Telegraph* were 'Laker's "No" Adds to day of Gloom at Lord's – Australian tour prospects hit by Spin bowlers' absence.' Its cricket correspondent E. W. Swanton wrote in his distinctive, almost pompous, style, 'It was announced by MCC this evening that J.C. Laker had notified them of his inability to tour Australia. The reasons were said to be personal. Coming on top of the recent news that J.H. Wardle was unavailable, this item did nothing to allay the gloom cast by another wet day and the complete absence of play in the Gentlemen *v.* Players.

'Wardle is, on his record, the most successful English slow bowler of the present day on wickets abroad while Laker, though naturally not so dangerous in hot countries [Jim would dispute that!] as he is at home, has such control and power of spin that he is a natural choice for any touring party, specially to Australia in view of his phenomenal performances against them here in 1956. Some sympathy for modern cricketers asked to spend a succession of winters away from home will be extended by most people, where the grounds as in these cases, are family ties. Laker has been away in 1947-48, 1953-54 and 1956-57. Wardle has done these three trips and also that of 1954-55 to Australia. The forthcoming tour would thus be his fifth in twelve years, and Laker's fourth. Many people will, however, feel that a professional cricketer who has obtained a substantial financial position in life as a result of the game, including a large tax-free benefit, is under a strong moral obligation, which has to be set against domestic inconvenience.

Laker's benefit two years ago, exclusive of a 'Shillings for Laker' fund, amounted to £11,086. Wardle last year collected £8,129.'

Swanton was the voice of the cricketing establishment and most of his readers would agree with his views at the time. The players were roughly treated then but the pendulum has now swung the other way with millionaire cricketers allowed to fly home to attend the births of their children. They are paid vast amounts for using their names and they live in houses that cost £1 million or more. In Jim's day he worked part time in various businesses and much of his annual income came from writing articles for newspapers. He wouldn't make too much money from the kind of anodyne articles that are produced today. Jim usually put over strong views and was well rewarded, although in *Over to Me* he went too far and found himself in trouble.

Other newspapers were equally critical of Jim's announcement about not touring Australia and in the *Daily Express* the normally restrained Pat Marshall, renowned for wearing city shoes, carried a highly damaging article under the headline 'No MCC tears – and no "change your mind" plea.' Marshall, who proved to be wrong on both counts, doubtless pressurised by his sports editor, wrote, 'It seems a pretty scurvy way to treat a game that has hauled him up from a junior bank clerk into super-tax class. Poor thanks to the fans who contributed to his £12,000 benefit. Certainly Laker is a family man, with all the family man's responsibilities. But cricket is his business, and a very good one.

'He owes the game his position in the world today. He owes a debt to MCC and England and to millions of cricket fans. A moral debt, to be sure, but a debt that demands that personal interests should be laid aside in the interests of the game that has given him his own particular place in the sun. I can assure Jim that his refusal will be accepted without quibble. No pressure will be exerted to make him change his mind again. His decision has shocked cricket's chiefs. But there will be no tears. They are more concerned about the Johnny Wardle situation. Experts agree that Wardle's absence is far more of a blow than that of Laker, whose overseas record is not too impressive. Wardle has an excuse for not making the trip. He told me at Lord's yesterday that when he returned from the South African tour in 1957 he found his wife Edna almost on the point of collapse. Of course, May does have Tony Lock, who took less than five minutes to make up his mind to say yes to the invitation.'

That night Jim attended an Eric Bedser benefit dance at the Dog and Fox Hotel in Wimbledon, one of countless obligational duties of a professional cricketer helping a colleague. Mike Langley of the *Daily Express* asked him, 'Did you say no because you were frightened of bowling on Australia's hard pitches?' 'No,' said Jim, 'if some malicious people think that they are free to do so. I am too old now to bother what anyone thinks. In any case, I've bowled and taken wickets on better pitches than they have got out there. I'm not saying the exact reason but it is not a cricketing reason.' Keith Miller, writing in the *Express* on the same day, defended his good friend, saying, 'Our lads are sorry you won't be coming. They would have liked their own back. But, good on ya! Against us in 1956 he built a reputation of being an unplayable bowler, with a record so fantastic that no other bowler is likely to equal it. If he came out to Australia, where no off-spinner has ever been successful, his reputation would have been lost overnight. He might have got his 1 for 60 or 2 for 70 but no more. He would have been useful to keep one end up, but he could not have been used as an attacking bowler.'

On 17 July Jim went to see his agent to discuss the whole affair and sitting in the office was Denis Compton, another client. He was regretting the whole affair but was still adamant that he couldn't play under a captain who thought he was a shirker. He told Compton, a good colleague and friend, he wanted to speak to Gubby Allen in person. 'I owed him an explanation,' said Jim. Denis Charles Scott (after Robert Scott, the Antarctic explorer) Compton shared a name, Charles, with Jim and they were dissimilar characters. While Jim was quiet and reserved, Denis was a warm, lovable and haphazard genius very similar to Keith Miller. Four years older than Jim, he was the most popular cricketer in the post-war years until he retired in 1956, saying farewell with 94 and 35 not out against the Australians at the Oval, the ground where he hit the winning run – from his trademark stroke, the sweep – to regain the Ashes three years earlier. Slowed by injuries to a knee playing football for Arsenal (he earned 14 wartime caps as a left winger) and almost round-the-year cricket, he had the kneecap removed. He was awarded the CBE, wrote for the *Sunday Express*, and worked occasionally for the BBC as a cricket commentator. In his final days before he died at the age of seventy-nine he could hardly get out of his armchair. He said to me, 'I can't play golf, I might as well sign me off. I've had enough.' But he was still capable of coming up with potent views about the state of cricket, particularly the wearing of helmets!

One of his tasks when he retired was to do some reasonably well paid PR work and at the talk with Jim about the Australian tour he came out with some good advice. 'You should ring Billy Griffith,' he said. 'He can bring the parties together and reach a compromise.' Billy Griffith was the assistant secretary of MCC at the time, later secretary between 1962 and 1974, and was famous for scoring 140 as an opener against the West Indies in Port of Spain on the 1947-48 tour and then being dropped. Christened Stewart Cathie Griffith, Billy played for Cambridge University, Surrey, Sussex and England and he was one of the nicest, most concerned, men who ever figured in English cricket. He was a glider pilot in the Airborne Division and was awarded the DFC for his services at Arnhem. One of his best friends was Brian Johnston, who was also at Arnhem.

Denis was the intermediary between Jim and the establishment at Lord's and he rang Billy and suggested a meeting of all the parties. Billy was keen. He telephoned Ronnie Aird, the MCC secretary, another decent, popular man, Gubby Allen and Peter May and they were asked to attend a meeting, along with Jim. A meeting was duly arranged at Lord's and it took place in secret. Jim was asked to give his side and finished up pleading to May, 'Your apology could resolve this straight away.' May refused to apologise. Jim said, 'I felt that Gubby was on my side, as far as he could. As a bowler himself, I fancy he knew just what it meant to be told that you are not trying. Perhaps, for a moment, he cast his mind back twenty off years and imagined how he might have felt if Douglas Jardine, say, had made the same comment to him.

I am certain that Allen's feeling was that May should never have said what he did.' The meeting ended with no agreement. Ronnie Aird and Gubby Allen urged them to reconsider.

Twenty-four hours later, Jim saw Peter May at the Oval and Jim repeated his plea. Once again May refused. A journalist, a friend of May's, told Jim the reason why May was so stubborn. 'If he said sorry he would lose face,' said the journalist. Jim was still being assailed in the newspapers and was beginning to accept that he would have to remain at home, instead of fulfilling his final ambition of touring Australia. Another day passed, and the two adversaries saw each other in the corridor downstairs at the Oval. May gave Jim the impression that he was prepared to reconsider, without actually apologising. Jim said in *Over to Me*, 'Without going so far as to say that he was wrong, he suggested I should forget he had ever said anything. With my hopes of the tour revived, this was good enough for me. Lord's were told that I was ready to go and there was relief all round. I must say I was very glad that the unpleasantness and uncertainty was over. It was a sad and sordid story but, like all the best ones, it had a happy ending.'

If the truth had come out, Gubby Allen and his selectors would have put pressure on May to climb down. It was yet another case of hiding the true facts to avoid controversy. A generation passed by before the cricket authorities started to explain the real reasons for certain happenings. With the new freedom of information legislation now in force, Governments have to be truthful. Cricket has been dreadfully slow to come out with the truth. In his autobiography, published in 1985 and written by Michael Melford, his best friend among the journalists, May didn't give any details about his row with Jim over his 'shirker' taunt. But he made a critical reference to another matter that annoyed Jim just before he died. He said that Jim sold a story to one newspaper announcing he would retirement from Test cricket, upsetting the other English journalists. He wrote, 'One other event which probably had an indirect effect on the tour was Jim Laker's announcement of his forthcoming retirement, made when we were scarcely out of the English Channel. This seemed a pity because it suggested to the opposition that he for one thought that he was past his best. He could never hope to approach his English menace on Australian pitches but I knew that he wanted to get through without damaging his huge reputation. His announcement was made exclusively to one paper. Its side effect was to increase the normal competitiveness of a section of the unusually large press party which we had with us.'

The bitterness between the two men lingered on but Jim wasn't a man to hold grudges for the rest of his life. In his book *Cricket Contrasts*, published around the same time as May's, he was generous about his former captain. 'There was no doubt in my mind that May was the best batsman we have had since the Second World War,' he said. 'He was a prime example that nearly all great batsmen are born not made. When George Geary was congratulated for his good job on him as a schoolboy, Geary replied, "I did nothing. He was such a marvellous, natural player that I could find very little fault in him from the first time I saw him." May played the game in a fairly simple manner and would never hook and seldom pulled. Playing straight was his greatest strength and it was small wonder that in his capacity of chairman of selectors he almost despaired of the number of England batsmen who seemed incapable of playing straight. He also hit the ball exceedingly hard, off both the front and the back feet and was probably the finest on-driver the game has ever seen. On top of that, he played the game very hard. There was nothing soft about his cricket and he had no mercy on any bowler.

'While I never considered him as a great captain, he was certainly a very good one. He was a fervent admirer of Hutton and he tried to captain England in a similar style to Leonard... rather cautious. He should have been more adventurous, though, and from my point of view, I got on much better with him than I had done with Hutton. Leonard was obsessed with fast bowling whereas May tried to give everyone a fair crack of the whip.' The way Ray Lindwall and Keith Miller battered Hutton's defences in 1948 had a profound effect on his captaincy. He wanted a tooth for a tooth.

Did Jim do himself justice on the 1958-59 series? He thought so. Topping the bowling averages with 15 wickets at 21.20, a figure not matched by Brian Statham, Peter Loader, Fred Trueman, Frank Tyson, Trevor Bailey and Tony Lock, who was bottom of the averages with 5 wickets at 75.20, was a remarkable achievement despite missing a Test and playing four with an arthritic finger that would have kept others out of action. At the end, he answered his critics who claimed he wouldn't succeed on Australian pitches. But if he had been given a chance to play in the two previous tours he could have further enhanced his already-high reputation.

SEVEN

A LAST CURTAIN CALL
AT ESSEX

Jim's fortieth birthday was looming and he had no thoughts of playing cricket professionally again. His business ventures, including running a ladies wear shop in Putney with Lilly, and his charitable work kept him busy but he still had a yearning for playing county cricket, as an amateur. The name 'amateur' used to upset him. Now his views had changed. In February 1962, he told the *Daily Mail's* Crawford White, 'I've volunteered to play as an amateur for Surrey but they turned the idea down. If any other county wants me, I'm available. I've practised two nights a week at Alf Gover's cricket school and the ball is turning as much as ever. I've got the urge back. I'd prefer county cricket to league cricket but I don't mind where I play. My finger is fine. Two seasons of very little cricket has done it the world of good and I think it will stand up to quite a lot of hard work again now.'

A few days later, having the traditional, unhealthy English breakfast with Trevor Bailey in the restaurant car of an express train coming from Manchester to Euston, he was asked by his friend, 'Do you fancy playing a few games for us? We're short of a spinner. It will be a different culture, more fun.' The two men had been speaking at a sporting dinner in Manchester the night before. Perhaps it had been a long night. Playing as a part timer on an amateur business was briefly discussed and no financial offers were made but Jim expressed interest. According to Alan Hill, 'His business colleagues were surprised since his views about amateurs were well known.' Jim was two years into his MCC and Surrey bans. No-one wanted him and he was still considered a pariah in the world of cricket.

On 23 March, 200 Essex members turned up at the annual meeting at Chelmsford, far more than normal, and half of them were strongly opposed to the recruitment of Laker. Pat Marshall of the *Express* wrote, 'Several stormed out. Others said that this decision would lead to resignations. One even said that he hoped the MCC would refuse to allow Laker's special registration to play for Essex. Doug Insole, the England selector and former Essex captain and a member of the committee, said, "Certainly there is a good deal of opposition to the decision but it is too early to say it will affect membership. I understand the committee decision was far from unanimous. In fact, it was almost as divided as the members."' The controversy dragged on and six days later Jim told his friend Alex Bannister of the *Mail*, 'If it is going to cause an upheaval I want nothing to do with it. I do not want to be mixed up in any more nonsense.' Arnold Quick, the treasurer, said, 'We want Laker and we need his experience. We need his drawing power.' As treasurers are powerful figures, his word went and Laker was signed up.

Looking back forty years later, Bailey said, 'Jim was prepared to do it for not very much money, petrol money really. It was hard to accept the criticism because I had acquired a great cricketer and personality for nothing. It was like signing George Best at the end of his career and persuading him to turn out without wages.' Essex went in for amateurs. That year they had five, Bailey, Insole, Sam Luckin and Eddie Presland, as well as Jim. Brian Taylor, who later became club captain, said, 'Jim had terrific influence over the whole club and we had three marvellous years with him. Bill Greensmith, the leg-spinner, had to bowl a lot of overs and there wasn't much more from the others. Our attitudes changed completely. Up to then we were a side with seamers bowling on green tops. It is well known that Essex is the driest county in county cricket and in the second half of the summer the ball turns there but I don't know why we had no spinners of quality, until he arrived. When I took over as captain we had three spinners and it made more sense. Jim's arrival got things going and it was breathtaking. And we had plenty of laughs.'

There were celebrated stories about Jim and perhaps the funniest came from the opening game of the season at St Valentine's Park in Ilford: 'The skipper said to him, "Do you fancy going out to the middle and taking a look at the pitch?" After a few minutes, Jim strolled back to the dressing room and Trevor said, "How do you think it'll play?" "I don't know," said Jim. "I couldn't find it!" It was, of course, an Essex green top. Gordon Barker, pressed into fielding at short leg, dropped a catch off Jim and was very upset. Jim calmed him down, saying, "Your boots were caught up in the long grass!"' *Wisden* reported, 'Laker bowled well but had no luck.' The Derbyshire seamers bowled his side out for a 7-wicket defeat.

'Some people, including the press, doubted whether Jim would be effective,' said Bailey. 'He hadn't played county cricket since 1959 and he was never over-enthusiastic about practice. He made his usual deceptively casual approach, over went his arm high, the ball dropped on precisely the right spot and turned enough to take the inside edge. Gordon Barker dropped it at short leg. I must say, in Gordon's defence, that he had never fielded at short leg to a bowler of that calibre. His only complaint, apart from his fury at missing the chance, was that it earned him bigger headlines than when he scored a century!'

Jim wasn't a watcher, according to Bailey. 'He read the papers most of the time,' he said. 'He drank a lot of tea and coffee and ate the traditional cricket meals of the day. I would call him, "an intelligent drinker".' One of the biggest characters in the side was the opening batsman Brian Edmeades, born in Matlock in 1941, who had the broadest Cockney accent although he hadn't been close to the Bow Bells. Doug Insole said, 'He was the man who pioneered the hair blower in cricket and they used to shout to him "Get that out of here, you tart." He wore winkle-picker shoes and sported extravagant sideburns and he wasn't a bad player. One morning he showed off his new watch and said, "It only cost me a fiver, a bargain." Jim said, "It looks a quality Swiss watch and worth far more than that. But it probably fell off a lorry!" The conversation turned to Jim's watch. "That's a nice one," said Chanson [that was his nickname, after the French song]. "How much did it cost you?" "Actually it was free, Brian." "Three nicker?" said Edmeades. "You've got a bargain there!" Surrey presented it to Jim when he retired in 1959.' The mood they were in when *Over to Me* was published, some of their committee members must have felt like asking for its return.

In Jim's third match, he failed to take a wicket against Worcestershire at Romford and his old adversary Tom Graveney scored 61. But 'Tonker' Taylor has strong memories of another incident about Tom when the players were discussing Tom's arrival at a match. 'Don't worry about him,' said Jim. 'He won't last an over. He doesn't fancy off-spin.' When Tom came in, Jim bowled him with his fifth ball. In his comeback season, Jim headed the averages with 51 wickets at 18.86. Mike Denness, the England and Kent captain, was given a testing debut at Dover by Jim, who had him lbw for a duck and caught for 3 in his second innings. *Wisden* commented, 'Several younger players were all at sea against Laker.' Jim took 7 for 73 and 6 for 86 and Bailey said, 'It was like a masterclass. He bowled beautifully.'

Keith Fletcher was eighteen when he first played with Jim and he said, 'The first thing I noticed about his bowling was the loud click of his thumb and bowling finger when he gave the ball a big rip. I played first-class cricket for twenty-six years and I encountered only one other off-spinner who did that – the Indian Erapally Prasana, who averaged almost 5 wickets every Test. I fielded at slip and I could hear the noise. In those days my hearing was pretty good. He was very good to me, helping with tips and he was a popular figure. I wouldn't say he liked going out on a riotous evening though. He could be a bit dour. He was a chain smoker and his preference was for Peter Styvescent. Trevor Bailey was a chain smoker too.'

Roger Harman, who played for Surrey in the 1960s and is now the club's cricket chairman, said, 'Jim bowled faster tham most off-spinners. He still had his loop, but batsmen were often bowled or lbw because the ball came onto them quicker tham they expected.' In 1963 Jim was less successful, taking 43 wickets at 19.25 and he experienced a pleasant interlude in the winter, playing two matches for the Cavaliers at Sabina Park, Kingston, and taking 5 wickets. Robin Hobbs, the former England and Essex leg-spin bowler, went on that tour and he said, 'Jim was a very courteous man but he didn't show his feelings. He tended to keep things to himself. Paddy Phelan was the other off-spinner and Paddy was in awe of him. He would have died to have had a good chat with him about off-spin but it never happened. He didn't help him at all which was sad. But in those days a lot of those cricketers were like that, the old-school type. They were eccentric cricketers who were playing for themselves more than the team. They didn't make a lot of money out of the game and they had to look after themselves.'

Hobbs was speaking the day after Gordon Barker died on 10 February 2006 and he said, 'The amazing thing about Essex is that all our bowlers of that era, Ken Preston, Barry Knight, Trevor Bailey, Roy Ralph and one or two others are still alive. It must be the air in Essex or our humour! At most of the counties they've lost a lot of bowlers in their sixties.' By the following summer Jim realised, at the age of forty-two, his powers had waned and after his final appearance at Northampton, one of the few pitches in the country that takes spin on the first day, he announced he was retiring. 'I think he realised the old bones were creaking and it was hard work,' said Fletcher. 'He sometimes spoke about his ban from Surrey and the MCC and he told us it was very unfair. "People should be allowed to write what they like within the law," he said.'

The match at Northampton was a high-scoring one and he took the wickets of two redoubtable and personable opponents, Albert Lightfoot and David Steele. His last wicket came from a caught and bowled off one of the game's straightest bats, wielded by the man who defied Australia in the 1970s. 'I can't remember that but I was out by a very fine bowler,' said Steele. 'I met him a few years later when he was a match adjudicator and on one occasion at a Benson & Hedges Cup tie against Cambridgeshire at March I scored a hundred. He gave me a good mention in his little speech and that really started me going up the ladder.'

Before joining Essex, Jim returned to the leagues in 1960, playing a season with Norton in the Staffordshire League, the club that hired Sir Frank Worrell and Sir Garfield Sobers. Worrell preceded him and Sobers followed him in 1961. 'I couldn't match them,' he said. He was paid £60 a game, £15 less than the Test match fee of £75. 'I thought I did reasonably well,' he said. 'And, far more important, I enjoyed the experience enormously.' His businesses were expanding and one season was enough. He had a brief spell in printing, learning the basics of letterpress and litho, and also worked for a company selling bronze heads of well-known celebrities. Yet another venture was working with his old friend Arthur Phebey, taking trade exhibitions on trains.

Jim took 270 catches in his 450 first-class matches, which is not an exceptional record but he didn't miss many. He fielded at gully – 'a better position than short leg' he said. Norman Preston, the Pickwickian figure who was editor of *Wisden* for many years, wrote in the 1952 edition when Jim was voted one of *Wisden*'s five Cricketers of the Year, 'Laker deservedly has the reputation of being a splendid fielder, particularly in the gully where he holds the hottest of catches.' That was a slight exaggeration. Jim spilled a few. Forty-six of his 270 catches came off the bowling of Tony Lock and out of his 1,944 wickets, 124 were caught by Lock, whom Fred Trueman called 'the greatest catcher I ever saw'. Lock's 830 catches in 654 matches was a far better record than Jim's and 202 were caught and bowled, an astonishing high percentage. No bowler fielded to his own bowling better than Lock.

After Jim died, Lock wrote a tribute for the 1987 edition of the Surrey CCC Yearbook and when the material arrived from Perth by post, Raman Subba Row said, 'It's a very nice piece but unfortunately there was no punctuation. Not one bit.' One of the staff said 'Do we keep it, or do we correct it?' Raman replied, 'We don't like to alter things but you can't ignore punctuation!'

But there were instances where Lock was stuck in the head and he recalled an incident at Hastings when he was fielding to George Cox of Sussex and Jim was bowling. 'George was one of the hardest hitters of all time,' he wrote. 'He picked one off his toes, middled it perfectly and before I had a chance even to duck, I was hit full on the ear. Jim walked over and said, "Bad luck, another catch dropped!" He was only joking, of course, and he didn't realise how badly I was hurt. I needed three stitches inserted inside the ear. In another game, I was struck on the top of my forehead by a hook from George Emmett, another fine hitter of the ball. Fortunately, I was wearing a cap and this took the brunt of the blow. I was dazed enough to go off for half an hour. When I returned, Stuart Surridge tossed the ball to me and said "See what you can do after your rest!"' Surridge was second in the list of catchers off Jim's bowling with 107. Jim caught 69 off his own bowling and there was a picture of him stretching out to his right above his head and it was one of the most spectacular of his catches. But there were fewer sensational catches close to the ground.

He claimed that one of his finest catches came earlier in his career, against the former Hampshire batsman and county umpire Sam Pothecary, who was well known for his wit. Christened Albert Ernest, Pothecary was always called Sam and Jim was playing for the Services side in 1946. Jim said, 'I beat him a couple of times and he was in a fearful quandary. At the end of the over he came over and studied my sore finger. Being an old professional up to the tricks of the trade he said, "I don't like the look of that. If I were you I would go off and have it dressed." I swallowed Sam's advice, hook, line and sinker. But in the end it rebounded against him. After being treated, I came back to the boundary and signalled to the umpire that I was ready to resume. No sooner had I stepped on to the field than Sam went for a big hit. He was 94 and it looked as though it was going to be a sixer. I sprinted after it, shot out a hand as I saw the ball sailing overhead, and it stuck. It stuck literally and I kidded him, saying, "That plaster on my finger stopped the ball bouncing out of my grasp!"'

Peter Walker of England and Glamorgan, one of the greatest fielders of all time, said of him, 'He was too bulky. Bulky people aren't athletic, like Colin Milburn and Colin Cowdrey, but Colin was a fine slipper and "Ollie" Milburn was a very sharp catcher at short leg. You need to be thin and lithe and quick. Jim was competent.' Graham Roope, one of England's finest fielders, disputes the contention that bulky fielders are handicapped in the field. 'I never played with Jim but I saw him in action and I wouldn't criticise his fielding,' he said. 'He was a very fit player and except with his problem with his finger, he never missed a game in nineteen years. He didn't pull any muscles or have surgery. In those days cricketers got fit by playing the game and Jim bowled an immense number of overs.

'People like Statham, Trueman and Bailey didn't keep breaking down like today's bowlers. I think today's crop of players are too fit. They do all this training and eat all the right food and they are frequently out of action. It's extraordinary! We had steak and chips and a pint or two of ale and we didn't miss many matches. When they first brought in tracksuits at Old Trafford, Brian Statham refused to wear one. "I'm not an athlete," he said. "I'm a cricketer." They left Ian Blackwell out after a tour once because he was overweight but I think he is a fine cricketer and needs persevering with because he's got some talent. If W.G. Grace was around today, they wouldn't pick him. I knew Tony Lock pretty well and he was rated as one of the greatest short leg fielders ever and he was, but he was a big bloke. He was an outstanding diver.'

Roope, who played 21 Tests, was a top-class goalkeeper and he perfected the art of diving in cricket. 'I think I was one of the first,' he said. 'I don't think Jim ever dived. Not many did. I remember one of my earlier games when I was at slip, standing alongside to Kenny Barrington and a catch came towards Kenny's boot and I dived across and caught it. I finished up between Kenny's legs and he was pretty upset. "That was mine," he said. "I know," I said, "but it's now in the book." Locky was another good diver but fielding at backward short leg the ball didn't come as quick to slip fielders and he had a bit more time to make some stunning catches.'

Roope now coaches at Woodhouse Grove, the public school in Yorkshire that helped produce the first British-born Asian cricketer to play for Yorkshire, Ajmal Shahzad. 'To be a coach you need patience and Jim was a very patient man,' he said. 'I spent a lot of time with him at the Oval and he helped me tremendously, especially with batting against off-spin bowling. Kenny Barrington was the same. Kenny could play off-spin as well as anyone. English cricket had a hatful of spin bowlers then but now they haven't got a good one, which is very sad. Shaun Udal is a lovely lad but if he was the number one last year, well, it's a frightening situation.'

Part of Jim's success was due to the outstanding catching of Surrey's close leg fielders. When Stuart Surridge took over from Michael Barton as Surrey's captain in 1952, leading them to five successive championships, he nominated himself as the short square leg expert. Just in front of square is the most dangerous position to field and more cricketers are injured there than any other. Surridge was never hit while Jim was bowling. 'Jim had the most marvellous command of length without ever neglecting to spin the ball,' he said. 'I fielded to him there for five years and I never got struck, not once. He just didn't give the batsman a chance to hit me. It was really remarkable. He was great, there is no doubt about it.'

'You've got to have two qualities in that position,' said Peter Walker. 'First bravery, and second confidence. And the guy has to have confidence in his bowler. Fielding so close as that you're like a tail gunner in a World War II bomber — you know you've got to be hit sooner or later. I always looked at the target and was only really hurt in the back as I turned away to avoid a full-blooded shot. My back still plays me up now, decades later.

'The worst injury I saw was playing for Glamorgan against Warwickshire at Cardiff. Roger Davis had taken the job from me and he was fielding four yards from the bat as Neal Abberley aimed to mid wicket with a short arm jabbing stroke. Roger had only time to half turn his head to the right before he was felled by a sickening, full-on blow to the left temple. We rushed to Roger's prostrate body. He was unconscious and the colour drained from his face. He started to twitch and turn blue, his breathing came in short, stifled gasps. None of us had any idea what to do but thankfully, among the small group of spectators present was a Dr Colin Lewis. He recognised the severity of the injury and ran on, turned Roger on his back, put his finger down his throat and pulled his tongue back into position, freeing his windpipe. He gave him the kiss of life and undoubtedly saved Roger's life.'

No-one was keen to take over at 'Boot Hill' and Tony Cordle, the opening bowler, seeing that a motor cyclist was parked nearby, asked him if he could borrow his helmet. It was the first time a fielder had worn a helmet in county cricket. Now, of course, no-one fields there without one and unlike Denis Compton, Jim's sometime fellow columnist working for Beaverbrook newspapers, Jim was a strong supporter of helmets. Compton worked for the *Sunday Express* for many years and Jim had a couple of seasons working with the *Daily Express*.

Jim was hit several times in the field, mainly on the boot and shins, and none of them had serious results. Micky Stewart took over from Surridge as the short leg specialist later in the 1950s and in 1957 he took 77 catches, including a world record of 7 in an innings at Northampton when the home side were dismissed for 111, the total most cricketers believe brings bad luck. Jim was unconcerned that Stewart held just two catches off his bowling while Alec Bedser and Lock caught three apiece. Some fielders recalled instances of Jim showing exasperation after seeing a chance dropped off his bowling but Stewart, who has spent most of his life playing and working for Surrey, said, 'He was expert at working out what the batsman was trying to do. It was easier to field there when I started than it is today because batsmen didn't whack the ball as hard. When I started batsmen still played with their bats in front of the pad and the inside edge more often than not went to Lock at backward short leg.

'Few batsmen swept when Jim bowled but an exception was Ken Grieves, the Australian who played for Lancashire. He was a magnificent sweeper and Jim wouldn't let me field there to him because he knew that Ken would sweep, with the spin, no matter where the ball pitched. I couldn't understand it because he was such a superb bowler. I was willing to stand there but Jim wouldn't have it. That was a side of him that too few people appreciated. He was a deeply caring and sensitive person in everything he did. Once I asked him if I could field just in front of square and Roy Marshall was playing a magnificent innings. Hampshire were following on and I said to Jim, "Let me get in there, he'll probably think it's cheeky, try to hit me and he might knock it up to mid off and be out." Jim looked at me and said, "You're bloody mad," but I got my way and Roy holed out.'

Ray Illingworth was never an immediate rival of Jim because he was born ten years later but their records are always being compared. 'I looked on Jim as the senior pro,' he said. In one field there were equals; they weren't lithe and agile fielders although they had safe hands. They just about got by in the Test arena as fielders. Jim's career was ending when Illingworth was starting. Illingworth made his Test debut against the New Zealanders in 1958 and he recalled, 'I might have played another Test in that series but Jim was complaining about his finger and when he heard I was about to be called up he changed his mind and played. I played all five Tests in the West Indies that winter and Peter May told me, "I would have preferred you instead of Jim in that other Test." Peter was a very straight guy and I think it was getting fed up with Jim. He felt that Jim suited himself a bit and some of the other players shared that opinion.'

Christopher Martin-Jenkins said in his highly-praised *World Cricketers*, brought out in 1996, 'Illy was every inch a professional, both in his fastidious attention to his own and his players' legitimate interests and his approach to the game itself. A formidable opponent, stubborn and fearless, he was a loyal and considerate friend. His batting was solid, rugged and utilitarian, and determined, especially in crisis. His bowling action started with a chasse, followed by a poised, relatively lengthy run and a classic delivery reminiscent of Laker. He varied his pace and mixed his stock off-break with the ball which floated away to slip.' Illingworth was born in Pudsey, four miles away from Fitzinghall, birthplace of Jim and a third great Yorkshire and England bowler, Bob Appleyard, who was born in Bradford in 1924. It was amazing that three of them were born within a few square miles and by the end of the century there wasn't a single world-class off-spinner in the cricketing world still bowling with an untarnished action. The configuration of Yorkshire and England off-spinners almost matched the three Ws – Sir Frank Mortimore Maglinne Worrell, born in 1924, Everton Decourcey Weekes, born in 1925 and Sir Clyde Leopold Walcott, born in 1926, all delivered by the same midwife in a square mile in Barbados.

Jim was a good friend of Sir Clyde and he was one of Jim's 'bunnies' – he dismissed him on twelve occasions. Sir Clyde said in his autobiography, 'West Indians like exotic names and apparently Everton Weekes was named by his father, who used to do the English football pools and was an Everton fan. When Jim asked me about it, he replied, 'It was a good thing that he wasn't a West Bromwich Albion fan!'

Speaking before one of his annual mid-winter trips to his house in the south of Spain, Illingworth said, 'It is difficult to compare off-spin bowlers. Jim had a similar record to Bob Appleyard and it was a good time for spinners. Not many batsmen were good against spin and the uncovered pitches enabled spinners to get plenty of it. Jim was very accurate but he didn't bowl the one that floats away to the off and these days if you can't bowl that one, you'll be murdered. He was a moody bugger and he wanted things to go his way.'

In Appleyard's biography, written by Stephen Chalke and Derek Hodgson, Illingworth was quoted as saying, 'Bob would be ahead of Jim. He was a big man and his arm came right over the top and he got tremendous bounce. He also had a wonderful change of pace. He bowled a loop ball, a slower ball that went up and bounced a bit, and he also bowled a magnificent quick leg-stump yorker.' In the same book, Fred Trueman was asked whether he preferred the Lock and Laker pair from the South to the Appleyard-Wardle combination from the North. 'Wardle was the best left-arm spinner on all wickets that I saw,' said Trueman. 'He could bowl it out of the back of the hand as well and, with Bob at the other end, it was a magnificent partnership. Locky wasn't as good a bowler as Johnny, and of course Locky had a very doubtful action. Bob was one of the all-time greats. I don't like to say it about Jim Laker, because he was a very fine bowler, but he had only half the heart of an Appleyard.'

Appleyard started his career with Yorkshire in 1950 when he was twenty-six and took 200 wickets in his first season, the first bowler to achieve the feat. Six months later he contracted advanced tuberculosis and had the upper half of his left lung removed and was out of action for two years. He played in only 9 Tests, taking 31 wickets at 17.87 compared to Jim's 193 in 46 Tests at 21.24. Trevor Bailey voted for Jim, not Bob. 'Laker was easily the best off-spinner in the world,' he said. 'He had a classic action, had wonderful control and he *was* an off-spinner. To my mind Bob really wasn't an off-spinner, he was an off cutter.'

Appleyard was asked what would have happened had he been picked instead of Laker in the 1956 Old Trafford Test. 'Who knows?' he said. 'I certainly don't think Jim would have taken 19 wickets if he had Johnny Wardle, rather than Tony Lock, as his partner.' Both Lock and Laker took 10 wickets in an innings and Appleyard's best tally was 8 for 78. Jim was generous in his praise about Appleyard, saying, 'He would have gone a lot farther but for his illnesses. With his brisk delivery, he was one of the most difficult bowlers in the world to collar, which is why, on a helpful pitch, he might take 6 for 15 whereas I might concede 40 runs in taking the same number of wickets.' In 1951 the two men were competing to be first to reach the 100 wickets and Jim said, 'There was a good deal of wagering in the Bradford area about it.' Appleyard reached 99 first but pleurisy kept him out for several weeks. When he returned against the South Africans on 30 June he laboured away without taking a single wicket, conceding more than 100 runs. The next day he was ill again and Jim's tally advanced to 94. On 11 July, he was back again while Jim was starting a game against Worcestershire at Dudley. Appleyard didn't bowl until late in the day at Hull and Sussex passed 300 without losing a wicket. 'I was lucky,' said Jim. 'I began taking wickets on a rain-affected pitch and took my sixth on the stroke of 6.30 to reach the hundred. I picked up the newspaper the next morning to discover that Bob had a difficult catch dropped off Don Smith minutes before I got my 100th.' Jim was a regular but cautious punter and many professional cricketers were the same. It kept up the competitive element between them.

Walcott had an interesting comment about the respective qualities of Sonny Ramadhin and Alf Valentine, the West Indian bowlers who were in their prime in the 1950s, and those of Lock and Laker. 'Sonny and Alf bowled more overs than Lock and Laker but I would nominate the Surrey pair,' he said. 'Ram and Val were successful on the softer, uncovered pitches of England; less so on the harder pitches of Australia.'

Was there a better pair than Lock and Laker in the history of the game? One doubts it.

EIGHT

AFTER CRICKET:
COMMENTARY, PROPHECIES AND PACKER

Jim's favourite book was *Wisden* and he loved dipping into the yellow-covered bible of cricket founded in 1864. When he died, *Wisden* had 1,296 pages. In the 2005 volume, it had 1,944 pages. No sport has a comparable book and it is one of the reasons why cricket remains in a healthy state. Jim was good on statistics and he liked a little flutter on quizzes about the game after matches.

Betty Surridge, the wife of Stuart Surridge, believes that modern players know little of the heroes of the past. 'One day at the Oval I was listening to some players and when the name of Peter May came up. One asked, "Who's he?" I ask you!' Lilly, a close friend of Betty, started the campaign to celebrate Jim's fiftieth anniversary of his 19 for 90 at Old Trafford. 'Another generation will be coming along and they wouldn't know of Jim,' she said.

Most of the people running Surrey County Cricket Club believe in honouring their heroes and there are dozens of pictures of former Surrey players of all ranks around the five-storey Victorian pavilion. But as 2005 was nearing its end, Jim's head-and-shoulders picture was stolen from a Hall of Fame corridor on the bottom floor and Trevor Jones, the club librarian said, 'We do have stuff removed and it's sad that Jim's picture has disappeared at this time. But we'll put up another one in the place. There is a growing market in buying memorabilia and we will have to be careful to protect what we have.'

Betty lived close to the Lakers in Putney and they were often in each other's houses as their children grew up. Lilly was pregnant when they were moving from their flat in Willesden and while they looked for a suitable house in Putney, the Surridges put them up for a few weeks. They settled on a big place just off the A3 and it suited them. The only recognition bestowed on the great off-spin bowler of all time was the naming of a road close by, named Laker Close. 'I think Jim should have been honoured,' said Betty. 'And Ken Barrington wasn't honoured either.'

Michael Atherton is one of the few leading English cricketers of the past decade who believes in honouring the heroes of the past. He wrote in his column in *The Sunday Telegraph*, 'Arriving at Old Trafford as a teenager I was eager to find out about Lancashire players and teams of the past. I learnt that the Lancashire teams were home grown, that they had strong links with the community they represented and that their players played hard but enjoyed themselves off the field. Such historical knowledge might help a present club that has gone awry. My knowledge of England openers post-Second World War was pretty good, too. I reckoned most of the best – Washbrook, Hutton, Boycott, Edrich and Gooch – had certain things in common: determination, a certain cussedness and pride in performance. Knowing I was part of that tradition didn't necessarily make me a better player but it was important to me.

'Outwardly, the England teams that I played in showed little interest in the past or the players of the past, except to sneer at the black and white action shown on TV during a rain break. "Look where the keeper's standing! He can't have been quick! Oh my God, check out the fielding!" And yet it was the same players who instigated the custom of having a number stitched on to an England shirt. Therein lies the importance of an understanding of the past for today's sportsmen. It won't make him a better player but it gives a link with both the past and the future; it provides some context and some meaning, so that, long after the bones have stiffened and the eyes have gone, it still matters.'

The Australians pioneered the idea of numbering their Test players and their Board insists that a current player with a knowledge of cricket history speaks to their international squad every year. Atherton was surprised to learn on a visit to the Manchester United training ground that there were no pictures on display of Denis Law, George Best and Bobby Charlton. 'Alex Ferguson said history was too much of a burden for his younger players who were then looking to break the championship voodoo,' he said. Nasser Hussain was another modernist, saying, 'It was a hindrance in the great quest – obsession in his case – to find a mystery spin bowler. What is a the use of knowing about Laker, Lock and Underwood, great finger spinners, from the time of uncovered pitches, when what you need is another Muralitharan?' Hussain was educated at Forest School in Epping and there are no pictures of him on show at the cricket pavilion.

Jim drew up a list of players to represent a World XI from the players with whom he played with in his career – four Englishmen, Len Hutton, Peter May, Godfrey Evans and Alec Bedser, five Australians, Arthur Morris, Keith Miller, Richie Benaud and Ray Lindwall, one from the West Indies, Everton Weekes and one from South Africa, Hugh Tayfield. 'The first thing you notice is the amount of talent I've had to leave out,' he wrote. 'Compton, Worrell, Walcott, Hassett, Harvey, Barnes, Statham and Bailey. Hutton stood out as the dominating figure of post-war cricket. He rose from the humble position of a pre-war Yorkshire professional to be the first professional captain of England. He was the greatest worrier I ever met. Just before Tests he was living on his nerves in a way that was alarming to watch and because of this he sometimes made wrong decisions under pressure. He had taken a battering from opposing fast bowlers and when he had fine fast bowlers in side, it was natural that he should relish the situation. I don't think he bowled me enough and I wondered why I was in the side under him. But I begrudge him nothing. He was a shrewd man and a clever talker. When I first met him at the Headingley nets in 1937 I was in awe of him. When he became England's captain, he never changed. He was never conceited and his players liked him.'

Choosing either Brian Statham or Fred Trueman ahead of Ray Lindwall might have bothered Jim for patriotic reasons but he was a lifelong friend of the great Australian fast bowler. Lindwall was of short stature – five feet ten inches, the same height as Trueman – as a genuinely fast bowler and with his low-slung approach to the crease and his control of swing his record of 228 Test wickets in 61 matches was one of the best in the history of the game. His first-class career lasted twenty years and he achieved that despite being a big drinker. Jim said of him, 'He was a great man at a party, and he played his part in ensuring that no English brewery went out of business through lack of patronage. When he went down with an internal complaint, he became teetotaller for two years and later on, when he was within sight of a few records, he adopted a strict training campaign to attain the targets.'

Jim had a high regard for Brian Statham. He said, 'He was phenomenally accurate and before the First Test at Trent Bridge in 1956 there were doubts about his fitness. The nets had been affected by rain and so it was decided that he should bowl at the stumps without a batsman in the way. It wasn't worth running a risk of injury. He hit the stumps more times than not and as he was walking off one of the selectors, said, "How is it?" "I should be okay," said Statham. But the selector wasn't satisfied. "Can you bowl three overs from your normal run?" he requested. Brian wasn't too happy but he bowled the eighteen deliveries at top pace and hit the stumps sixteen times.' Jim Cumbes, the Lancashire chief executive who started his career at Old Trafford, had a good story about Statham. 'Brian was a very heavy smoker and he'd just decided to give up,' he said. 'I was in the dressing room on my own when he came in and I asked if that was true. "Yes lad," he said. "I've stopped but unfortunately I've f—ing well stopped bowling as well!" A few days later he resumed smoking. Jim was a pretty heavy smoker. Later on Rothmans and John Player, sponsors of the Sunday League, and their girls were giving out packets out to the players ad lib.'

Dickie Bird, a fellow Yorkshireman, resisted the temptation and he recalled a story about Jim taking 7 for 89 at a doctored pitch at

Leicestershire for Essex in 1963 and still being on the losing side. Essex were beaten by an innings and 48 runs after scoring only 225: 'I was playing for Leicestershire and Maurice Hallam, their captain, said, "We haven't won a game for ages and we have to win to get off the bottom." So they tinkered with one end, making the soil rough and putting down sand to cover it. Jim bowled beautifully and we thought we were going to lose but we had two useful spinners in John Savage, the off-spinner and Ray Smith, the left hander, and we ran through Essex.'

'In the sense that English cricketers are ambassadors of their country, Statham should be foreign secretary,' said Jim. He was an excellent tourist and his name was held in the highest regard wherever he has played. When he was on tour, he used to hibernate and, like one or two other colleagues in the England side, he was a famous sleeper. His contribution to English cricket is the greatest of any fast bowler since the Second World War. This isn't only true of his bowling but of his whole cricket philosophy, which has acted as an inspiration to others in times of strain. I don't think I've ever met a more placid or pleasant character, and I cannot remember Brian showing any serious signs of annoyance on the field, or off.'

Jim was less complimentary about Peter May in *Over to Me*, but he had no reservations about May's ability of cricket. 'A true great,' he said. 'There is no argument about him and Don Bradman being in the World XI. Hutton had to open and I have no doubt Arthur Morris, a fine player, must go in with him.'

Four years earlier, Jim praised May's strength of character, saying, 'In the autumn of 1955, he was offered a £20,000 contract to write for a well-known newspaper. The offer was so wonderful that May, who was not over-endowed with worldly goods, thought deeply and longingly over it. He was strengthened in his desire to accept by the newspaper guaranteeing that his views would not be stunted, and thus could contribute much good to the game. Furthermore, advice from Lord's was, I understand, that Peter should accept if it would enable him to stay in cricket. After the most careful deliberation he turned it down. Off his own bat, he waved goodbye to £20,000. His reason was simple: as England's captain he didn't wish to commit himself in print to observations and criticise his colleagues. That shows how highly he rated the captaincy. And it showed his self discipline and determination.'

In today's terms, that sum would be more than £600,000. Jim once worked out how much he made from his cricket career – from 29 Tests in England he received £2,370 and from five overseas tours another £2,700, thirteen years with Surrey earned him £10,000 and a benefit, a good one of the time, £11,000. The overall total was £26,370 and, having played 30 matches for Essex as an amateur between 1962 and 1964 the figure might have passed £27,000. It worked out £1,500 a season. But he was a shrewd man and he had various jobs out of season and made a reasonable sum from newspaper articles. As a Yorkshireman, he looked after his money and didn't squander it.

Jim had good relationships with most of the journalists, friendships sealed from long sea voyages to the other side of the world. He had got on well with the feared *Evening News* correspondent E.M. Wellings, who was known as Lyn. Perhaps that was because Wellings was an off-spin bowler earlier in his life. Jim worked for the *Daily Sketch* and the *Daily Express* and sold several serialisations to Sunday newspapers. Most cricketers court certain reporters to help their chances of having a successful benefit. The writers are usually receptive when the cricketer asks if the journalist can write an article for his benefit brochure. During the 1958 tour of Australia, most of the England squad were petrified of Jim Mather, the Australian cricket writer, but Jim often passed on tips to him to keep him sweet. After writing his own copy for several years , Jim applied for membership of the National Union of Journalists, an organisation that has strict rules, and he was delighted to be accepted.

When Jim wrote his book *Spinning Around the World* he included a chapter entitled 'The Year AD 2000', containing prophecies about how cricket would evolve. Most of them turned out to be eerily correct. Lilly has always been interested in astrology and her husband shared her enthusiasm for it. 'I'm a Taurus, steadfast in mind, unshaken in adversity and quietly persistent in the face of difficulties,' she said. Jim's star sign was Aquarius – 'Not in awe of tradition or authority. He will never refrain from turning on those in higher office, particularly when in search of the truth.' Both readings accurately summed up Mr and Mrs Laker.

Jim did some research in his *Wisdens* and came up with some appropriate star signs for many of his Test match colleagues. Under Aquarius were the South Africa off-spinners Athol Rowan, the man who he always said was number one in the field and Hugh Tayfield, a more abrasive character, was fourth in Jim's list. He produced a team of eleven Aquarians who all had a stubborn streak – Australians Bill Lawry, the left-handed opener who scored that defiant 132 on the 'ridge' at Lord's in 1961, Bobby Simpson, who sweated through two-and-a-half days to score 311 at Old Trafford in 1964, Norm O'Neill, who was hailed as the next Don Bradman, the nuggety wicketkeeper Don Tallon and Neil Hawke, the brave pace bowler who finally died of cancer after a terrific long fight, New Zealander Bev Congdon, whose character-filled innings of 176 and 175 against England in 1973 were separated by playing in a village match on a Sunday, England's John Hampshire, the sturdy batsman from Yorkshire who scored the first hundred on debut for England at Lord's, the South African 'Toey' Tayfield who always kissed his cap before every over, the menacing and determined West Indian fast bowler Andy Roberts, the only one among them who was a teetotaller, England's rebellious Freddie Trueman and the equally strong-minded Jim Laker.

The more he looked, the more he found revealing signs appearing. He discovered that Peter May and Colin Cowdrey were Capricorns ('takes life earnestly and is generally an upholder on tradition and authority'). Denis Compton and Alan Davidson were Geminis ('charming types with many friends, impatient with repetition and with a great desire to express themselves'). Aries ('known for leadership') – was Bill Edrich, who had a distinguished wartime record in the RAF. Len Hutton and Sunil Gavaskar were Cancer ('patience').

It was surprising that Jim nominated Athol Rowan as his second-favourite off-spinner because the South African from Johannesburg, born in 1921, played in only 15 Tests and his 54 wickets cost 38.59. One of his legs was hit by a bullet fired by a soldier of Rommel's Afrika Corps in the Western Desert and occasionally he had to play wearing his leg in irons. He had to retire at the age of thirty and if the roles had been reversed and Jim was serving in the front line with Rowan stationed at Cairo, the course of cricket history might have been drastically changed.

Jim had plenty of respect for Hugh Tayfield, nicknamed 'Toey' because he stubbed his toe into the ground before bowling or receiving a ball, but he wasn't keen on his acerbic comments out in the middle. Jim played only one Test in the 1955 series against South Africa at the Oval, and his personal duel with Tayfield ended in an honourable draw with England winning by 92 runs. Jim had an aggregate of 6 for 127 and Tayfield bowled an unchanged spell of 53.4 overs to finish with 5 for 60. Tayfield's record of wickets per Test was slightly better than Jim's, with 170 wickets at 25.91 apiece in 37 Tests. In the tour of South Africa in 1956–57 Jim came well second to Tayfield, taking 15 wickets against Tayfield's 37. Tayfield's tally remains one of the highest of a South African in Tests and his wickets only cost 17.18 runs each. Jim said, 'He was the most accurate off-break bowler I ever saw and had many other virtues. But he came to the fore at the time when the Springboks [now known as the Proteas for politically correct reasons] had an outstanding fielding side. I should say half of his victims were attributed to their fielding.' His form deserted him on the tour of England in 1960 with England's batsmen using their feet to get after him. He retired at the age of thirty-four, a young age for a spin bowler.

Jim placed Gloucestershire's Tom Goddard first ahead of second-placed Athol Rowan in his list and he modelled himself on his style of bowling. Six feet three inches tall and with huge hands, Goddard started his career at the age of twenty-two bowling fast but five years later he switched, like Jim, to off-breaks and in his new style he took 186 wickets in his first season as a spinner. He had a wonderful career up to his fifty-third year, taking a colossal number of wickets – 2,979 wickets at 19.84. However, he played in just in 8 Tests. Jim said, 'He had a rolling, burring West Country accent and appealed saying, "How were it?" With the slightest help, he spun the ball like a top and he took the game very seriously. He could take punishment but he hated being hit unscientifically. Once I went in to face him and I drove him high over mid off for a couple of fours. I thought they were good strokes but Tom, arms akimbo, looked darkly down the pitch and in his familiar accent exclaimed, "You should know better than that!"' Goddard died at the age of sixty-six. It seems a bad age for spinners.

John Pretlove, the former Kent left-handed batsman who played for Cambridge University (1954-56) and Kent (1955-59) was coached by Jim when he was at Cambridge and said, 'I think Jim was the greatest of all time but the fans of Tom Goddard would support Tom. I liked Jim a lot and we would listen to him talking cricket for as long as he was prepared to speak. He made mental files on most batsmen he bowled to, also batsmen of other countries. He coached at Fenner's for two seasons – pre-season of course – and was gener-ous with his comments and advise. His immense knowledge of the great game came across when commentating on radio and TV. He was clear and concise at the microphone and had a great following from cricket lovers all over the world. The only time he was short of words – as with Stuart Surridge – was when I took them both to the Cambridge Jazz Band Ball. Humphrey Lyttleton and his band were in fine form but somehow we couldn't persuade Jim or Stuart to take to the floor!'

Jim's third choice behind Goddard and Rowan was Sonny Ramadhin. He liked him as a man and he enjoyed his duels with him in the 1957 series, when he dismissed Walcott five times. Peter May and Colin Cowdrey put on 411 at Edgbaston, with Cowdrey putting his left pad just outside the line without playing a shot to thwart Ramadhin's off-spin. Ramadhin wasn't the same bowler after that. 'He never did well against the Aussies,' said Jim. 'They attacked him ruthlessly and Keith Miller waged a successful mental war against him. "Good morning, Ram," he would announce, "I'm just in the mood to give you some stick today, so watch out." This may have sounded like bravado, but it was calculated planning which nearly always threw Ram out of gear. He could never bowl properly at Keith.'

Asked once what he would do if he had his time over again, Jim said, 'My choice would be a left-arm spinner in England or a leg-spinner anywhere. There are times when off-breaks are more successful than the left hander's natural leg-break. But day in and out, the left hander has the better chance of taking wickets in good cricket, with the ball leaving the bat. If the ball is turning several inches, the off-spinner can be most deadly. But we don't strike many pitches where the ball can be turning appreciably. Where it will turn only the bare inch or so the left armer is in his element. The ball then does just enough to find the outside edge of the bat, and batsmen, certainly the better players, find more trouble with that delivery than those turning into them slightly.

'As for leg-spin, there are not many pitches on which that type of bowling will not bite. Leg-spin is the most difficult type of bowling to learn to control but if a cricketer has the gift of spinning the ball in the unorthodox way, it is his own fault if he does not practice and persevere so that he combines his spinning talent with great accuracy. Being a leg-spinner gives so much satisfaction to the bowler because, although he may be more expensive than the off-spinner or the left hander, he is constantly on the attack and liable to remove the best batsmen.'

Now in 2006 he has been proved right. The off-spinner is virtually extinct, slaughtered by batsmen advancing their front foot outside the line of the off stump and wielding heavy bats that propel the ball with immense power into the leg side. It is almost impossible for an umpire to give them out lbw. And with fielding restrictions on the leg side, everything is now against the off-spinner. The Test match-winners are Shane Warne, Stuart MacGill, Anil Kumble, Danish Kaneria and the magical non-conformist Muttiah Muralitharan. Though looked on as an off-spinner, Murali's most successful wicket-taking delivery is the 'doosra', the one that goes the other way. Or, as the cynics say, the one he throws. If another Laker emerged, youngsters might take up the art of off-spinning again but it is doubtful. The all-rounder, which was fading from view, has been revived in England due to the interest created by Andrew Flintoff's success. Jim always thought that Hutton was right, that fast bowlers win Test matches. 'Runs on the board, or flying stumps, those are things spectators can see clearly with their own eyes,' he said. 'It is the reason why the successful batsmen and the demon fast bowlers are the glamour boys of cricket. I had a long battle in my career. I was never an automatic choice for England until the 1956 series and they thought I wouldn't be effective in Australia.'

In his prophecies about the year 2000, Jim forecast that scoreboards would be electrically controlled with every phase of the player registered on it, even the number of balls each batsman has received. He also mentioned numbered shirts and the new development that the ICC has experimented with in one-day cricket – substitutes to come on and take part in the match. He recommended bowlers to be rested after 8 overs and given a rub down. Well, Duncan Fletcher's bowlers did that in the last Ashes series in England. Jim came up with another, more controversial idea – reducing boundaries to 60 yards. It is surprising he should have said that because it denies the spin bowler a chance to take wickets from catches on the boundary line. In his day, boundaries at the Oval were up to 90 yards. Now with the rebuilding one boundary is little more than sixty yards. The ICC have encouraged bringing in boundaries for one-day cricket in an effort to bring more excitement to the game. He was in favour of fielding restrictions and the inner circle was introduced after he died.

Jim was an innovative thinker about the game and he wanted a bowling rate of 100 balls an hour, slightly quicker than the current Test rate of 15 overs an hour. But fines for slow play were introduced after he first wrote that. One of his more contentious views was the idea of 'hotting things up', insisting that each batsman had to make three scoring strokes in every 10 balls. If not, there were penalties. You cannot imagine the harassed modern day scorer, working at a Twenty20 match, having to calculate the penalties with any confidence. He had the foresight to predict that more countries would take up cricket. In *Spinning Around the World*, he wrote, 'There is always the possibility of Americans, Russians and Chinese taking up the game. The Chinese? Well, unless they have completely changed their quiet philosophies, they should be well suited to cricket.' He was right about the Chinese: there are now fourteen clubs playing cricket in Shanghai and the game is spreading to other cities. In 2005, China were admitted to the ICC as an associate member. The USA have been members for some years and though cricket is played in a number of cities in Russia, there aren't enough players to justify an application for membership.

He prophesied that ex-cricketers would be running county cricket clubs in 2000 and though some of them serve as committee members it is disquieting that some clubs, including the MCC, give powerful roles to non-cricketers. He thought that boards would be set up to handle young cricketers – they are now in place. As for the laws, he was in favour of the old lbw law being resurrected, with umpires giving batsmen out when the ball pitches outside the leg stump and would have gone on to hit the wicket. It would stop batsmen padding the ball away. He wanted boundaries standardised (that still hasn't happened) and he favoured the creation of a panel of experts advising on the preparation of cricket pitches. He wrote, 'Within a few years I would wager that practically all first-class wickets in England would offer a better balance between bat and ball.' The ECB have tried to do that, without too much success.

He wanted covered stands with provision of rest rooms and toilets and proper facilities for refreshment and for general comfort. 'And there should be an undertaking that the public will get their money refunded if there is no play, and get half of it back if there is less than, say, two hours.' He was spot on with that – the ECB introduced money back facilities some years ago. He had another idea to bring in more revenue, urging the counties to stage athletics and horse-jumping festivals. 'With quick-growing grass and 21st century methods of cultivation, there is no end to the possibilities,' he said. He was accurate in some respects. For example, Australian Rules Football matches are held at the end of the season at The Brit Oval but athletes and horses have yet to appear in the outfield. Pop concerts have been money spinners although some grounds have had their outfields damaged. He concluded, 'No matter how many distasteful incidents mar the great international matches, nor how many county treasurers have seasonal seizures, cricket as it was known in 1900, as we know it in the 1950s, and as it will be known in the year of 2000, will remain an essential part of our way of life.'

Jim thought cricketers around the world were downtrodden and grossly underpaid so it was something of a surprise when he opposed Kerry Packer's hijack of international cricket. In his book *A Spell from Laker* he wrote, 'I took a violent objection to the underhand manner in which it was announced and introduced in May 1977 and in which, from the English point of view, Tony Greig, England's captain, played the lead. Hard as I searched and hoped for some sort of compromise, it seemed inevitable after a while that one was not forthcoming, and nobody can lay the blame fully for this on Packer's shoulders. Due totally to the way establishment cricket had been stabbed in the back, I opted to stay with the people who had provided me with a life of full excitement, great joy and world travel, and who had made me the envy of so many people.'

He was in favour of night cricket in Australia – he was soon proved to be right with that – and he also approved of the use of the white ball, helmets and coloured clothing. He thought the drop-in pitches – pitches produced somewhere else and taken by massive transporters out to the middle and hoisted into the middle of the square – made sense, especially in Australia where their big grounds had to be played across the square for other sports. But he hated the dumbing-down of the game, the incessant advertisements, shown almost at every over, the non-critical commentaries of his friends, the emphasis on intimidatory bowling and the high workload provided for the sixty cricketing mercenaries from around the world. The bulk of the cricket lovers of the West Indies were particularly upset, depending on their age and gender, by seeing their greatest cricketers forced to wear pink garb.

Kerry Francis Bullmore Packer, the big, rough, tough, self-confessed bully died at the age of sixty-eight on Boxing Day 2005, forty days after Lord Robert Alexander of Weedon, the QC who helped him to win the celebrated High Court action in September 1977, died from a stroke at the age of sixty-nine. Some of the newspapers hailed Packer as cricket's saviour but the case was about television rights in Australia, not so much about the genteel sport of cricket. The TV rights were vested with the Australian Broadcasting Commission (now Corporation), the terrestrial equivalent of the BBC, and when the contract expired, Packer's Channel 9 outbid the ABC only for the Australian Board of Control to reject Packer's offer and give the contract to ABC. The cricket Board's main reasons were the inability of Channel 9 to extend their coverage to reach the whole of Australia and second, the members, mostly ex-cricketers who ran it, disliked Packer's ruthless business methods and suspected he would downgrade cricket to the status of wrestling. Sir Frank Packer, Kerry's austere father, launched Channel 9 in Sydney in 1956 and won the support of Sir Robert Menzies, the Australian Premier between 1956 and 1972. Bob Menzies, a good friend of Jim Swanton and a host of other English cricketing members of the establishment, had Packer knighted for his services to journalism.

In *The Times* obituary of Kerry Packer, the author wrote, 'Packer had a name as a bully to his employees, not least his executives, and extended his profanity-spattered truculence to politicians and businessmen. But he could also exude rough-hewn charm, and long-serving staff, valued friends and good causes could benefit from his extraordinary (and sometimes anonymous) generosity.' Packer's latest international business project was to plan more gambling casinos in England to accompany the ones where he often won and lost huge amounts of money. Fortunately the plan ran into stronger opposition than the International Cricket Council managed to muster twenty-seven years earlier. Packer was a regular visitor to England and paid out £5 million in 1989 on a 1,000-acre estate in West Sussex, now owned by Roman Abramovich. He spent a further £1 million to import Argentinian horses to further his hobby of the rich man's sport polo and he had to ensure the animals could carry his girth. In 1990 he collapsed with a heart attack while playing polo and claimed he was technically dead for eight minutes. When he was revived he said, 'I've seen what's on the other side and believe me there's nothing there.' A quintuple bypass followed and in 1986 he had a diseased gall bladder removed, and also a cancerous kidney. His personal pilot gave him one of his kidneys for a transplant. Jim Laker died in 1986 after the removal of a gall bladder.

The Packers, staunch Royalists, were living in Berkshire 300 years or so ago and Kerry's great-great-great grandfather was the organist of St Mary's Minister, Reading and his great-great grandfather Frederick Alexander Packer was a musician. He married Augusta Gow, daughter of Neil Gow, one of Scotland's best-known composers. With a family that loved classical music, it might have continued down the line but when Frederick emigrated to Tasmania around 1850, not as a POM or as an assisted passage, he fathered to Robert Clyde Packer who launched the family into journalism and gambling. Robert claimed that he found his fortune by finding ten shillings in the street and putting the money on a horse that won. Frank, Kerry's father, was the heavyweight boxing champion of New South Wales he built up a newspaper empire 'with a combination of hard work and devil-may-care bravado'.

Although Kerry had polio as a boy, he insisted he should take up boxing. Kerry grew to six feet three inches, weighing more than Andrew Flintoff when the England all-rounder was in his binging days. *The Daily Telegraph* obituary said, 'On one occasion, when Kerry returned from Geelong to Sydney for the school holidays without his tennis racquet, his father, anxious to inculcate a sense of the value of possessions, sent him straight back by train – a 1,200-mile journey – to retrieve it. "Arrived Melbourne safely," the miscreant telegraphed, "No love, Kerry."' A biographer wrote of Sir Frank, 'He devoted up to twenty hours a day to business and his two young sons paid the price with unhappy childhoods.' Kerry's brother Clyde was primed to take over the newspaper empire but he had a fierce row with his father and fled to Los Angeles, where he became a successful impresario. Kerry brought out Clyde's share and when Sir Frank died in 1974, he took over at the age of thirty-seven. In a short space of time he became the richest, most powerful and, possibly, the most hated man in Australia.

Packer started planning the World Cricket Series to coincide with the ending of the ABC television contract. Thirteen of Greg Chappell's seventeen tourists to England for the ill-fated 1977 tour of England had signed up and the team manager, Len Maddocks, Jim's old friend, wasn't let in on the secret. The first three matches played by the Australians were washed out and the third one, against Sussex at Hove, gave added time for Greig to hold a party at his home on Sunday 8 May to explain the background. Greig's agent was Reg Hayter and Alan Lee of *The Times* was Greig's ghost writer at the time. He said, 'Reg's face fell as fast as the business he was about to lose, but his shock was not mercenary. Hayter, my employer at the time, was a traditionalist.' When Maddocks heard the news he came out with one of the most unfortunate remarks of the summer – 'I do not envisage that this will have a detrimental effect on the tour.'

The first published hint of the recruitment of thirty-five leading cricketers, whose salaries, on average, were increased ten times by Packer, came from the magazine *Bulletin* in South Africa. The news swept around the cricketing world the next morning and the shock struck like a tsunami. The players were called traitors. Friendships were severed and Rod Marsh, one of the Australian squad, spoke out about the way it had been handled and had his contract torn up. Don Bradman castigated the role of Benaud and put the phone down on him. And Neil Harvey, one of the five 1956 Old Trafford survivors, came out just as strongly. In his role as chief recruiter, Greig offered Geoff Boycott a contract and when he suspected that he wouldn't be allowed to play for Yorkshire when the ICC eventually banned the rebels, Boycott turned down the offer from WSC. Packer was able to bully most people he met but not Boycott. The two men failed to get on when Packer introduced him to his son James, suggesting he had a future as a cricketer. 'He wasn't a bad player,' said Boycott. 'Packer had strong views about him and I disagreed. Dad thought he knew more about cricket than me. I told him that making money was his job and playing cricket was mine.'

But there weren't many cricketers who said no to Packer. Among the few were three others, Chris Old, Derek Randall and Bob Willis.

Boycott had other reasons and had just returned from a three-year exile from Test cricket and wanted to show the authorities that he was now the master. In one of the worst Ashes series, won by England 3-0, Boycott reached his 100th century in the Headingley Test and found himself mobbed at the crease, losing his cap to a souvenir hunter who later returned it. Jim called Boycott 'Fiery', like many of his contemporaries, and doubtless made a pertinent quip at the expense of the thirty-seven-year-old maestro. In one of his books, Jim described him as 'selfish and a loner.'

At Lord's the men in charge wanted England's recruits – Tony Greig, Alan Knott, John Snow, Derek Underwood, Bob Woolmer and Dennis Amiss – banned and the ICC members felt the same way. Jim wrote in his last book, 'On reflection this new cricket revolution should not really have been such a complete surprise. For years one had listened to dressing room murmurs of low pay and poor conditions. The ideas of a players' union and privately organised games and tours were being mooted thirty years ago.'

He fell out with Greig and he said, 'Never at any stage had I criticised him as an England cricketer or indeed on his appointment as England's captain. With the demise of the unfortunate and unlucky Mike Denness, he was the natural for the job and brought to England's Test match scene a flair and charisma which made him both popular and successful. His record for England as captain, as batsman and indeed as bowler, was beyond reproach. He spent the winter of 1975-76 in Sydney most lucratively and no one could blame him for that, yet prior to his return I sensed that he felt his future lay Down Under. In fact, he announced his intention of returning to Sydney the following winter despite the fact that the MCC were due to tour India. I took him to task in the *Daily Express*, querying his statement that he was not certain to be selected for India and suggesting that as England's captain his first priority should be to English cricket. He was incensed with my article and he was allowed to reply in the paper in the following week. In the strongest possible manner, he refuted any insinuation I might have made, going on to say what an honour it was to be England's captain and that if selected he would be ready and willing to tour India. Most important of all, he went on to say that he would seek approval from Lord's for any decision he might regarding his future and keep them informed. Within twelve months he had played a leading part in secret negotiations which could do nothing but harm to the very people he had earlier promised to support.

'From the moment the story broke, Tony was hounded from pillar to post by the Press and television. He is a very good and plausible speaker and persuaded many that what he had done was for the benefit of cricket and cricketers in general, emphasising time and again that the benefit would be felt by the lowest-paid player in the poorest county side. No one would argue that WSC has greatly improved the financial lot of the chosen few, but I would take a lot of convincing that cricketers such as John Barclay of Sussex, David Acfield of Essex or Harry Pilling of Lancashire are any better off. There was little doubt that Greig had sold himself body and soul to Kerry Packer, had sworn allegiance that there would be no leak until the appropriate time and I was equally sure that Packer would stand firmly by Greig. But the same token I am sure that if Lord's had been fully in the picture as promised by Greig, they would have attempted to find a solution, though they would have met fierce opposition from the Australian Cricket Board, who it seemed would not concede any inch of the way.'

Imran Khan, one of the outstanding performers in the hard grind cricket of WSC, made some good points about Greig and Packer's kind of cricket when he said, 'It was the toughest test of skill and stamina but it lacked the tension of Test matches and the adrenaline that flows when one plays for one's country. Some reputations were damaged beyond repair, particularly Tony Greig's. His bowling was innocuous and his batting technique was exposed by short-pitched bowling. Ironically, one of the main organisers of Packer cricket was quite unsuited to meet its special demands.'

Henry Blofeld thought Greig had some kind of hold on Packer and he may have been right. Greig is still a big name in Australia, still making a good living. Greig was known for his prophecy about the

West Indians, saying, 'We will make them grovel,' and these days he would have been taken down to the nearest police station and charged with inciting racism. As he was born and educated in South Africa, he claimed he didn't know the full meaning of the word 'grovel'. Greig was one of the outstanding self-publicists in English cricket and one of its leading ambassadors and spokesmen. Overnight, he was now the PR for World Cricket Series on the other side of the trenches. The establishment at Lord's needed someone like him to speak for it and Jim was one of the first to be approached. He was invited to speak on the *Frost* programme when Sir David Frost's viewing figures were among the highest of the day. Packer had arrived with his entourage and he was ready to explain himself on TV.

'I was looking forward to it,' said Jim. 'It seemed to me an admirable opportunity to discuss seriously and intelligently the whole complex situation and secretly I nurtured the thought that some good might come of it. These hopes were dashed when Robin Marlar [the MCC president 2005-06] arrived on the scene to make up the quartet. Robin had been a good friend of mine ever since he was captain and I coach to Cambridge University. He had tremendous potential as an off-spin bowler but never quite reached the heights that his ability warranted. For many years he had been in the top flight of cricket journalism and is certainly the first I turn to when the Sunday newspapers arrived on the mat. Periodically he has an outburst, either verbally or in print, and unhappily he chose the *Frost* programme for one of them. His temper reached boiling point as he confronted Packer, and he completely lost his self-control and was quietly and clinically taken apart by the cool professionalism of Packer. Worst of all he received little sympathy from David Frost and none at all from the studio audience, the majority of whom probably believed that I ran an airline [a reference to Freddie Laker]. In the end all I could do was to attempt to bring some calmness and common sense to the proceedings and the programme ended with Packer winning by an innings.'

Marlar was still causing controversy twenty years later when he assumed the presidency of the MCC. In an interview he said he opposed women playing in mixed games because it was dangerous for them to face fast bowlers bowling at 80 mph. It was a sensible point but Michael Atherton tore into him in his column in *The Sunday Telegraph* and the female columnists joined in the chorus of protest. Jim wasn't against women's cricket. He was a good friend of Rachael Heyhoe-Flint, the most renowned England women's captain. One of her best lines in her public speaking days was about the protective box and Jim often used it in his speeches. 'We didn't call them that,' said Rachael. 'We called them manhole covers!' She always insisted that she hadn't thought of it herself. 'It came from a game in 1963 when a Colin Cowdrey team played against an England women's side at Chislehurst and Peter Richardson and Peter Parfitt concocted the line while chatting in the slips between deliveries,' she said. 'It was inaccurately attributed to me by a well known women's magazine and that almost led to a libel writ.'

Jim was a moderate drinker and he was surprised to discover that Packer was a teetotaller. 'I've got to have some vices to enjoy in my old age,' said Packer. 'I don't do it through any sense of conviction though. When I was twelve my father bribed me not to drink before I was twenty-one. He said he would give me a big new car if I didn't. When I reached twenty-one I thought I held all the cards but I was out-negotiated. All I got was a second-hand Triumph.'

On 23 June Packer, accompanied by Richie Benaud and his aides McNicholl and Taylor, attended a meeting at Lords with the delegates of the ICC. 'Tadge' Webster, the chairman of the UK Cricket Council, presented five points to Packer and he conceded on each of them. A solution was in the offing until Packer demanded the right to own the ABC exclusive cricket rights from 1981 when the current contract expired. Jim said, 'Bob Parish and Ray Steele, the Australian representatives and both managers of Australian tours to England, would never submit to that condition. The other delegates backed them and the meeting ended with an angry Packer striding out to face a barrage of journalists in what was a declaration of cricket war.'

I was among the throng. Packer was red faced, looking like an angry bull elephant. Alan Lee has now revealed that Packer's office in Sydney used to be filled with pictures of elephants. Perhaps Packer had a sense of humour! Packer made a short statement and as he turned and strode towards the W.G. Grace Gates he shouted the famous words, 'Now it's every man for himself and the devil take the hindmost.' Webster emerged and said, calmly, 'Wars are not won by appeasement.' It was a miserable summer and the only person who seemed to like it was Boycott. On 10 August, the ICC changed their rules to prevent WSC players from playing in Test cricket without its approval after 1 October. Packer's lawyers pounced. They realised it was an unfair restraint of trade. On Monday 26 September a High Court action started and thirty-one days later Mr Justice Christopher Slade ruled that the ban was unreasonable. The individual plaintiffs were Greig, John Snow and Mike Procter, the great South African all-rounder and now ICC Referee.

After the *Frost* programme Jim had a chat with Packer and he found him rather engaging. Packer spoke about his plans to revolutionise the televised coverage of cricket. Up to then, the BBC used only four cameras at a Test match, with only one behind the arm. 'We'll have eight,' he said. In England in 2005, Channel 4's Sunset & Vine company used thirty-two cameras in the Ashes series. 'Coverage has advanced light years,' said Richie Benaud.

Jim recalled their meeting, saying, 'With a wry smile, Packer hinted to me that he would like me to be involved as a commentator. If it was possible, I produced an even wryer smile in return. Within a few days and thanks to a recommendation from Richie Benaud, a most lucrative offer was handed to me by my agent. In essence the terms for roughly an eight-week engagement in Australia were approximately the equivalent of a full three-year contract with the BBC. It took me less than twenty-four hours to thank him for his offer and decline it without offering a reason. Fred Trueman, who had been waiting anxiously in the wings, accepted the offer with alacrity.'

Packer was an accomplished golfer, a useful tennis player, an enthusiastic game hunter and fisherman and a supporter of rugby league, so how good was Packer as a cricketer? While on that trip to England he volunteered for a friendly 40 overs Press game at Harrogate on 14 August between the English Cricket Writers and the Australian

Press. Jim used to play benefit matches after he had retired but this time he was too old and was probably playing golf that Sunday. Ian Chappell was captain of the Australians and the Thursday before the game he rang me to say he had another player. 'Who is it?' I said. 'Kerry Packer,' he said. 'We can't have him,' I said, jokingly. Naturally we welcomed Packer because the occasion would provide immense exposure and attract a good attendance. 'He's bought the whole lot,' said Ian. 'Pads, box, helmet, everything, in Harrods.' 'He'll need his helmet,' I said. Peter Lush, a likeable teddy bear of a man who had the difficult task of being the media manager of the Test and County Cricket Board, was in the England squad and in the Australian side was David Lord, the agent for several Aussie players who refused Packer's overtures. Lord and Packer hated each other and Lord appeared as a witness in the High Court.

Twenty minutes before the start there was no sign of the tycoon. The spectators were complaining. 'I've taken a day off to come here and it's cost me hard-earned brass,' one said. Packer had hired a light aircraft to bring him from London. As he walked in to the wooden pavilion, he was surrounded by dozens of media men, some of whom were dressed in their whites ready to take the field. 'Look,' he said, 'we're all here for a civilised afternoon. Cricket is a very civilised game.' He admitted he hadn't played cricket for eight years – 'although I've had a net this week.' At the toss up, Chappell decided to bat first and he scored 60 out of his side's 220. There was an amusing moment when Chappell drove a full toss straight back to Scyld Berry, the cricket correspondent of *The Sunday Telegraph* and Berry, who was a leg-spinner of sorts, dropped the ball. Earlier, Berry was refusing to bowl against such a great cricketer but having been forced to, he missed the biggest chance he'd ever had to take the wicket of a famous Test captain. Instead, he picked the ball up and held it high aloft, shouting, 'That's the hand that dropped Ian Chappell!' When Chappell was bowling, he stopped when he was about to release the ball and the umpire, Jack Fingleton, the former Australian Test opener who was an acerbic opponent of Packer and the Chappell brothers (brother Greg was at the game) shouted 'No ball!' Realising he had been made to look a fool by Chappell's actions, the angry Fingleton snarled, 'Don't ever do that to me again!'

Because of his late arrival, Packer was down at eight in the order and the innings was coming towards the end. The television and radio people were becoming anxious – Packer might not get in. The twelfth man was sent out to pass on a message from Chappell. 'Can you extend the overs to 45?' it said. 'Tell him we can't,' I said. As the man started to leave, I said, 'Okay, but I hope he will give me a free trip to WSC!' Packer finally reached the crease in the forty-third over and he faced 7 balls. He played forward and missed his first delivery. Then he completed a forward defensive shot of some merit. The third delivery hit him on the pad and went down to fine leg for a single. There were loud cheers from all around. At tea Packer sat upstairs and none of our players had the opportunity to speak to him. Most of the people who had dealings with him reported that he was 'a bit rude and curt'.

Keeping wicket for the Australian Press team was Alan Shiell, the cricket writer who was credited with breaking the story of WSC Down Under and standing next to him at first slip was Packer. Lord, who was a fast bowler but now was marginally quicker than Reg Hayter's medium-paced swingers, bowled to Lush, who had just passed his fifty. There was a nick and Packer caught the ball in front of his expansive chest. The fielders screeched and waved their arms as they congratulated the man of the day. It couldn't have been fixed better – Lush (from the English Cricket Establishment XI) caught Packer (Australian Pirate XI) bowled Lord (The Australian Gent) 52. As Lush came from the South, there was no collection for him.

The Australians won by 63 runs and without changing, Packer went off to the Dragonara Hotel in Leeds for dinner with Greig. In the scorebook they had him down as scoring 2 runs. I asked the scorer, 'What's going on? He didn't score from the bat. It was a leg bye and it wasn't two it was one!' He said with a laugh, 'He needed a bit of a leg up!' Afterwards, John Parker, the English ITV sports correspondent, discovered that someone had nicked £50 out of his pocket in the home dressing room. I checked my wallet. My only fiver was gone too. A Yorkshireman said, 'You can't trust these bigwigs from Down Under!'

Two winters later, Jim went to Australia and watched World Series, where the emphasis had been switched from unofficial Super Test matches to night limited-overs games. 'If I harboured any doubts as to the wisdom of the action I had taken, they quickly disappeared,' he said. He found the television commentaries 'loaded, biased and non-critical'. Fred Trueman, so strident when he appeared on television in England and on *Test Match Special,* followed the party line by praising rather than being objective. The average attendance at Tests in the first year was 5,311 but the figure at night cricket was more than trebled, reaching 52,000 in the inaugural game at the Sydney Cricket Ground. Benaud said, 'The ground authorities closed the gates but Mr Packer threw them open, having helped to man the turnstiles when it became obvious that the night was going to be a sell out. It was a marvellous evening, full of emotion even for the more cynical observers who had watched with interest the comings and going of the previous eighteen months when establishment cricket and WSC had been at loggerheads. It worked and it changed the game forever.

'The English county player was able to earn a decent basic wage and Test players suddenly saw his match fee jump from £300 to £1,000. Umpires, the financial outcasts of the game, were paid in more reasonable fashion.' One of the chief reasons why the English players were better paid was the £1 million a year sponsorship introduced by Cornhill Insurance in 1978 following an initiative from the Conservative MP David Evans. He started a campaign to keep England's best players available for Tests and appealed for £1 million to fund it. Every time the subject of the emancipation of England's cricketers comes up, the credit goes to Packer's revolution. Evans, who was once chairman of Luton Town Football Club, is forgotten.

Jim reckoned that there were thousands of children in the old ground at Sydney in the second and last year of WSC, another encouraging sign for the future of Australian cricket. He sat in a private box of the trustees and his old friend Arthur Morris, the former Test opening batsman, said, 'If this sort of cricket is going to pull them in, we should not discount or discredit it.' Jim also believed the organisers had pulled in the boundaries in WSC to help improve the run rates. Well, that happened in England in 2005, which explained why so many sixes were struck. Jim's final verdict on Packer cricket was, 'From the Test players' viewpoint, whether they were pro or anti, they all should give Packer a vote of thanks. He certainly put a firecracker under the tables at Lord's and Melbourne.'

The major plus resulting from Packer's innovations was to introduce successful one-day, limited-overs night cricket that brought in bigger crowds and extra income. But after two years, in which he lost £1.5 million, he brokered a peace treaty with the authorities and disbanded WSC. He had won his argument over the TV rights. The downside viewpoint came from Michael Henderson, the freelance writer who loves classical music and classical cricket. He wrote, 'What was Packer's bequest? Confrontation, for a start. Cricket had never been whiter than white, no matter what its guardians said about "fair play", but, in his eagerness to bump up TV audiences and attract younger viewers, Packer's tastes pandered to the lowest common denominator. Cricket, like most sport today, is louder, more insistent, more aggressive. More players are imbued with "attitude", that peculiar term which really means people find less shame in behaving like petulant adolescents. It is inconceivable that England cricketers of previous generations could behave with the lack of restraint that Kevin Pietersen displayed last year, promoting himself to stardom before he had actually accomplished much of real significance. For better, for worse, we are living in a world created by men such as Packer. Professional sport is now a multi-million dollar business, where image can count for as much as talent – witness David Beckham, a footballer of decent, though hardly unique, talents. Games are now played principally for TV audiences and the easy, pliable tastes of the multitude. Packer, we have heard, was "a great friend of the game". What tosh!' Few people did more than Packer to live up to Oscar Wilde's definition of the cynic – 'A man who knows the price of everything and the value of nothing.' Yorkshireman Jim might well agree with the Lancastrian Henderson.

At Packer's state-funded memorial service, which had a distinct lack of religious content, 1,800 people turned up at the Sydney Opera House on 18 February and John Howard, the Australian Prime Minister, said, 'He was a larrikin [rascal] but he was also a gentleman and that's a description that any Australian would be proud to have.' The Sydney Symphony Orchestra struck up a version of 'C'mon Aussie, C'mon', the catchy advertising jingle that first broadcast Packer's WSC into Australian homes. Instead of choirs, there were ranks of children from some of Australia's most exclusive schools singing lustily along as they unfurled banners. One said, 'We love you Kerry.'

JIM AS A COMMENTATOR

In the last eighteen years of his life Jim took up another job that brought him immense satisfaction, as a TV and radio cricket commentator. He did it so well that he was often compared to Richie Benaud, who was generally accepted to be the finest worldwide commentator of them all. Great rivals on the field when both men were at their peak as cricketers, they became friends and working colleagues in press boxes all over the country. They shared one outstanding attribute – the ability to speak only when words were required to back up the pictures. Jim wasn't garrulous and his low-key approach suited the technique of broadcasting at the time. There were silences when they appeared in front of the microphone and the viewers appreciated that in a more leisurely era, before the gabblers took over. Benaud said, 'Jim was outstanding where economy of words and the ability to fit the story into a space are so important. He was always a level-headed cricketer and he carried that into his broadcasting. He had a wonderful knowledge of the game that he was able to impart in an interesting fashion, whether in conversation or on the box.'

Jim was the first to admit that Benaud was the top man. In the early 1950s after he took over as captain of Australia at the age of twenty-one, Benaud signed up as a news reporter, doing the police beat working for the *Sydney Sun* and was one of the few cricketers who qualified as a journalist. His father Lou once took 20 wickets in a second-grade game over two weekends at the Penrith Showground in Sydney, outdoing Jim, obviously at a lower level of the game but still a remarkable feat. Jim had no practical training as a journalist but he was intelligent enough to write his own material in the *Daily Express* and when a microphone was put in front of him he followed the advice of John Arlott, who told him, 'Just talk as though you are sitting with a mate in a bar.' Later Jim was given membership of the National Union of Journalists, although he never underwent the journalistic courses.

Alan Davidson, the great Australian all-rounder who spent most of the 1956 tour of England recovering from a fractured ankle, believes that Laker was superior to Benaud. Davidson visits England most years and stays with his friend Raman Subba Row, and he said, 'In my view, Jim was *the* best. Jim's analytical pieces were spot on. He was always calm and he never spoke more than he needed to. I switch off the sound when most of today's commentators start up. They babble on and it puts you off.'

After retiring at Essex, his various business commitments kept him busy and he spoke at dinners and events all over the country, generally without payment but at bigger events he received modest fees from the organisers. In 1967 his re-admittance to the Oval and Lord's enabled him to renew friendships. He was ready to give advice to younger players and he had a habit of sending congratulatory notes to ones whom had performed creditably. Raman Subba Row recruited him as a member of Surrey's public relations committee and the healing process continued apace. But it was the offer from the BBC that transformed his life and revived his reputation as a national figure, helping to absolve him from his earlier sins. When he was first asked, he said, 'With my voice, I'd put everyone to sleep.' They were less concerned with his voice, more interested in his deep knowledge of the game. His first job was second man behind Sir Learie Constantine, the great West Indian all-rounder who became Lord Constantine of Maraval and Nelson, at an International Cavaliers' XI fixture at Fenner's in Cambridge. Learie was a governor of the BBC and a much-admired man before he died in 1971. Nick Hunter, a former BBC director who grew up as a Surrey fan at the Oval, said, 'There was an aura about Jim although he never played the VIP. Anyone who has taken 19 wickets against Australia can walk on water. I was certainly keen to make sure we got things right for him. We treated him with considerable respect, as was his due.'

Arlott proved to be a great friend and advisor of Jim and he recalled, 'Jim had a deceptively fast reaction to any movement or action on the field. Among long distance observers of an incident, he was more likely than anyone to read it accurately.' Bill Frindall, the long serving and arguably the best scorer in the history of the game, reckoned that Jim could be stubborn. In his recently published book *Bearders – My Life in Cricket* he said, 'I worked for BBC Television for the first seven seasons of the John Player Sunday League, at first commanding the caption hut and feeding presenters Frank Bough and Peter Walker with the scores of other matches being played that day, before succeeding Ross Salmon as scorer for Jim and John Arlott. If Jim made an error he would never correct himself. At the start of one of these 40-over thrashes, he confused the identities of the two opening batsmen and wouldn't correct his error even when one of them was dismissed. The other opening partner survived and he still ignored my note pointing out the mistake. Not until John took over after 20 overs was the correction made.

'We first worked together at Cheam Cricket ground in 1965 when I made my scoring debut for television at one of the last of the Rothman's Cavaliers matches. Gary Sobers had just struck three balls from Surrey left-arm spinner Roger Harman high over the line of poplar trees separating the ground from a railway line. Commentator Neil Durden-Smith asked Jim where he would bowl to Sobers in this form. Jim paused for ten seconds before growling, "Three feet outside the off stump, turning sharply away!"'

Peter Walker, the England and Glamorgan all-rounder, took some time to get to know Jim after several rebuffs when he played against him. Born in Bristol, his father Oliver, a journalist and club cricketer, moved the family from Cardiff to South Africa and at the age of six-teen, Peter ran away to sea and the 11,000-ton tanker going northwards ended at Barry in South Wales. His book *It's Not All About Cricket*, yet to be published but well worthy of exposure, recounted, 'Jim took a lot more knowing than John Arlott. Essentially a private man, once Jim had sized you up, if he liked you, he was delightful company with a sense of humour as dry as anything in John's 2,000-bottle cellar in Alderney. I'd played against Jim during his twilight days but I wouldn't say more than a dozen words had passed between us in that period. When I replaced Frank Bough on Sundays, Jim was somewhat wary of me. With typical Yorkshire bluntness he swiftly taught me a lesson in broadcasting etiquette that a lot of sporting commentators and radio interviewers these days would do well to emulate.

'It came at the start of one of my earliest appearances fronting the BBC2 Sunday cricket programme. The match was at Tewkesbury and, as always, we went on air five minutes before the starting time of 2 p.m. I'd prepared what I thought was a marvellously descriptive piece about the area and I was still in full flow when the umpires came out and with time running out before the start I then expounded on each player. By the time I finished, the bowler was about to run in and I said, "And now for commentary, here's Jim Laker." I sat back smugly, pleased with my opening until Jim responded, "Thank you Peter, you've said it all." And he never spoke for a few min-utes. It was a hard lesson − never steal the main man's thunder. But things improved and later he was immensely kind to me. He wasn't a chit-chat man, or a very social guy. He had a huge belief in himself. He was very similar to Richie Benaud. They were solitary guys in a cocoon. Not easy men to know but when you did, you admired and respected them.'

The highlight of Jim's television career came in 1971 at the Gillette Cup semi-final between Lancashire and Gloucestershire at Old Trafford. Like in 1956, the weather interfered, with ninety minutes lost at the start. At 6.30 p.m., with the lights switched on in the pavilion and also on the scoreboard, umpires Arthur Jepson and Dickie Bird were ready to call it off at 7.30 p.m. to the relief of Jim and Nick Hunter. But the cricket authorities were reluctant to abandon play for the day on a televised match and, against his natural instincts, Dickie Bird agreed with Jepson to allow the game to go on, despite the rapidly deteriorating light. Jepson said to the Gloucestershire players, 'You can see the moon. How far do you want to see?'

Paul Cox, the BBC Controller in London, gave the order to go live for the rest of the game, which left Jim trapped in the commentary box for two-and-a-half hours. Lancashire skipper Jack Bond wanted to continue and Tony Brown, the Gloucestershire captain, also saw a chance of victory. With 7 wickets down and needing 25 more runs at the start of the fifty-sixth over – with car lights switched on the roads outside – David Hughes took 24 runs off John Mortimore's next over. Bond, facing the fearsome Mike Procter, managed to squeeze the winning run in the next over and there were scenes of bedlam, with 23,350 deliriously happy home supporters cheering and shouting. The decisive run was scored at 8.50 p.m. and the programme ran five minutes into the 9 o'clock News. Millions saw and heard Jim's performance, marvelling at his calmness. Asked how he did it, he replied 'Well, it could have been worse. I could have been out there bowling!' Along with his producer Nick, he dashed to the closest toilet. They weren't able to leave their positions.

Jim Swanton, such a strong critic following Jim's indiscretions in *Over to Me*, was generous when he spoke about Jim's work in front of the cameras. 'He talked over the air rather as he bowled,' he said. 'Precisely, accurately, shrewdly, with no fanciful flights.'

Jim was anticipating a close series Ashes series in 1981 until he was struck down with illness in March, just before he and Lilly went to Barbados to watch the Test between the West Indies and England. Severe pains in the lower body, accompanied with a high temperature was diagnosed as a viral infection. He responded to treatment and was given clearance to go on holiday. But a few days before, watching the televised news, he learned that his great friend Ken Barrington had died of a massive heart attack. It turned out to be a nightmare instead of a holiday. Two months later, Jim was laid low again while attending the Surrey Old Players' dinner at the Oval. He was in such great pain that he could hardly move. Back at home, Lilly rang a family friend, Mr Lance Bromley of St Mary's Hospital in Paddington, and the doctor had him checked into the hospital within three hours. The diagnosis was aortic aneurism, an excessive enlargement of the artery. Next day another consultant, Dr Eastcott, operated on Jim and the operation lasted five hours. It was a close call and he needed a few weeks to regain strength. Christopher Martin-Jenkins took over his position in the commentary team while he watched on TV and, on the final day, listened to *Test Match Special* to follow the Botham-Willis inspired victory at home from Headingley. On 2 August, almost exactly twenty-five years after the 19 for 90, Bill Frindall interviewed him and there were some interesting observations from Jim. Part of Bill's interview comes from his latest book.

'I recorded a chat with him following major heart surgery,' said Bill. 'He had missed the first three current Ashes Tests, returning for the Fourth at Edgbaston to commentate for BBC TV and write for the *Express*. I began our chat by asking him how it felt to be back.

JL: "It's good to be back. Basically one is thankful to be there. Physically, I feel fine."

BF: "Did you miss being at the matches? Or was it a novelty to relax at home and watch from a distance?"

JL: "It was interesting on one count. Of course, I had never watched TV for such a long time and it was nice to look at it from the other end. Probably the point that will amuse you is that my TV set broke down on the final and great day of that Headingley Test so I was listening to the radio boys all day!"

BF: "Can we ask what you thought of it?"

JL: "I enjoyed it. People ask me what I feel about radio commentary and I never know because you never hear it. Obviously we are next door the whole time. I don't think I could do it for one thing. When you get some of these dull, dreary days we can get away with it with a picture but you've got to talk the whole time and I don't think a lot for that."

BF: "Your return has coincided with the twenty-fifth anniversary of what will always be known as Laker's Match. In fact, you rather look like that slim line Laker of 1956! How clear are the memories?"

BF: "Well, I think they will always stay pretty vivid in my memory, Bill. It was, as you say, a fairly unique occasion and one is constantly reminded about it even twenty-five years on. I reckon I get stopped, perhaps twice a month, by people in the street, often strangers, who still talk about it. All these reminders do keep it fairly fresh. I can remember most of the dismissals."

BF: "If my memory is correct, all the wickets fell from the Stretford End. Is that right?"

JL: "No, Tony's wicket was taken from the other end, the Warwick Road End. Certainly all 19 of mine were taken from the Stretford End. The interesting thing was, of course, that we switched about continually, particularly in the second innings when I bowled 51.2 overs. Tony in fact bowled 55 and I suppose he bowled 20-30 from the Stretford End. This is the most remarkable thing about that whole match. It was a freak. It could never happen again. There is no way that Lockey and I could bowl and share wickets like that. Couldn't happen in a million years."

BF: "How long was it before he spoke to you after the game?"

JL: "He was a bit upset [chuckle]. I think possibly I would have been if I had been in his position. And I thing one think I never possibly will forgive myself for, because amid all the glorification that was taking place afterwards, I didn't spare enough time for him. It was only in later years that I realised that he must have felt desperately unhappy. But fortunately he and I were never very close in those days and it is only in later years that we became far more bosom pals than we were then."

BF: "In fact, during the Centenary Test at Lord's he stayed with you, didn't he?"

JL: "Yes, I was returning a bit of hospitality because I stayed with him the previous year in Australia."

Jim made a good recovery after his heart surgery and was soon back working at the Edgbaston Test. But he was never the same. His pace of living, never too fast, slowed and he preferred to stay overnight than drive himself home after matches. On New Year's Day 1986 he was taken ill again and spent three weeks in hospital. This time it was severe inflammation of the pancreas, a gland near the stomach. The doctor in charge recommended the removal of the gall bladder, one of the ways to cure the problem. Both Jim and Lilly had reservations but the surgery went ahead. He rallied but became increasingly ill and was admitted to the Parkside Clinic in Wimbledon. On 23 April he died of septicaemia, or blood poisoning. Close friends knew he was ill but they were shocked to lose him so suddenly at the age of sixty-four. Only a few weeks before he was working as usual in the commentary box.

His service of thanksgiving took place at Southwark Cathedral on Friday 11 July, the same place where Ken Barrington's service was held four years previously. On both occasions, the cathedral was filled with 800 people, most of the same people. Former England captains Peter May and Len Hutton led the host of cricketing stars and Raman Subba Row, newly appointed chairman of the Test and County Cricket Board, spotted the former tennis champion Fred Perry who had flown in from the US. 'I had to come,' said Perry. 'He was such a great man.'

Richie Benaud gave the Address and Micky Stewart read the Second Lesson. The Revd Alan Sirman, Vicar of Holy Trinity, Putney, Jim's church, said, 'As an international cricketer Jim gave immense pleasure to the many thousands who saw him on the field of play. For millions throughout the world his quiet and knowledgeable broadcasts brought the action and subtleties of the game he loved into their own homes. His family life was a source of warmth and joy to him. We pray this life, with its love of family, the gentlemanly behaviour and honesty that marked it both on and off the field, will be an inspiration and example to us all. Most especially we pray that the young people of our nation should see his way of life as a standard by which to measure their own.'

John Arlott captured the feeling, saying, 'His daughters love him and his wife Lilly adored him. If he took a quizzical look at the world, he missed very little. To work with him, and to be accepted by him, was something of an accolade. It was an admission to a school of cricketing thought that was often quite bewildering in its depth. The off-break is not merely the bowler's bread and butter, it is the staff of his life. And in that school Jim Laker was the past master.'

In 1952-53 he joined with some of the England team to play small parts in the film *The Final Test*, written by Terence Rattigan, filmed at Pinewood Studios. It was shown to coincide with the 1953 Australia tour. 'We were paid by the day,' said Jim. 'One of the cricketers kept foozling his lines. Some of the others were annoyed with him, as it showed up our "acting" ability, until he leaned over and said confidentially said, "Don't worry. The more re-takes the better. We're paid by the day!" Jack Warner, the star, lived near to me and often drove me to the studio.' *The Final Test* wasn't a very good film. A much better one, made today, would be about a tormented genius, born out of wedlock with his father abandoning him when he was two years of age, who rose to become the greatest off-spin bowler of all time. A man who was brave enough to speak out of the feudal way cricket was run and his bitterness spilled over into a book that led to him being sentenced to two concurrent bans, four and seven years. He changed his approach to life, became more compassionate – cricket itself changed too, abolishing the distinction between amateurs and professionals – and he emerged as one of the finest cricket television commentators, up alongside Richie Benaud who was there on the field at Old Trafford at his peak. That would really be a compelling and absorbing film.

Roger Knight, the MCC chief executive and former Surrey captain, said, 'I am sure that the present England team, especially given that Ashley Giles wasn't fit for the tour to India, would love to have a spin bowler with half of Jim's talent. I remember in my very early days at Surrey meeting him and being impressed with his straightforward approach to life and cricket. By that stage he was commentating and, perhaps because he was a Yorkshireman, he was always blunt and to the point.'

We will never see his like again but in the summer of 2006 we were fortunate to see his feats re-shown on television in black and white. Sitting up in commentary box on high he would probably say, 'It wasn't that good!'

STATISTICS

THE FIRST-CLASS CAREER (1946-1965)
OF JAMES CHARLES LAKER

Born: 9 February 1922 at Frizinghall, Bradford; died at Wimbledon, 23 April 1986

Debut: Surrey *v.* Combined Services at the Oval, 17 July 1946

County Cap Awarded: Surrey *v.* Middlesex at Lord's, 26 August 1947

England Debut: *v.* West Indies at Barbados, 21 January 1948

Final Day in Tests: England *v.* Australia at Melbourne, 18 February 1959

Final Day in First-Class Cricket: Cavaliers *v.* Barbados at Bridgetown, 27 February 1965

CAREER BATTING AND FIELDING

SEASON	M	I	NO	R	HS	100	50	Ave	Ct
1946	3	3	1	3	3	—	—	3.00	1
1947	18	26	4	408	60	—	1	18.54	13
1947/48 (WI)	8	12	2	212	55	—	1	21.20	4
1948	29	44	10	828	99	—	3	24.35	16
1949	28	39	7	548	100	1	—	17.12	25
1950	30	42	6	589	53	—	1	16.36	22
1950/51 (IND)	10	10	1	171	61	—	1	19.00	5
1951	28	38	6	624	89	—	4	19.50	22
1951/52 (NZ)	4	4	0	77	35	—	—	19.25	3
1952	30	34	5	310	26	—	—	10.68	15

1953	31	34	3	502	81	—	1	16.19	25
1953/54 (WI)	7	9	1	123	33	—	—	15.37	4
1954	29	33	9	607	113	1	1	25.29	29
1955	30	38	6	706	78*	—	4	22.06	26
1956	25	34	5	320	43*	—	—	11.03	8
1956/57 (SA)	14	16	6	79	17	—	—	7.90	3
1957	28	28	11	210	44	—	—	12.35	10
1958	28	29	6	325	59	—	1	14.13	10
1958/59 (AUS)	10	13	3	107	22*	—	—	10.70	1
1959	24	30	7	301	28	—	—	13.08	15
1962	12	11	2	43	13	—	—	4.77	5
1963	10	12	5	95	24*	—	—	13.57	4
1963/64 (WI)	2	1	1	0	0*	—	—	—	1
1964	8	6	1	110	28	—	—	22	2
1964/65 (WI)	4	2	0	6	5	—	—	3	1
TOTALS	**450**	**548**	**108**	**7304**	**113**	**2**	**18**	**16.6**	**270**

CAREER BOWLING

SEASON	O	M	R	W	BB	Ave	5wi	10wm
1946	60	12	169	8	3-43	21.12	—	—
1947	575.5	135	1420	79	8-69	17.97	5	—
1947/48 (WI)	388.5	117	973	36	7-103	27.02	3	—
1948	1058.4	251	2903	104	8-55	27.91	4	—
1949	1192.1	419	2422	122	8-42	19.85	8	1
1950	1409.5	522	2544	166	8-2	15.32	12	5
1950/51 (IND)	315.2	131	579	36	6-23	16.08	3	—
1951	1301.3	400	2681	149	7-36	17.99	13	5
1951/52 (NZ)	228.1	88	379	24	5-44	15.79	3	1
1952	1071	342	2219	125	7-57	17.75	9	1
1953	1165.5	383	2366	1.35	6-25	17.52	7	1
1953/54 (WI)	333.5	113	756	22	4-47	34.36	—	—

1954	966.2	315	2048	135	8-51	15.17	13	5
1955	1091.1	362	2382	133	7-95	17.90	9	3
1956	959.3	364	1906	132	10-53	14.43	8	3
1956/57 (SA 8b)	388.7	121	875	50	6-47	17.50	2	—
1957	1016.5	393	1921	126	7-16	15.24	5	—
1958	882.5	330	1651	116	8-46	14.23	7	2
1958/59 (AUS 8b)	282.1	63	655	38	5-31	17.23	3	1
1959	797.2	246	1920	78	7-38	24.61	5	2
1962	379.5	96	962	51	7-73	18.86	5	1
1963	374	128	828	43	7-89	19.25	2	1
1963/64 (WI)	72	13	221	5	2-50	44.20	—	—
1964	226	55	577	17	4-41	33.94	—	—
1964/65 (WI)	133.4	23	434	14	5-54	31.00	1	—

TOTALS

(6b)	16000.2	5238	35791	1944	10-53	18.41	127	32
(8b)	671	184						

TEST CRICKET BATTING AND FIELDING

SEASON	M	I	NO	R	HS	100	50	Ave	Ct
1947/48 (WI)	4	7	1	109	55	—	1	18.16	1
1948 (AUS)	3	6	1	114	63	—	1	22.80	—
1949 (NZ)	1	1	0	0	0	—	—	0.00	—
1950 (WI)	1	2	0	44	40	—	—	22.00	—
1951 (SA)	2	3	1	46	27	—	—	23.00	1
1952 (IND)	4	4	2	44	23★	—	—	22.00	3
1953 (AUS)	3	4	0	64	48	—	—	16.00	—
1953/54 (WI)	4	5	1	44	27	—	—	11.11	3
1954 (PAK)	1	1	1	13	13★	—	—	—	—
1955 (SA)	2	0	14	12	7	—	—	7.00	—
1956 (AUS)	5	6	1	37	12	—	—	7.40	—
1956/57 (SA)	5	9	3	40	17	—	—	6.66	1

1957 (WI)	4	3	1	18	10*	—	—	9.00	1
1958 (NZ)	4	3	1	27	15	—	—	13.50	2
1958/59 (AUS)	4	7	2	62	22*	—	—	12.40	—
TOTAL	**46**	**63**	**15**	**676**	**63**	**—**	**2**	**14.08**	**12**

TEST CRICKET BOWLING

SEASON	O	M	R	W	BB	Ave	5wi	10wm
1947/48 (WI)	186.4	48	548	18	7/103	30.44	1	—
1648 (AUS)	155.2	42	472	9	4-138	52.44	—	—
1949 (NZ)	32	6	89	4	4-78	22.25	—	—
1950 (WI)	31	9	86	1	1-43	86	—	—
1951 (SA)	111	30	208	14	6-55	14.85	1	1
1952 (IND)	90.3	33	189	8	4-39	23.62	—	—
1953 (AUS)	58.5	11	212	9	4-75	23.55	—	—
1953/54 (WI)	221.1	84	469	14	4-71	33.5	—	—
1954 (PAK)	32.2	17	39	2	1-17	19.5	—	—
1955 (SA)	60.4	31	84	7	5-56	12	1	—
1956 (AUS)	283.5	127	442	46	10-53	9.6	4	2
1956/57 (SA 8b)	145.1	46	324	11	2-7	29.45	—	—
1957 (WI)	246.2	99	448	18	4-119	24.88	—	—
1958 (NZ)	131	67	173	17	5-17	10.17	1	—
1958/59 (AUS 8b)	127.6	24	318	15	5-107	21.2	1	—

TOTALS

	O	M	R	W	BB	Ave	5wi	10wm
(6b)	1640.4	604	4101	193	10-53	21.24	9	3
(8b)	272.7	70						

HUNDREDS (2)

100	Surrey v. Cambridge University	Guildford	1949
113	Surrey v. Gloucestershire	Kennington Oval	1954

SCORE OF 99

| Run out | Surrey *v.* Kent | Kennington Oval | 1948 |

PAIRS

| Surrey *v.* Gloucestershire | Kennington Oval | 1949 |
| Surrey *v.* Yorkshire | Kennington Oval | 1950 |

The pair against Yorkshire was followed by another duck – against Worcestershire at Worcester.

TEN WICKETS IN A MATCH (32)

5/51 & 7/47	Surrey *v.* Kent	Kennington Oval	1949
8/2 & 2/44	England *v.* The Rest	Bradford	1950
4/42 & 6/56	Surrey *v.* Gloucestershire	Kennington Oval	1950
8/45 & 4/41	Surrey *v.* Gloucestershire	Bristol	1950
4/36 & 7/61	Surrey *v.* Worcestershire	Worcester	1950
6/52 & 4/37	Surrey *v.* Essex	Chelmsford	1950
4/15 & 6/19	Surrey *v.* MCC	Lord's	1951
5/74 & 6/49	Surrey *v.* Somerset	Kennington Oval	1951
4/76 & 6/65	Surrey *v.* Essex	Kennington Oval	1951
5/79 & 7/65	Surrey *v.* Worcestershire	Kennington Oval	1951
4/64 & 6/55	ENGLAND *v.* SOUTH AFRICA	Kennington Oval	1951
5/53 & 5/68	Auckland *v.* Wellington	Auckland	1951/52
6/64 & 4/55	Surrey *v.* India	Kennington Oval	1952
6/38 & 4/67	Surrey *v.* Yorkshire	Kennington Oval	1953
7/46 & 8/51	Surrey *v.* MCC	Lord's	1954
5/33 & 5/59	Surrey *v.* Essex	Kennington Oval	1954
6/58 & 5/36	Surrey *v.* Northamptonshire	Kettering	1954
5/37 & 5/53	Surrey *v.* Middlesex	Lord's	1954
6/41 & 4/41	Surrey *v.* Lancashire	Kennington Oval	1954
5/39 & 6/28	Surrey *v.* MCC	Lord's	1955

5/53 & 5/68	Surrey v. Glamorgan	Swansea	1955
7/95 & 3/90	Surrey v. Warwickshire	Coventry	1955
10/88 & 2/42	Surrey v. Australians	Kennington Oval	1956
5/58 & 6/55	ENGLAND v. AUSTRALIA	Headingley	1956
9/37 & 10/53	ENGLAND v. AUSTRALIA	Old Trafford	1956
5/34 & 5/42	Surrey v. Middlesex	Kennington Oval	1958
8/46 & 4/32	Surrey v. Sussex	Hove	1958
5/31 & 5/70	MCC v. South Australia	Adelaide	1958/59
3/28 & 7/38	Surrey v. Sussex	Sydney	1958/59
5/53 & 6/27	Surrey v. Gloucestershire	Guildford	1959
7/73 & 6/86	Essex v. Kent	Dover	1962
6/69 & 4/57	Essex v. Northamptonshire	Romford	1963

PRINCIPAL BOWLING FEATS

Most wickets in a Test Series:

Only S.F. Barnes, for England v. South Africa in 1913/14, has taken more wickets in a Test Series than Laker did against Australia in 1956.

Their respective figures are:

S.F. BARNES

Tests: 4	Runs: 536	Wickets: 49	Average: 10.73
Balls per wicket: 27.67	5wi: 7	10wm: 3	

J.C. LAKER

Tests: 5	Runs: 442	Wickets: 46	Average: 9.60
Balls per wicket: 37.02	5wi: 4	10wm: 2	

Best Bowling Figures in a Test Innings: 10–53 England v. Australia, Old Trafford 1956

Best Bowling Figures in a Test Match: 19–90 England v. Australia, Old Trafford 1956

(Both unequalled records)

HIGHEST WICKET AGGREGATES FOR ENGLISH SPIN BOWLERS

	M	Runs	Wkts	BB	Ave	5wi	10wm	S/Rate
D.L. Underwood	86	7674	297	8/51	25.83	17	6	73.60
J.C. LAKER	**46**	**4101**	**193**	**10/53**	**21.24**	**9**	**3**	**62.31**
G.A.R. Lock	49	4451	174	7/35	25.58	9	3	25.58
F.J. Titmus	53	4931	153	7/79	32.22	7	–	98.81
H. Verity	40	3510	144	8/43	24.37	5	2	77.59
J.E. Emburey	60	5105	138	7/78	36.99	6	–	103.09

FIFTY OR MORE WICKETS IN A MONTH

May 1951	Innings: 16	Wickets: 60	Average: 13.53
	BB: 7-36	5wi: 7	10wm: 3

June 1950	Innings: 16	Wickets: 55	Average: 13.80
	BB: 8-45	5wi: 4	10wm: 3

BOWLERS WHO HAVE TAKEN 1,000 CHAMPIONSHIP WICKETS FOR SURREY

	Runs	Wkts	Ave
J.C. LAKER	**20528**	**1203**	**17.06**
G.A.R. Lock	25255	1458	17.32
T. Richardson	27371	1531	17.87
W.H. Lockwood	18395	1001	18.37
A.V. Bedser	23753	1241	19.14

TEN WICKETS IN AN INNINGS TWICE IN ONE SEASON

J.C. Laker 10/88 and 10/53 in 1956
(This is the only instance in the history of first-class cricket)

MODES OF DISMISSAL

Batting:

Caught   279 (50.91 per cent of all innings)
Bowled   120 (21.89 per cent)
LBW   31 (5.66 per cent)
Stumped   4 (0.73 per cent)
Run out   6 (1.10 per cent)
Not out   108 (19.71 per cent)

Bowling:

Caught   1068 (54.94 per cent of all dismissals)
Bowled   530 (28.29 per cent)
LBW   248 (12.76 per cent)
Stumped   74 (3.81 per cent)
Hit wicket   4 (0.20 per cent)

Principal victims:

14   C.A. Milton
13   D.J. Insole, W.J. Edrich
12   R. Smith, K.R. Miller (Australia), C.L. Walcott (West Indies)
11   J.F. Crapp, R.G. Marlar, C.C. McDonald (Australia)
10   T.E. Bailey, L.H. Compton, R.T. Simpson, F.J. Titmus, J.J. Warr, J.W. Burke (Australia)

9   A.V. Avery, D. Kenyon, J.G. Dewes, I.W.G. Johnson (Australia), K.D. Mackay (Australia), R.T.D. Perks, P.E. Richardson, R.T. Spooner, J.H. Wardle
8   R.G. Broadbent, D.C.S. Compton, E.D.R. Eagar, G.O. Dawkes, G.H.G. Doggart, F.C. Gardner, W.E. Jones, G.E.E. Lambert, D.C. Morgan, A.S.M. Oakman, L.F. Outschoom, K.C. Preston, D. Shackleton, H.W. Stephenson, F.H. Vigar, J.V. Wilson, R.C. Wilson

FIELDERS WHO HELPED LAKER ACHIEVE MANY OF HIS DISMISSALS:

Most catches:

124	G.A.R. Lock
107	W.S. Surridge
77	A.J.W. McIntyre
69	J.C. Laker
63	M.J. Stewart
44	A.V. Bedser
31	E.A. Bedser
30	P.B.H. May
29	J.F. Parker
28	K.F. Barrington
27	T.H. Clark
26	D.G.W. Fletcher
25	B. Constable

Stumpings:

39	A.J.W. McIntyre
16	T.G. Evans

Other titles published by Tempus

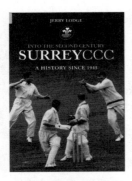

Into the Second Century A History of Surrey CCC Since 1945
JERRY LODGE

Celebrating their centenary just seven days after the Second World War, Surrey has won more County Championships than anyone else since 1945. This delightful book contains comprehensive statistical information and over 100 superb illustrations.

0 7524 3177 3

Surrey County Cricket Club Fifty of the Finest Matches
JERRY LODGE

Surrey CCC have been involved in many titanic struggles over the years and fifty of the best encounters are relived here. With match reports, scorecards and illustrations it recounts vital and historic encounters against rival first-class counties and touring sides from around the world. This book celebrates the great achievements of Surrey CCC over the years and is entertaining reading for any supporter of the club.

0 7524 3786 0

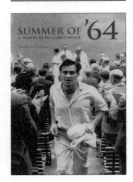

Summer of '64 A Season in English Cricket
ANDREW HIGNELL

The halcyon summer of 1964 saw Graveney, Boycott and Wilson all make over 2,000 runs, while Shackleton, Harman, Cartwright, Titmus and Illingworth were the most lethal exponents of the art of bowling. After one of the hardest fought contests in living memory Australia very narrowly took the Ashes while Worcestershire finally saw off intense competition to take the County Championship. A nostalgic look at one of the finest seasons on record.

0 7524 3414 4

Victory England's Greatest Modern Test Wins
ALAN BONE

With a foreword and commentary from the inimitable Christopher Martin-Jenkins and a wealth of illustration, this book highlights the most memorable occasions on which England has triumphed, be it a consummate thrashing of the opposition or an epic against-all-odds comeback from the brink of defeat. Featuring match reports and scorecards from thirty fine victories this is a source of great nostalgia and delight for all England cricket fans.

0 7524 3415 2

If you are interested in purchasing other books published by Tempus, or in case you have difficulty finding any Tempus books in your local bookshop, you can also place orders directly through our website:

www.tempus-publishing.com